The Origin of Ideas

The Origin
Of Ideas

*Blending, Creativity,
and the Human Spark*

MARK TURNER

OXFORD
UNIVERSITY PRESS

OXFORD
UNIVERSITY PRESS

Oxford University Press is a department of the University of Oxford.
It furthers the University's objective of excellence in research, scholarship,
and education by publishing worldwide.

Oxford   New York

Auckland   Cape Town   Dar es Salaam   Hong Kong   Karachi
Kuala Lumpur   Madrid   Melbourne   Mexico City   Nairobi
New Delhi   Shanghai   Taipei   Toronto

With offices in

Argentina   Austria   Brazil   Chile   Czech Republic   France   Greece
Guatemala   Hungary   Italy   Japan   Poland   Portugal   Singapore
South Korea   Switzerland   Thailand   Turkey   Ukraine   Vietnam

Oxford is a registered trademark of Oxford University Press
in the UK and certain other countries.

Published in the United States of America by
Oxford University Press
198 Madison Avenue, New York, NY 10016

© Oxford University Press 2014

Library of Congress Cataloging-in-Publication Data

Turner, Mark, 1954-
The origin of ideas: blending, creativity, and the human spark / Mark Turner.
pages cm
Includes bibliographical references and index.
ISBN 978-0-19-998882-2
1. Creative ability.   2. Idea (Philosophy)   I. Title.
BF408.T845 2014
153.2—dc23
2013015132

1 3 5 7 9 8 6 4 2

Printed in the United States of America
on acid-free paper

Contents

Acknowledgments

I am grateful to the Norwegian Ministry of Education and Research and to its Centre for Advanced Study at the Norwegian Academy of Science and Letters for a fellowship year in 2011–2012. This book was written during my residency in that superb company.

I thank Joan Bossert, my editor at Oxford University Press; the many members of her staff who assisted in the publication of this book; Arthur Evenchik; and several very helpful anonymous reviewers.

This book draws on a number of articles, chapters, and online presentations I have published previously, including the following: "The Art of Compression" 2006, in *The Artful Mind: Cognitive Science and the Riddle of Human Creativity*, edited by Mark Turner (Oxford University Press); "The Scope of Human Thought" August 17, 2009, *On the Human* (target article in an online forum run by the National Humanities Center); "The Origin of Selkies" 2004, *Journal of Consciousness Studies,* volume 11, numbers 5-6; "The Mind is an Autocatalytic Vortex" 2008, in *The Literary Mind,* Volume 24 (2008) of *REAL: Yearbook of Research in English and American Literature*, edited by Jürgen Schlaeger (Tübingen, Germany: Gunter Narr Verlag); "The Ghost of Anyone's Father" 2004, in *Shakespearean International Yearbook*, volume 4, edited by Graham Bradshaw, Thomas Bishop, and Mark Turner (Hants, UK: Ashgate Publishing Limited); and "Double-scope stories" 2003, in *Narrative Theory and the Cognitive Sciences*, edited by David Herman (Stanford: Center for the Study of Language and Information).

The Origin of Ideas

I

The Human Spark

The human contribution to the miracle of life around us is obvious: We hit upon new ideas, on the fly, all the time, and we have been performing this magic for, at the very least, 50,000 years.

We did not make galaxies. We did not make life. We did not make viruses, the sun, DNA, or the chemical bond.

But we do make new ideas—lots and lots of them. They arise constantly in human minds, and sometimes tumble out of our minds to influence other minds and change the world. We have creative insight and we recognize new possibilities. Our new ideas are not fixed instincts—like a beaver's instinct for building a dam or a bat's instinct for echolocating and ingesting an insect. We have such instincts, certainly, but they are not the subject of this book. The subject is our amazing ability to come up with new ideas that go far beyond our local situations.

When we come up with a new idea, we can carry it with us and share it with other people. When someone teaches us a new idea—through learning that goes well beyond instinct—we can do the same: We can carry it with us and share it with others. We use these new ideas to make new sense of the world and to make new sense of each other. We can use these new ideas to make yet newer ideas, and then we can use those newer ideas to make even newer ideas: We can have an idea that builds upon an idea that was built upon an idea that was built upon an idea . . .

Our new ideas sometimes seem to come to consciousness fully formed, at a speed that makes biological evolution look as if it is standing still, or even as if it is going backward. We all know that some of these ideas are superior to our old, deep instincts, which remain powerfully with us. We can have ideas that our ancestors 10,000 years ago did not have. We can have ideas that our parents did not have. Every child knows this. We can have ideas that even we did not have, indeed that nobody had, just yesterday. The human pace of creativity completely outstrips any process of evolutionary change in the descent of any species, even those that breed fast.

We are the origin of new ideas. This is why we have human culture, so various and powerful and quick. Each of us is born with this spark for creating and understanding new ideas. But where exactly do new ideas come from?

The claim of this book is that the human spark comes from our advanced ability to *blend* ideas to make *new* ideas. Blending is the origin of ideas. If you have not heard of blending, that is not a surprise: The first full presentation of research on blending appeared only 10 years ago, in *The Way We Think,* a book which Gilles Fauconnier and I wrote.[1] Blending, I claim, is the big lever of the cognitively modern human mind. This is a controversial claim, but I think it is true. More important, I think it is an idea anybody will want to know about. The blending hypothesis is, to my mind, the best scientific hypothesis we have for the special powers of the cognitively human mind, for the origin of ideas. I will lay out evidence, questions, challenges, and possibilities as we go along. You be the judge.

I emphatically do not mean that everything in human thought is blending or that blending is a great leap. On the contrary, blending depends on all the mental and bodily abilities that came before it, and relative to that great suite of abilities, it is small, perhaps even tiny. Life proceeded superbly before the evolution of advanced blending, and could have done very well, thank you, without it. But sometimes a small step makes all the difference. Sometimes a small difference in causes makes a huge difference in effects, and that is what happened, I propose, when we evolved the capacity for advanced blending. Most of the way we think existed before the rise of advanced blending, but once advanced blending arose, it touched and altered almost everything that preceded it. The way we think now is not a linear sum of everything that preceded advanced blending plus a separate, additional process of blending. Now, for us, advanced blending and the ways of thought that preceded it are inseparable.

I think of the human brain as constantly trying to blend different things, unconsciously. Every human brain is making many attempts to blend at every moment. Yours is doing so right now. Any two things activated simultaneously in the mind are candidates for blending. Most of these attempts fail, I imagine, almost immediately, because no good blend arises, or if it does arise, it attaches to no purpose, and so is allowed to pop, like a transitory bubble. Relatively few attempts at blending succeed, and almost none of those ever enter consciousness.

Almost all blending happens below the level of consciousness. We almost never see blending at work, and it is hard for us to see it. The reason for the invisibility of blending is simple: The human mind is not built to look into the human mind. To look at blending is unnatural, perverse, weird. To look at it, we must trick powers of mind that were meant for other jobs into looking at what they were not built to look at.

To see the human spark, we will need to take a journey through some territory that we know well at the unconscious level but poorly at the conscious level. This may seem like a strange thing to say. How is it possible that we would not know our own minds? When we pick up a book on a technical subject—like income taxes or algebraic topology—we expect it to be difficult to follow. Yet we are in the grip of the illusion that we know our own minds and know how we think, and so we expect any book about the human mind to be simple and easy to understand. This is the biggest barrier to understanding the human mind. The one thing the mind is least equipped to understand is itself. The one thing the mind is least equipped to explain is itself.

On our journey to understand the origin of ideas, we will see terrain that will strike us as both familiar and alien. We will learn that people do a great deal more than abstract from perceptions or make connections between ideas. Instead, people *blend* what they already know and thereby create new, tractable ideas. (I have not yet said what a blend is, but we are barely a thousand words into this book, and I will say what blending is in just 1 second.) We will see that blends are very handy for thinking: They are small enough and tight enough to be carried within the limits of our minds, and they can be expanded as needed later on to help us think about things we otherwise could not grasp.

Blends are all around us. We make them and remake them all the time. Very young children are geniuses at blending, and their favorite stories—*The Runaway Bunny, The Cat in the Hat, Harold and the Purple Crayon*—contain blend after spectacular blend, and children have no trouble understanding and even extending these blends on the fly. The same is true for *The Lord of the Rings,* Greek and Norse mythology, Superman and Spiderman. It is not just that these stories have a blend or two, but rather that they could not begin to get off the ground without blending. For the most part, blends make up our ideas. This is true in science, in mathematics, and in our understanding of each other. It is true of parenthood and childhood, of law and economics, and of almost anything else we want to think about. If I am right, then the job of this book is to provide a field guide to our most basic human world, a world that in one sense we know but in another sense we do not recognize at all.

Let's start with an example, something in the real world—a *stockbroker*. This is a very common idea. It belongs to a little mental package, a stereotyped bundle of ideas, sometimes called a "mental frame," or just a "frame."[2] We have a mental package for buying and selling, and a more limited mental package for the special case of buying and selling securities, particularly stocks and bonds. In that mental package, that little frame for buying and selling securities, there are roles for the buyer, the seller, what is sold, and the broker who arranges the transaction. When someone says, "I have to call my stockbroker," everyone can activate the appropriate package, the appropriate bundle of related elements. When someone says that sentence, we imagine, unless we are told or have reason to believe otherwise, that the telephone call is about *buying and selling securities*. Nobody needs to explain that the call is about buying and selling, because the word "stockbroker" calls up that little mental package. To understand "I have to call my stockbroker," we activate information from that frame to build a small mental array containing the speaker, the phone call, and the broker. These mental arrays are often called "mental spaces," a term invented by Gilles Fauconnier.[3]

So suppose someone says, "Luke is a stockbroker." We can take this as a prompt to build a little mental space, which has a man named "Luke," the role *stockbroker,* and a relation between them. The relation between them is obvious: Luke is a stockbroker.

Actually, the mental space in which Luke is a stockbroker arises from the simplest form of blending, one we never even recognize as a blend: We take one mental space with Luke and another mental space with the role for *stockbroker,* and make a blend in which Luke is a stockbroker. *Stockbroker* is a familiar frame-element, and Luke is just the kind of thing to which the role *stockbroker* naturally applies. So now we have a little blend in which Luke is a stockbroker.

This kind of framing may be possible to an extent for other species. For example, although other species cannot achieve the idea of a *stockbroker,* nonetheless it is not implausible that dogs have some basic mental frames— like *playing fetch*—which they can use for some simple blending. For example, they might be able to blend different people with the role of "person who throws the ball in playing fetch."

And yet, this simple blending can become impressive fast. If we hear, "Luke is a stockbroker and a jazz guitarist," then we are blending Luke with two different frames, both of which are built to apply to people, but we might start to develop some interesting new ideas in the blend of what kind of stockbroker is also a jazz guitarist, and we might come to conclusions about whether we would like Luke the stockbroker-jazz-guitarist to manage our securities.

"Luke is a stockbroker. He is my brother-in-law." These two sentences prompt us to activate not just the mental space for "Luke is a stockbroker" but also another mental space, which contains *I,* the speaker. We build relations between the space with the speaker and the space with Luke. To build these two mental spaces, and the relations between them, we need to draw on the mental frame of *kinship* and its relation *brother-in-law,* which connects three people. One of the things we know, once we have built these relations, is that either I am married to Luke's sibling or Luke is married to my sibling. This knowledge comes from the mental frame for *kinship* and its unspoken structure.

Mental spaces are sewn together in what we might think of as a mental web. A mental web has mental spaces and connections between them, and we build more mental spaces and more connections as we think about something. For example, "My brother-in-law, the stockbroker, and his family will be traveling from San Francisco to Cleveland for Thanksgiving for a massive family reunion, and we need to learn the time of their arrival so that we can drive down to pick them up" will prompt for many mental spaces. There might be one mental space in which I drive my car through complicated holiday traffic, another in which I stop at the appropriate gate at the arrival deck of Cleveland Hopkins International Airport, and so on. Typically, we cannot hold all these spaces equally active simultaneously in mind. As we think, we focus on one or another mental space in the mental web at a time. The mental spaces that we have activated recently will remain latent, which is to say, easier to activate.

A mental web will have many conceptual connections between its mental spaces. For example, in the mental web about my picking up my brother-in-law and his family at the airport for the massive family reunion, there will be an element in several of those mental spaces corresponding to *I,* and all of those elements in all of those mental spaces will be connected by *identity* relations. The pickup at the airport is connected by a *time* connector to the Thanksgiving feast so that the pickup happens before the Thanksgiving feast. But the pickup is also connected by a *time* connector to the mental space for the speaker in the moment of speaking, so that the pickup happens later than the moment of speaking. The mental space for the pickup at the airport is connected by a *space* connector to the home where the Thanksgiving feast is held in the vast dining room, so that we understand that the airport is distant from the home.

Now comes the crucial step for the origin of ideas, and the focus of this book. Here is the point that will carry us from here to the last sentence: We can *blend* mental spaces in a mental web in highly creative ways.

A *blend* is a mental space. It results from the mental act of *blending* other mental spaces in a mental web. The blend is not an abstraction, or an analogy, or anything else already named and recognized in common sense. A *blend* is a new mental space that contains some elements from different mental spaces in a mental web but that develops new meaning of its own that is not drawn from those spaces. This new meaning emerges in the blend. For example, suppose I say, "My brother-in-law, the stockbroker, lives in San Francisco. The stock market opens on the East Coast at 9:30 a.m., when it is only 6:30 a.m. on the West Coast. So my brother-in-law must awaken every weekday at about 5 in the morning if he is going to be sufficiently alert to start serious and risky work at 6:30 a.m. If I were my brother-in-law, I would be miserable." Take that last sentence. It asks us to *blend* me and my brother-in-law. To understand the passage, we need a mental space that has me and a mental space that has my brother-in-law, and we need to *blend* those spaces. The result, in the blend, is a man imbued with some of what we think about me and some of what we think about my brother-in-law, but only some in each case. In the blend, I am my brother-in-law, in a way: There is an element in the blend that has my personal identity, but no longer my job. It has my emotions, but my brother-in-law's competence and business activity. This new idea of the blended man is not available from any other space in the mental web. It is unique to the blend. There is a new idea here, one that emerges only in the blend. I-am-my-brother-in-law is a new idea, and a very complicated one.

We have just seen the origin of a new idea. This blend has many elements and properties that are not available from other spaces in the mental web. In the mental spaces that have the brother-in-law (living in San Francisco, arising at 5 a.m., and so on), he is not miserable; quite the contrary. In the mental space that has me, I am not miserable; quite the contrary. But in the blend, there is a person who is miserable. This person and his misery emerge in the blend.

Elements and relations are projected to the blend from the other mental spaces upon which the blend draws. There are many words to describe these projections: "gifts," "offers," "loans," "endowments," "copies," "booty," ... Whatever we call them, they are always *partial* or rather *selective*. For example, in the case of "If I were my brother-in-law, I would be miserable," we project to the blend the speaker, but only a small part of what we know about the speaker. We do not project the speaker's current employment, for example, because then the speaker could not be a stockbroker. We do not project the speaker's currently living in Cleveland. We project from the mental space with the stockbroker brother-in-law the role *stockbroker* and perhaps even *living in San Francisco and accordingly rising every weekday at 5 a.m.,* but not of course the physical appearance of the brother-in-law, or his family relations, and so on. Otherwise, in the blend, I would have to be my own brother-in-law, and that's taboo. We might project his lodging to the blend, but then again, we might not, and this variation in projection shows that what we project to the blend is mostly left up to members of the conversation as they explore new ideas. People often try out different projections from the same mental spaces, trying to find a good blend. Disagreements and misunderstandings arise. Blends are sometimes hotly contested in culture, as we see in the current legal wrangling over how to conceive of the blend *intellectual property,* which, at last count, was the subject of over 5,000 court cases.

In the I-am-my-brother-in-law blend, there is a person who is a stockbroker and is miserable. In no other space is it true that anyone is miserable. The misery emerges in the blend. It is new stuff. The new stuff arises as a consequence of making the blend. Crucially, there is also new stuff in the mental web outside of the blend. For example, once we have the blend, then we think of the speaker in his own actual life as averse to rising early. This is new stuff we build for the speaker in his own reality that we did not have in those mental spaces before we made the mental blend. We build this aversion for the speaker as a consequence of what we learned by building the blend. There is also new stuff in the connection between the speaker in his mental spaces outside the blend and the stockbroker in his mental spaces outside the blend, namely a disanalogy connection between them. Of course, there always were disanalogies between them in the mental web: The brother-in-law lived in San Francisco but the speaker presumably lived somewhere else, like Cleveland; the brother-in-law was a stockbroker but presumably the speaker was not; and so on. But now there is a *new, emergent* disanalogy connection between these mental spaces, having to do with personal preference and disposition: The stockbroker-brother-in-law likes rising early and I hate it. It could have been different, and would have been different if the sentence had been, "If I were a stockbroker, like my brother-in-law, who lives in San Francisco and so must rise at 5 a.m., I would be happy." As we will see, when we project what we have built in the blend back to mental spaces outside the blend and to connections in the mental web, we do not always project exactly what has arisen in the blend.

Some bundles of thought are tractable and manageable by the human mind. They are at human scale. Other bundles of thought are not tractable, because we cannot wrap our minds around them easily all at once. Most mental webs would be utterly intractable for us to grasp except that we can make a human-scale blend, drawing on different mental spaces in the web. The mental web is not at human scale, but the blend is, and so the blend gives us a way to think about the mental web. The blend gives us a handy, tractable thing to think about. It helps us access, organize, manipulate, and adjust the mental web that the blend serves. For example, in the vast mental web of thinking about life and possibilities, I can have a little blend in which I actually am a stockbroker, going through the motions and being miserable, and since this is something I want to avoid in life, the blend is useful to me. The blend in this case is a human-scale mental simulation. I can now do my best to steer clear of both it and anything like it.

A blend is not a small abstraction of the mental spaces it blends and is not a partial cut-and-paste assembly, either, because it contains new stuff, new ideas. It is a tight, packed little compression. It contains much less information than the full mental web it serves. From it, we can reach up to manage and work on the rest of the vast mental web.

One way to get a feel for the idea of a tight, compressed blend is to think of a map, not one on paper, but a map held in the mind. I have available to me from memory little maps of various Metro systems in the world: Washington, DC; Paris; London; Oslo; Rome; Cleveland; and the San Francisco Bay Area. They are very partial. My mental map for the Metro in Washington, DC, for example (I have not cheated by looking it up on the Internet), includes the fact that there is a red line shaped something like a U and running through Metro Center, an east-west orange line that begins in Virginia, and a blue line and a yellow line that both run past National Airport, with the blue line heading up to Rosslyn in Virginia and the yellow line diving across the Potomac River toward L'Enfant Plaza. From the little bit in that mental map, I can expand mentally to think about a trip in Washington, DC.

That little compressed blend of the DC Metro leaves out very many things in the mental web it serves, and it also has some new structure of its own not found in the rest of the mental web it serves. For example, in the blend, I can actually see the entire extent of a particular Metro line, like the red line, and each line is in fact a color, and different lines are different colors, with separate geography for each line even though I know (in the mental web) that in some locations, trains serving different "lines" use the same physical tracks. My mental map also has special geographical circles for the transfer stations. None of that is true in reality, and perhaps none of the mental spaces other than the blend has quite those features. The mental map for the Metro is a compressed blend, something at human scale, something I can think about and wrap my mind around easily. Using it, I can begin to draw inferences, connecting up mental spaces far removed from that mental map of the Metro system but indispensable to my thinking about an actual trip. The mental map of the Metro I can actually call up on the fly is very partial, very tight, but it gets me going. It offers connections to a vast mental web I can build by expanding from the blend. Best of all, I can carry all these little tight blends, these compressions, around with me in my mind, wake them up, and start to expand them.

We use compressed, tight, tractable blends to help us think about larger mental webs. We might say that we carry small, compressed blends with us mentally, and *unpack* or *expand* them as needed to connect up to what we need to think about. For example, the pithy, compressed little blend with the miserable stockbroker can be used to help the speaker think about any job in a time zone other than the Eastern time zone (GMT −5) and lead him to be vigilant for downsides. Enlightened by the blend, and expanding from it, he might now, any time he is offered a new consulting job, become cautious about problems that might arise from the need to coordinate across multiple time zones. He might study the offer closely in order to learn what demands the new job might impose upon him that stem from the fact that people in other time zones have different sleeping patterns. Anybody who does a lot of videoconferencing to coordinate research groups will understand immediately that the difficulties are no longer a matter of technology; the difficulties come from conflicts in people's daily rhythm of sleep and work.

I offer the example of the I-am-my-brother-in-law-the-stockbroker blend to launch us, but it is dangerous to generalize from it more than a little. Although the me-as-my-brother-in-law example is clearly a blend, and even leaps out at us as a blend, essentially all blending is invisible to consciousness and does not look at first like blending. The counterfactual "If I were…" is only one linguistic prompt for blending. There are many prompts like it, of various kinds. In fact, blending is a mental act and does not require any communication, or signals, or language. On the contrary, our ability for full human language is a product of our ability for blending. Also, blends do not have to be counterfactual, hypothetical, false, or fictional. On the contrary, many blends constitute what we feel to be utter fact, ground truth, and common sense. We will see several such blends in the following chapters.

Now for the map of coming attractions:

In chapter 2, "Catch a Fire," we will see in more detail what a blend is and how it arises, with examples.

In chapter 3, "The Idea of *You*," we will see ways in which blending makes it possible for us to have ideas about other people, about how to work with them, and about how to interact with them.

In chapter 4, "The Idea of *I*," we will see ways in which blending makes it possible for us to have ideas about *ourselves.* This may seem to be a topic that needs no discussion. But even a few seconds' reflection will make it clear that it is miraculous that we can have an idea of the self that stretches far over time, space, and causation. Who are you? That's not such an easy question. It is one of the most challenging open questions in science. We spend much of our lives thinking about it.

In chapter 5, "Forbidden Ideas," we will see some of the most complicated results of blending, wherein two quite different complex *entire stories* that conflict very strongly with each other on basic structure are blended to create powerful and memorable new ideas.

In chapter 6, "Artful Ideas," we will see some standard and powerful patterns of how we blend visual images, especially in art and film.

In chapter 7, "Vast Ideas," we will confront the age-old question: How can people, who live in the here-and-now, have vast ideas that run over enormous expanses of time, space, causation, and agency? The subject of this chapter is not biological instincts that have long-range consequences—every mammal has those—but, instead, active new ideas that people put together on the fly to understand ranges of information no other animal is even remotely able to handle.

In chapter 8, "Tight Ideas," we will see some patterns of blending that produce tight, human-scale ideas, just the kinds our minds are built for.

In chapter 9, "Recurring Ideas," we will study the general blending pattern that creates a *cycle* in the blend, and investigate which kinds of cycle blends are congenial to the way we think.

In chapter 10, "Future Ideas," we will consider opportunities for future work.

Time to look at the origin of ideas.

2

Catch a Fire

The Lionman

To illustrate the origin of ideas and the antiquity of blending, let's start with an unforgettable example from archaeology—the lionman. The lionman is a 32,000-year-old ivory figurine found in 1939, smashed to bits in a cave in southern Germany. When it was found, it did not look like a lionman, and its shards lay neglected for decades. But since its full reassembly in 1998, scientists have pointed to this figurine as evidence that creative human culture came from a major evolutionary change, an expansion in "working memory."[1] Is there such a thing as "working memory"? Most researchers think so. There are debates over what it involves, but it is thought to be a mental system that lets us hold transitory information active in the mind while we work on it. The idea that researchers have put forward of this major evolutionary change is this: If there was an expansion of working memory in our ancestors several tens of thousands of years ago, then they would have been able to hold more concepts simultaneously active in mind, concepts like *lion* and *man*. The idea is that the artist needed to do that in order to be able to come up with the idea of a *lionman*.

Perhaps the lionman is a result of expanded working memory. Perhaps this figurine is evidence of a moment when our ancestors could at last hold active in mind both *lion* and *man*. But that is a little hard to swallow, because it is difficult to believe that earlier people could not have thought of a lion attacking a man, which all by itself holds both *lion* and *man* in mind, in a little emotion-packed story. Be that as it may, what the figurine of the lionman most clearly shows us is the mental ability to *blend* different concepts: *Lion* and *man* are not merely held in mind at the same time; they are also used to create a new, blended concept, a *lionman*, which is neither a lion nor a man, exactly.

As David Brooks says,

> Any child can say "I am a tiger"—pretend to be a tiger. It seems so elementary. But in fact it is phenomenally complicated to take a concept *I* and a concept *tiger* and blend them together. But this is the source of innovation. What Picasso did, for example, was take the concept *Western Art* and the concept *African Masks* and blend them together; not only the geometry, but the moral systems entailed in them.[2]

The origin of new ideas through blending is my subject. What is the human spark? When we look at it, this simple question turns into two hard questions: (1) What is the spark that every newborn has that lets it create and understand a flood of ideas that are new to its mind? (2) What happened in the evolutionary descent of people that gave us this human spark? Why are we so good at coming up with new ideas? Why are we so good at carrying new ideas with us mentally, to awaken and deploy in new situations?

One thing is clear: We all have the human spark now. And in our evolutionary descent, not necessarily at a single stroke, our ancestors acquired that human spark. Once they did, they had the ability to come up with new ideas on the fly. In the course of human culture since then, we have used that spark to invent new things and pass them on. It is how we live every second.

It's really too bad that we do not have a time machine to carry us back to look at people and brains 50,000 years ago. Those people and their brains are utterly lost to us. They do not survive at all in the archaeological record. If I had a time machine, I know right where I would take it: 50,000 years ago.

In my view, if we had a time machine and could go back 50,000 years and pick up a newborn baby and fly it right here, right now, it would grow up just like us, and we would never know the difference. It would fit right in—cognitively, at least. It is true that there have been some evolutionary changes in the last 50,000 years (sickle cell condition, relative ability to bind oxygen, relative ability to metabolize alcohol, relative presence of melanin in the skin, ability to metabolize lactose, maybe differential attention to the environment among Northern tribes). None of these, however, is a cognitive change. So my guess is that babies today and 50,000 years ago could do advanced blending, in the same ways. This hypothesis could be wrong, and we have no time machine to let us check it, but it seems to me on the available evidence to be the most likely guess.

People can put together mental blends that contain new ideas. The idea of the *lionman*, for example, is a blend of *lion* and *man*. The blend calls upon the idea of *lion* and the idea of *man*. Each of these is an "input mental space" that the blend uses. We could call them "inputs" or "contributors" or "donors" or "ingredients" or use a range of other words, and any of these words is probably as good as any other. The blend takes parts of each of these input mental spaces, but only parts, and puts them together into a single new idea, a simple, tight idea that fits the mind nicely. The *mental web* for this thinking contains a mental space for *lion,* a mental space for *man,* and a mental space for their blend, the *lionman.* The *lionman* has elements that belong to neither *lion* nor *man.* We can carry that blend with us, hold it in mind, and use it to think about our identity and our place in the world.

Vast Ideas in Here-and-Now Minds

Human thought stretches across vast expanses of time, space, causation, and agency. Think of the idea of a *lionman.* People are one sort of thing, and there are many of them, spread out over the land. Lions are another sort of thing, and there are, or were, many of them, spread out over the land. Human thought is able to range over all those things, to see connections across them, and to blend them, as we see in the *lionman.* The world contains more lions and men than we can count or hold in working memory, but in the blend there is just one thing, something we can wrap our minds around all at once. Making the blend of the *lionman* gives us *one thing.*

This one thing, this *lionman,* does not replace the vast mental web of all the people we can think about and all the lions we can think about. Instead, it gives us a new idea, a tight, manageable idea, and we can use it to help us think about the vast, intractable, uncongenial mental web it serves, with all those people and all those lions. We can use it to help us hold onto the vast mental web while we work on this bit or that bit. Focused on the *lionman,* our thinking can arc across the vast scope of all people and all lions, without actually having to think about them all at the same time. This vast scope is common in human thought. We appear to be the only species that has it. Again, I am not talking about instincts. Evolution can build an instinct that has consequences across time, space, causation, and agency—instincts like lust and hunger. I am instead talking about *thinking* at vast scale.

Consider, for example, ideas in law. Although the way people interact with each other is affected by our instincts, the complexity of our systems of law goes far beyond instinct, and these complex systems of law have been with us for only a few thousand years. Law depends on far-reaching ideas. Let us consider a few. A statutory law is meant to apply across vast ranges of time, space, causation, and agency. Legislators assess similar situations that are distributed over time and space and that involve many different causes and agents, and they invent laws—statutes—that are meant to influence future situations, way down the road, mostly unforeseen. Judges and juries establish case law, common law, on the basis of past complex events, and the laws so established, although not enshrined in statutes, are meant to apply across future complex events. A contract stretches across time, space, causation, and agents. Testimony from witnesses stretches across memories and inferences. Judges and juries form opinions and determinations and make rulings or findings about the reliability and accuracy of testimony concerning past events. These judges and juries reach conclusions and make findings about causality that stretch over vast expanses.

Lots of animals can have specific, individual memories—that is, thoughts not entirely bound to the time and situation in which the animal finds itself. But human thought goes incomparably beyond such pinpoint memories in its scope. We can conceive of the entire 20-year history of a friend we saw most recently 20 years ago. We can think of the progress of democracy since the eighteenth century. We can think of the future of democracy over the next century. We can imagine alternative futures for the next century.

Far-reaching concepts are indispensable for our lives. Dogs, ferrets, frogs, and ravens have instincts, but they do not invent far-reaching new ideas. What makes far-reaching concepts possible in the first place is our ability to blend. Blending lets us create a tractable new idea that serves to organize a vast mental web and its far-reaching concepts.

Limited Human Brains

To achieve big ideas and concepts—which stretch across vast ranges of time, space, causation, and agency—we must use advanced mental operations, like *blending*. The results are not perfect; our challenges in trying to put together big ideas, and our failures, are well known.[3] The challenges arise from the fact that we are trying to use here-and-now biological processes, which is all we have, to produce and hold big ideas that go sweepingly beyond our here-and-now biological processes. Our biology is always local and transient. As Sir Charles Sherrington famously expressed it over a century ago, the brain and the central nervous system are an "enchanted loom" where "millions of flashing shuttles weave a *dissolving* pattern, always a meaningful pattern, though *never an abiding one*."[4]

Here-and-now is all we have. It may seem as if memory provides there-and-then to supplement here-and-now, but that is an illusion. Memory does not actually produce an intersection of past times and the present time, although it seems to us as if it does. Past times and conditions are not here now and cannot be here now. Memories are of course nothing but here-and-now biological events. We do not have anything like videocamera memories—far from it. We do not have a mental crystal ball with which to see the future. We do not have a mental time machine to range forward and back. It is true that we use the world around us to help us think and remember, and that we even manufacture items to help us do so—items such as writing and pictures—but still, all we have with which to make sense of these items is our present, here-and-now biological processes.

Thought is biologically here and now. That is not to be confused with a separate question, the question of whether thought is "internal" or "external" or both. We don't care about that question in this book. The cartoon of the "internal" view is that thought is isolated computation, running everything on its own—a lone mind thinking inside itself, a poet in a garret, a brain in a vat, a computer in the night. The cartoon of the "external" view is that there are no truly internal thoughts because there is no dividing line at all between what is in the mind and what is outside the mind. But this book is not about the internal versus external debate.

There is no doubt that human thought is built for the wild, built to work in context, exploiting and relying upon whatever conditions we inhabit. We need what is external. Vision does not work without light from the world. We cannot use our knowledge about sundials to tell time unless we can find a real sundial, in the world, and then pay attention to what the sun is actually doing with the actual sundial. We are built to think with each other, and all those other people with whom we do our thinking are external to our nervous system and our skin. People have always used what is readily available, such as the night sky, and, more than that, they have manufactured ranges of artifacts in the world upon which to rely: writing, calendars, computers, the Internet.

Where is the "thinking" occurring? That question is definitional: It all depends upon how you want to define "thinking," and we can define "thinking" any way we like. Do you take the view that the sundial's work or the night sky's work or the work done by the person you are talking to is part of your thinking? Cool. No matter, all we have for interpreting and exploiting those "external" events and relying on them is the here-and-now biology of our body. We can get a lot of help, but it is all in the category of help.

The research question we are considering in this book is not a definitional question, like the question of internal versus external thought. Instead, the research question is: "What processes are at work and how do they operate?" How can people use local biological processes to handle vast ideas that span great ranges of time, space, causation, and agency, ideas that are not at all restricted to the local scene? How can there be law, or any large ideas that stretch over time, space, causation, and agency? How do we fit the big world into the human mind?

I offer the answer that blending, the origin of ideas, lets us fit the big world into the human mind by making new, tight, manageable ideas that we can exploit, like little mental tools, to help us deal with and manage the big world. The blend is a new idea with newly created parts, and it fits our minds, and we use it to grasp big mental webs. Blending lets us create I-am-my-brother-in-law. Blending lets us create the *lionman*. There is no really good term to describe a blend—it is a platform upon which to stand, an anchor for a vast web of thought, a wrangler on a big mental ranch, a rich package that can be unpacked, a portable mental gem, a touchstone, a...bunch of jargon. There are no words for it, so I have picked one that I hope is suggestive: "blend." It's just a word. Labels are unimportant. What we want to know are the *processes* that go into the origin of ideas, and that is what this book is about.

Thanks to blending, we do not need to hold an entire mental web active all at the same time. The power of blending is three-fold: (1) blending lets us create new ideas in the blend that are congenial to our minds—it is the origin of ideas; (2) a blend gives us a handy tool for working on the vast mental web it serves; (3) the blend is small enough to be carried around mentally and to be expanded to connect to our current situations.

Now for some serious examples and serious analysis.

What Is Blending?

Blending jumps out when we look at arresting and pyrotechnic monsters, gods, chimera, and therianthropes like the lionman. Karl Duncker,[5] who did not call it a "blend," provided a spectacular and arresting example of a blend in "the Riddle of the Buddhist Monk's Travel," later analyzed by Arthur Koestler.

A Buddhist monk begins at dawn one day walking up a mountain, reaches the top at sunset, meditates at the top overnight until, at dawn, he begins to walk back to the foot of the mountain, which he reaches at sunset. Make no assumptions about his starting or stopping or about his pace during the trips. Riddle: is there a place on the path that the monk occupies at the same hour of the day on the two trips? [6]

The riddle is challenging because it asks us to draw inferences over a mental web involving dynamic events. It reaches over time and space. Many people have trouble wrapping their minds around the riddle. That's why it is a riddle. But we can draw the right inference if we blend the monk's ascent with his descent. In the mental theater of your imagination, superimpose the ascent and the descent. Run those internal movies at the same time, on the same screen, so that it looks as if there are two monks moving on the same path. This is a great compression of time.

In imagination, we have the ascent and the descent. But now we have projected from them to a third, "blended" scene. In this imaginary scene, at dawn, the monk is at two positions: One monk is at the bottom of the path, and another monk, who is identical to the first, is at the summit. So the monk in the ascent and the monk in the descent are blended to identity, but not to uniqueness: There are two monks, not one, even though in the mental space for the ascent, and in the mental space for the descent, there is always, of course, only one unique specific monk. In the blend, by dusk, each monk has traveled to the opposite position. Of course, the monk must meet himself somewhere during the day. That location on the path, where the monk meets himself, corresponds to the same spot on the path in the ascent and the descent, and to the same time of day during the ascent and the descent. It is a point where the monk is located at the same time of day during the two separate days. The riddle is solved. Mathematical proofs are easy to adduce, and in fact, they all use blending![7]

It is natural to wonder whether the existence or nonexistence of the point the monk occupies at the same hour of the day on the two successive days depends on how the monk moves, that is, at what speed he moves at any time, or whether he stops or backtracks or whatnot. But in the blend, no matter how the two monks move, so long as they start at dawn, end at dusk, and traverse the path without leaving it, the monks must always cross, or meet, somewhere, at least once, and that meeting point will be the location that the monk occupies at the same hour of the day on the two successive days. We do not know what point it will be, but we know that there must be at least one such point.

"The Buddhist Monk" has become a chestnut of blending research. It is important to see that the projection from the ascent and the descent to the two-monk blend is partial: We do not project from the ascent and descent the date, for example, or our knowledge that a person can be in only one place at one time. It is equally important to see that the blend has all-important new stuff: The meeting, for example, is not in the ascent or the descent.

These unforgettable examples of blending—*lionmen* and Buddhist Monks—help get the discussion rolling. They make blending visible, at least. But they mislead us if we end up thinking that blends are always visible, clever, and unforgettable. Everybody likes a figurine or a riddle, but no one thinks a figurine or a riddle is essential to life. Nothing goofy seems fundamental. These spectacular blends can mislead us into thinking that blending is rare, obvious, and striking, the kind of thing we find in entertainment, or in a museum. But, on the contrary, blending is not a curiosity. It is a common, everyday process indispensable to the most routine workings of the modern human mind. Blending is not something special or costly. Blending operates almost entirely below the horizon of consciousness. We usually never detect the process of blending and typically do not recognize its products as blends. Very rarely, the scientist can drag a small part of blending onstage, where we can actually see it. But the mind is not made for looking into the mind, and as a result, we see blending only infrequently, and poorly.

The figurine of the lionman, for example, leads us to focus on the concepts *lion* and *man,* and their selective blend into the idea of a *lionman.* If we do not look closely, that is all we will see, even though much more blending runs invisibly through the mental web. Once we think about it, it is clear that the lionman depends on several ideas that we had not picked out. To think about the figurine, we also must have in mind the idea of a piece of *ivory* that is 28 centimeters high. We must also have in mind the idea of human manufacture, specifically *carving.* Our concept of the actual figurine involves ivory, an act of carving, a span of 32,000 years, a height of 28 centimeters, and so on. Obviously, lions and men are not 28 centimeters tall or made out of ivory. Obviously, neither lions nor men come into existence through carving. Obviously, men and lions are dynamic, but the figurine is permanently static. The lionman is actually an inert solid object we can hold in our hand. It has no life or death. It does not know it is a lionman.

Our idea of the figurine and our idea of the *lionman* are far from being the same. We must hold them both in mind. A *lionman* is not a figurine. A *lionman* might be large, powerful, full of motion, flesh and blood, scary, wise, or threatening. Our idea of the figurine itself has none of these features.

Creating complicated mental webs of ideas like this, with many mental spaces and various blends, all related mentally to each other, is easy for us. Consider, for a moment, representations—sketches, photographs, sculptures. All representation involves blending the idea of the representational medium (such as *ivory*) and the represented concepts (such as *lionman*). Blending like this happens not only in the case of the lionman but also in the case of simple sketches like stick figures in the sand. Making stick figures in the sand is a simple act for us. It is the easiest thing in the world. Using the stick to make the sketch goes without saying. Yet, remarkably, making such pictures seems to have been impossible for the human mind until very recently in evolutionary time, maybe 50,000 to 100,000 years ago or so, depending on how one interprets some ambiguous artifacts that are dated to a time slightly prior to the Upper Paleolithic.

It is stunning that the archaeological record before the Upper Paleolithic provides no examples of sketches, pictures, figurines, or other iconic representations. Think of it. All over the world today, children perceive animals and objects in clouds, and people of all ages use twigs to sketch figures in the sand. Any person with a cognitively modern mind (jargon: that means any one of us whom we would take to be even close to normal) perceives figures in the clouds. Any person with a cognitively modern mind can sketch representational figures in the sand. A human being before the Upper Paleolithic with the mental ability for representation should have had no difficulty whatever actually carving a face in stone—a petroglyph. The tool needed has been around since at least the Oldowan toolkit, in the Lower Paleolithic Age, maybe 2.6 million years ago. And all along the way, over the course of maybe 2.55 million years, our ancestors, at a pace so astonishingly slow as to be unimaginable, eked out now and then a little advance: bifacial stone tools, composite tools that join stone points to wood shafts, heat-treated stone tools, and projectile tools. But none of these tools was even necessary for carving a petroglyph: A naturally-occurring rock edge would have served the purpose easily.

Everyone alive today has had the experience of seeing part of a face in natural stone—a boulder, a cliffside, a bank of a river. Imagine a cliffside or boulder with two natural indentations that look like eyes. Hop in the time machine and swirl back to somewhat before the Upper Paleolithic, where we see one of our bored ancestors with a stone tool in hand, standing in front of a boulder with two indentations that look like eyes. Why does he not while away his time by making a smiley face? He can do it just by carving a smile below the eyes. Nothing to it. Yet not a single instance of a representation of a face—or anything else—has been found in the entire archaeological record much prior to the era of the cave paintings in Europe. Even if such a representation is ultimately found, perhaps among the Blombos Cave artifacts in South Africa, it will date from perhaps a mere 100,000 years ago.[8] There are other sites, much more recent, with interesting and promising artifacts, such as Border Cave in South Africa, dating from about 44,000 years ago,

FIGURE 1 The Recency of Representation

showing a process of relatively quick change that might have begun as early as 53,000 years ago.[9] In any case, the fundamental question remains: How did we go from no representing *at all* to its being so easy? (See figure 1.)

One might object that even animals communicate with symbols, and that what the animals are doing should count as representation, so we should think that representation stretches way back, to the bees at least. No doubt, we may sometimes want to use the word "representation" in this sweeping way, to refer to even the kind of instinctive, nonconceptual activity bees perform in a "waggle" or "round" dance. We take these "dances" to be blends of the bees' bodily actions and geographical distance and direction in the bees' environment, and that is the point: *We* see it as a blend, as a representation. We can use our advanced blending ability to form an idea of what the bees are doing. But there is no evidence that the bees have any such idea. The bees themselves seem to have only a fixed, special-purpose, instinctive response behavior, instead of a general cognitive ability for advanced blending. It took no mental understanding by the bees for evolution to build such behavior into the bees. It took no apian culture. No scientist imagines that the bees think that they are using representations. No scientist imagines that the bees buzz around trying to come up with better representations. It takes an almost unimaginably long time for biological evolution to build something like a bee dance, and once it is built, it is relatively rigid. Human blending has no such limitations. Human blending operates in cultural time rather than evolutionary time. Blending can happen in one second, and be adjusted and transformed a few seconds later. For quick creativity, the human capacity for blending blows biological evolution out of the water. Blending raises thinking to an entirely new level. It is like introducing nuclear bombs to a tribe that barely knows how to make a proper fist.

To be sure, the capacity for blending is an evolutionary product. Once biological evolution hit upon making brains that could do advanced blending, people possessed the capacity to make new ideas on the fly, to invent and maintain culture. Cultural innovation, based on these evolutionary capacities, could then progress incomparably faster than biological evolution itself.

There are other cases in the animal world of fixed, instinctive, special-purpose behaviors that look to a person like blending, such as chase play,[10] in which conspecifics (jargon: it means "members of the same species") take on the roles of predator and prey for the purpose of training in predation. For example, a female jaguar and her offspring look as if they are pretending to be predator and prey. To people, it looks as if the animals are "practicing." It also seems to us that cats "practice" hunting when they "play" with a mouse. What these predators are doing is evolutionarily fit, but no scientist proposes that the animals share our full understanding that they are practicing. Cats do not seem to say to themselves, "Time to practice hunting if I want to keep my skills sharp! Today, I need to come up with a better practice routine, because it didn't work so well yesterday. What shall I change? After all, I want to keep my paw in so that later on at some unforeseen time, I won't get hungry!"

The hallmark of modern human cognition is the general, flexible ability to blend concepts that have fundamental clashes—*lion, man, ivory, flesh, birth, carving*. We do this widely across all our ideas, quickly, flexibly. This ability for blending runs across all our thinking. Compact blends do not replace the mental webs they serve. Instead, they give us tools that we can use, platforms where we can stand to reach up to manage, search, and manipulate those mental webs. The *lionman* is just one thing—an agent, with a form. This simple form can help us think about a vast web of connected ideas that might otherwise be mentally intractable for us.

The Cyclic Day

I have noted that striking examples like the *lionman* and the Buddhist Monk can mislead us into thinking that blending must be unusual and noticeable, instead of commonplace and below the horizon of observation. Let us look at one very common example. We will consider it again in more detail later. It is the *cyclic day*.[11]

In our experience, there is actually just one day and then another day and then another day and then another day, in a sequence that stretches out indefinitely, forward and backward. The days in that sequence are all quite different. They do not repeat. If we woke up today and it was exactly the same as yesterday because it was in fact the same day in every detail, we would be sure we had lost our minds. And then it would not even be the same day, because yesterday we did not think we had lost our minds. Day after day after day indefinitely, with all those differences between days, is too much to comprehend, too much to fit inside working memory, too much to carry around and manage. It is not mentally portable.

So we blend these different days into a conception of a cyclic *day*. We do this by using a general template for creating cyclic blends. As we will see later, this template is widely used across human thought.

There are analogies and disanalogies across the different days in our experience. The analogies are packed into one thing in the blend: the *day*. The disanalogies are packed into change for that thing: The day is *cyclic*; it *starts over* every dawn and *repeats*. It is important to recognize that the *cyclic day* blend is not just an abstraction. There is new stuff in the blend that is not in any of the individual days in the mental web to which the blend can be applied. Indeed, almost no blend consists exclusively of structure that is equally shared by all the mental spaces upon which the blend draws.

The *lionman* is not an abstraction of what is common to *lion* and *man*. On the contrary, some parts of it do not belong to *lion* and some parts of it do not belong to *man*. The riddle of the Buddhist Monk is not solved by abstracting what is common to the ascent and the descent: In the blend for the Buddhist Monk, we need both the ascent (which is not in the mental space for the descent) and the descent (which is not in the mental space for the ascent). Even more, each of these blends has new stuff—like the meeting, and the monk's being in two places at the same time—that is not in any of the input mental spaces, so surely the blend is not an abstraction of what is shared by all the input spaces.

For everyday blends like the *cyclic day*, we might need to look twice to recognize the new ideas that emerge in the blend, and to understand why the blend is not an abstraction. Still, once we look a little closer, it is easy to see the new ideas, and to understand why the blend is not an abstraction. For example, no one of the individual input days to the cyclic day blend is cyclic; no one of those individual input days repeats or starts over. But because of blending, all the days that have ever happened or will happen can be packed into a single idea, a tight, tractable, manageable, human-scale idea—the cyclic *day*, which *repeats*. Thinking of the cyclic day, we can say, "dawn is coming around *again*," or "It's time for my *morning* coffee" or "this park closes *at dusk*." We know how these words and concepts apply to the compact blend, and we can expand from that blend to any parts of the mental web that interest us, to any day at any time, and even to a tractable stretch of days. The cyclic day is a compact touchstone, a congenial blend for thinking about the vast sequence of days. This vast sequence of days is of course itself too big for working memory. The compact blend—the single *cyclic day*, a new idea—makes it possible for us to work with concepts of time that stretch far beyond what we would otherwise be able to manage.

Time for a vocabulary review. We have talked about *packing* and *unpacking* ideas. We could instead have talked of *compressing* and *expanding* ideas. A blend like the cyclic day is a compressed, packed, tight little idea. We can wrap our minds around it and carry it with us. It is at *human scale.* Here is a way to think about mental packing and unpacking, mental compression and expansion: When we travel to a foreign country, we cannot take with us our houses, our full wardrobe, our kitchen, our car, our scooter, the city we live in, our relatives and friends, all the connections we have established. Instead, we take what can be packed to human scale, for ready transport. We wear some clothes, festooned with small, human-scale items like mobile phones, pens, keys, wallets with money and identification cards, and iPods. We take glasses, a laptop computer or tablet, perhaps earplugs, and a rolling bag containing some alternative clothes, some tools, a sewing kit, a toiletry bag. If we were suddenly dropped down into the wilderness, most of this would be useless. But we do not drop down into the wilderness. We go to some other cultural environment where we can unpack our stuff to serve our needs. We expect that in that other environment, what we unpack will hook into the new situation, not only for the purpose of remembering the world we came from, but, more important, for the purpose of acting in the world we have joined. There will be water, somehow, somewhere, if only from a pool or a bottle, so we can use the toothbrush. There will be electric current, though perhaps not exactly the electric current we have at home, but no matter, the power brick we carry can hook up to ranges of voltages and frequencies. The power brick is a packed little tool, just right for our hands and our electronic devices, built to connect to various environments and to work within them.

Our packed, human-scale kit for travel must be designed for easy and effective unpacking. This is the main requirement. Our travel kit is not an archive or a museum or a display case. It is designed to be hooked into our surroundings. But this is a two-way street. We alter new environments by unpacking what we have carried and hooking into them; at the same time, what we unpack is changed by the new situations in which we deploy it. Our kit, as it is, hooks into new environments and enables us to operate there. When we are finished in that environment, we repack. But often the repacked kit, although similar to the one we left home with, is a little changed. It has a new item, or a replacement, or wear, or alteration in some of its elements. We might even repack our kit using a way of arranging the items in it that is not exactly the one we originally used. And off we go to the next country.

Our ideas work like that. We carry with us compressed, human-scale ideas—like the cyclic day. We bring them out when we need them, unpack them, and deploy them for help as we travel through life and situations. We carry our ability to expand them and connect them to mental webs. Some of the mental webs we build resemble mental webs we have built many times, but some are interestingly different. We operate with these webs in the moment. The effect goes both ways: We alter the moment by unpacking our ideas to hook up to what we are thinking about, but we also sometimes alter our blends a little when we unpack them, so that they will fit the new environment in useful ways. These alterations are only rarely deliberate, or even conscious. But as a result, we develop some new ideas. We repack everything and move on, but what we have repacked is not exactly identical to what we unpacked in the first place. Our ideas carry with them the vestiges of a lifetime of this packing and unpacking. Mental packing and unpacking makes mental travel possible.

I have given a sketch of human thought as always involving dynamic compression and expansion of ideas, always connecting elements up in mental webs and blends. This sketch differs from the usual picture of thinking as "retrieving" what you "have" and "using" it. In an earlier book,[12] I surveyed the scarcity of answers offered by cognitive science for explaining where ideas come from and how they change. For now, let's contrast the "pack, carry, unpack" view with the "retrieve and apply" view. On the "retrieve and apply" view, how would our ideas change? How would new ideas originate? The answer offered is that if we try to "retrieve" and "apply" an idea to the world but it fails, then we have negative feedback, and we adjust the idea. But this "feedback" view is a weak answer, for obvious reasons: (1) Many of our ideas are not about something that already exists in the world, something to which we are trying to apply our ideas. On the contrary, much of what exists in human culture was put there because *first* we had an idea and *then* we used that idea to guide us in manufacturing or establishing something new. Although it is true that we might have to adjust our idea of *telephone* or *Halloween* because of some negative feedback that arises from our experience of a particular telephone or a particular Halloween, that cannot be the explanation for how we got the idea of *telephone* or *Halloween* in the first place. (2) Negative feedback might tell us that something is wrong, but it doesn't tell us what to do about it. It does not tell us how to build a new idea. (3) Plenty of times, our idea worked just fine when we applied it, but then we came up with a new idea anyway. For example, the system of modal verbs in English (*shall, should, will, would, can, could, may, might, must,* and perhaps *have to, ought to…*) has changed over the centuries, but not because the system wasn't working, not because of negative feedback. If we were simply "retrieving" ideas of grammar we have, and "using" them, and they worked, then why would the modal system have changed?

With the "unpack, deploy, repack" view of thought, things look different. On that view, when we hear someone use a linguistic pattern, we unpack our compressed ideas of grammar so as to build a mental web that renders the expression intelligible, and then we repack from that mental web, and small differences in the mental web we constructed have a chance to be repacked into the knowledge we carry.

Blending lets us take diffuse *mental webs* that are not at *human scale* and *compress* them to ideas that are at human scale. The compressed idea is congenial to our minds, even though the diffuse mental web it serves may not be tractable for us without the blend. A compressed blend, at human scale, can then serve as the basis for yet another round of blending. The result is something like placing a stepping-stone where one can stand, and stepping to it, and then placing another stepping-stone farther on, and stepping to it, and so on up the hill. Blending allows ideas to bootstrap themselves. The result is that we can handle mental webs that are many removes away from what we are built to understand. Mental webs that were not originally at human scale can be drawn into human scale because the blend makes it easier.

Working from a blend that serves a mental web, we can manage, handle, connect to, and change the rest of the web. For example, we can carry the congenial, human-scale idea of the cyclic day with us, and expand it to hook up to the temporal dimension of something we are thinking about. If we read a religious text or science fiction story about some supernatural or technological power that lengthened or shortened a day, we can activate our idea of the cyclic day and scale it differently for that one day in the mental web. Similarly, once we have the blend for the *cyclic year,* we can make adjustments in the mental web: We can "add" a day during a leap year we are thinking about.

I am typing this paragraph aboard an international flight. Hundreds of people are packed into clothes with assorted technologies (belts, passports, pencils, eyeglasses). They are packed into seats. Beneath their seats are little packages, constantly being unpacked and repacked. In front of them are small back-of-the-seat pockets, with more packing and unpacking, some of it involving objects the passengers brought, some of it involving items provided by the airline. When we all packed ourselves in, each seat had a pillow, a packaged blanket, and an envelope (proudly announcing its recycled content) containing other packages, one holding a toothbrush and toothpaste, another holding a mask and ear plugs, another holding headphones, and so on, all labeled "for the long haul." The overhead compartments are full of varieties of luggage designed to be packed into overhead compartments of just that size. The compartments have little images instructing us on the most efficient disposition for each piece of luggage. Most of this luggage can be rolled into the airplane, and when that job is completed, the handle can be packed back into the luggage. There are baby bags of baby stuff, and there are baby beds, packed away in other compartments, which the flight attendants open so as to unpack and unfold the bed so the baby can sleep.

Because of advanced blending, we can make blending webs that let us understand movies (just as we can understand the little images in the overhead compartments instructing us in how to pack those compartments) and deal with the little screens packed all over the airplane, in the backs of seats. Rolling service carts, packed with food, packed inside locking chambers in the galleys, which have been packed into this airplane, are unpacked, rolled out, and the packed food extracted, so we passengers, packed in seats, can unpack the tray table on which to unpack the food so we can pack it into us. And while this is going on, we are involved in numerous social packings and unpackings—it's a routine characteristic of really long flights. Before long, we will all pack up, roll off, unpack into the airport, and go through it all again (customs, boarding cards, wallets, ATM machines).

Almost none of this was here during the Upper Paleolithic—which was only a moment ago, evolutionarily speaking—but our minds almost certainly were, so perhaps my blend of how we pack and unpack for travel and how we pack and unpack for thought tells us something about both travel and mind.

What's So Special About Us?

Long ago, it used to be common to encounter what we might call "Great Chain of Being" views of the human mind. According to these views, our species sits at the top of the terrestrial order: glorious human beings, bathed in a light divine. We are higher, better, special, possessed of all the good qualities of "lower" animals but distinguished by additional godly capacities.

Great Chain of Being views are scientifically dead. Clearly, other animals have abilities that we lack, and they often display rudimentary forms of some of the abilities at which we are exceptionally adept. Various nonhuman species seem to be able to do rudimentary forms of blending. In general, human beings are no more "special" than other animals. It might even be, for example, that other animals aside from human beings have very powerful working memories.

In some ways, we look simpler than even plants. The individual genome (jargon: it means the totality of genetic information carried by a particular organism) for an individual spruce tree is, according to recent reports, about ten times the size of an individual human genome.

But the rejection of Great Chain of Being views is beside the point here. Plants can photosynthesize; bats can echolocate; we cannot do either; and science wants to know both why other species can do the things they can do and why we can do the things we can do. Human beings are spectacularly adept at the origin of ideas. This is the great human contribution to the miracle of life around us. We do rapid, creative, and innovative thinking on the fly, in the moment, in cultural time—that is, in time spans from a few moments to several generations. Our thinking spans vast mental ranges. For us, it's the easiest thing in the world, and for every other species, it is utterly, wildly, radically out of the question. I love dogs, dolphins, spiders, New Zealand rooks, and lots of other animals, and lecture from time to time about their amazing abilities. These riffs are real crowd-pleasers. But we must not lose sight of facts. Our thought arches very widely and powerfully over time, space, causation, and agency. Biologically, we resemble other species. Mentally, we leave them in the dust. Why?

Nonhuman animals handle the sorts of things for which they are evolved. Frogs handle frog stuff. Rodents handle rodent stuff. Bats handle bat stuff. Chimpanzees handle chimpanzee stuff. Most important, these animals master things that have limited scope in time, space, causation, and agency. No species except our own, even with constant and dedicated support from human handlers, appears to be able to move more than a fraction beyond its natural evolutionary mental landscape.

There are hints that dogs have some human-like social skills[13]; that rats have some recollection-like memory retrieval[14]; that scrub jays have some episodic-like memory[15]; that chimpanzees have some understanding that conspecifics (you saw that jargon before) have goals, intentions, perceptions, and knowledge[16]; that Santino, the Swedish zoo chimp, stores rocks as part of a plan to throw them at human visitors tomorrow[17]; and so on. There is considerable evidence for the suspicion that animals have some abilities of which we are not yet aware. Science will presumably inch forward significantly here and there to extend our conception of what other species can do mentally. Nonetheless, there is no evidence that we are not the only ones with the ability to extend the scope of our thought creatively, systematically, abidingly, quickly, repeatedly. We are the origin of ideas. Our capacity for the origin of ideas is unparalleled. For us, such extension and innovation is a normal, minute-to-minute feature of thought. The highly impressive performances by members of other species have severe limits in regard to the origin of ideas that people everywhere indisputably blow right past, effortlessly, from an early age, without help from another species.

Consider dogs, born with superb hearing and motor abilities, domesticated for thousands of years to work closely with people, and often raised from birth inside attentive and helpful human families, housed in environments filled with elaborate material anchors to support creative thought. Lots of love, too. Despite all this, no dog conceives of making percussive music along with Mozart. We know why dogs do not burn to be rock stars. It is because it is not in their nature to think widely in novel ways. To be sure, we can build a welcoming sound studio and bring in all the equipment and encourage and reward the animals to do what they can, and that is interesting, even impressive, not least for the ways in which those animals are so good at following our lead, but these performances present no model for what we are doing mentally when we set a key and time signature and compose bar after bar of music to create a cohesive tune. Dogs cannot stretch to come up with a system of major keys and relative minor keys. There was a time—and very recently, too, on the evolutionary scale—when human beings had not yet invented this systematic understanding of music, either; but now that idea has had its origin: We invented it, and children everywhere can learn to extend their thoughts to master it. The human spark for the origin of ideas produced our understanding of music, just a few centuries or mere millennia ago, and every child, born with the human spark for the origin of ideas, can put that idea together, with a little guidance.

No animal routinely expands the scope of its mental understanding, except for us; that is, except for us since perhaps the Upper Paleolithic or somewhat before. We might refer to people since that era as "cognitively modern," to distinguish them from our "anatomically modern" ancestors. "Anatomically modern human being" includes any ancestor who had your gross form, in skeleton, muscle, and organs. Our speciation (jargon: it means the time at which our ancestors looked "anatomically" like us) happened perhaps 150,000 to 175,000 years ago. But we do not know in any detail how the wiring of the human brain and its operation back then compared to what we have now. At what point did our ancestors have *minds* like ours? As of now, there is no compelling archaeological evidence for any cognitively modern human minds before 50,000 to 100,000 years ago, which is not to say that there were no impressive rudimentary achievements before that, often coming at a pace so slow as to be incredible to cognitively modern human beings.

Our ability for advanced blending makes us routinely adept at understanding concepts that are not at our ordinary evolutionary human scale. Advanced blending makes possible *mental compression and expansion,* which we have also called *packing and unpacking.*

What is "advanced blending"? Advanced blending has been called by a variety of names, such as "double-scope" blending and "vortex" blending. These names are feeble, and I wish I could come up with better ones. All these synonymous labels—all of them unsatisfying—are meant to point to a level of blending that seems to be routine for human beings across all domains of thought, and yet, to all indications, unavailable to members of other species. Other mammals seem to be capable of various rudimentary forms of blending, such as blending individual events close in time and space into one event arc. But when it comes to the mental operation of blending, human beings go incomparably beyond them. We perform the most powerful form of blending, which from now on I will call "advanced blending." What is it?

Advanced blending occurs when two mental spaces have basic organizing structures that are in fundamental conflict, or the relations between them make a fundamental distinction, but they are nonetheless blended so that the blend has parts of each organizing structure and develops a new organizing structure of its own.

What is *organizing structure*? Organizing structure includes causes, intentionality, participants, time, and space. It includes "modal" structure—that is, the structure of possibility, counterfactuality, hypotheticality, necessity, permissibility, and negation. We will discuss these kinds of structure as we go along. In advanced blending, sharp differences in the basic organizing structure of mental spaces, or sharp distinctions in the relation between the mental spaces, offer challenges to the imagination, and the resulting blends often turn out to be highly creative. Far from blocking the origin of ideas, these sharp differences and distinctions seem to foster new ideas, at least for human beings.

Advanced blending is the great human talent. In mental webs with advanced blends, different mental spaces might have different organizing frames; they might conflict utterly; but those conflicting frames can make central contributions to the blend. For a crystal-clear example of an advanced blend, take our very first example: "If I were my brother-in-law, I would be miserable." Clearly, his intentionality and mine, his emotions and mine, his preferences and mine, his identity and mine, and so on and on and on, are profoundly different. The conflict is extreme on central structure. But far from stopping the blend, the conflict fuels the blend! In the advanced blend, we have a new result not contained in the mental spaces the blend draws upon: That is, in the blend, we have *misery*. Similarly, the conflict between *man* and *lion* is deep, but this does not stop us from imagining a *lionman*. In the riddle of the Buddhist Monk, we have one mental space in which the monk is going *up,* while in the other mental space, he is going *down*, but no matter, we can make a blend in which he is doing both simultaneously, and in this blend, we have not one monk in one place but the *same* monk in two places going in *opposite* directions. It is a fabulous blend, and it solves the riddle. Good for us.

3

The Idea of You

It is only shallow people who do not judge by appearances.
OSCAR WILDE

Who are all these people? How do we understand them? Or animals, for that matter?

These questions may seem strange, until we begin to reflect that we have no direct access to the minds of other people, or the minds of animals. We cannot share their pain, though we may empathize with them. We cannot read their minds, or feel what they are feeling. We have perceptions, but what do we perceive? Some photons strike our retinas, some longitudinal waves fall upon our eardrums and skin, some smells come to us, some sense of touch is activated. Even these perceptions are largely driven by our own conceptions.

Where is the "other person" in any of this? What is the origin of the amazing idea that there is another full person out there, one like us, one who thinks as we do, more or less? To be sure, there is language, there are pokes. Eyes move, heads turn, bodies walk. We perform autopsies after people die, we measure some blood flow inside their skulls to make colored pictures, or we record some electrical phenomena happening inside their brains.

But none of this is a perception of mind or soul or personhood. We have no direct access *at all* to other minds. Here is an analogy for what is happening when we look at other people: A computer screen gives us an *interface* for interacting with the computer system. On the screen we see little two-dimensional representations of folders and files, so that we have a way of dealing with the inner workings of the computer, where of course there are no folders or files of the sort we see on the screen. Just so, consciousness gives us an *interface* for dealing with reality, an interface populated with cartoons that have been honed to contribute to our evolutionary fitness, and part of that interface, one of the best cartoons, like the pictures of folders opening and closing on the computer, is our idea of *other minds*. We can watch this cartoon all day and all night. We can watch it in our dreams.

What is the origin of our idea of other minds? To be sure, there is substantial research on what ideas an animal—a chimp, a dog, a raven—can have of other agents. The evidence is complicated. It includes evidence that some animals can think of agents as goal-directed or good for imitation. But no researcher on mind contests that human beings have by far the most robust and complicated ideas of other minds, ideas stretching over time, space, causation, and agency.

Other Minds

Consider, for example, our perception of a seal. The eyes of a seal are remarkably like the eyes of a person. When we see a seal at the seashore, it is impossible to resist the conclusion that we and the seal share a category, that we are alike, that the seal is in some way like us. Compelling and evident analogies, between the seal's appearance and ours, between the seal's motion and ours, between the seal's anatomy and ours, leap out at us. Our human eyes align toward an object as our limbs propel our bodies toward it, and it seems to be little different for the seal.

Working from such analogies, we immediately forge a mental blend of ourselves and the seal. The result is a conception of a seal that has not only all of the seal's appearance and motion but additionally a feature we know only of ourselves—the possession of a mind (figure 2).

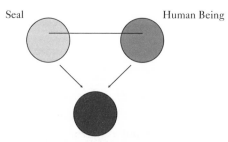

FIGURE 2 A Blend—Seal with a Mind

In the mental blend, we conceive of a seal as having a mind something like ours, lying behind its appearance and motion. In the mental blend, the seal's eyes are not merely open, round, clear, and active, but also alert, intelligent, inquisitive, and perceptive. The seal *inspects* us with wide-eyed, penetrating *attention*. It *intends* to *pursue* an object. It has perception, appetite, and memory. We believe in this blend long before we have any tested scientific evidence for it. As we will discuss later, there are researchers who propose that "mirror neurons" are especially useful in helping us achieve this particular blend.

It takes no frisky seal frolicking in the spume to prompt us to conjure in our brains a mental blend in which another creature has a mind. On the contrary, this is the sort of blend we assemble unconsciously, from early childhood, for any other person. In the standard blend that we use for conceiving of another person, the person has not only all the organismic appearance and movement that we routinely perceive when we pay attention to the person, but also something of ourselves that we project to it—the possession of a mind. It has perception, sensation, and intention behind its appearance and movements, just as we have perception, sensation, and intention behind ours. In the blend, the person whom we watch has mental states that accord with what we see.

Aristotle, Hume, and Darwin all recognized that the way we conceive of other minds depends on projection from what we know of ourselves. In *De Anima* (*On the Soul*), Aristotle points out that when we see something that appears to be self-moving, including moving in a way that suggests that it is moving in response to a sensation, we are apt to regard it as minded, or in his terms, having a soul.

David Hume, in "Of the Reason of Animals," a section of *A Treatise of Human Nature*, reviews how automatic it is to project what we know of our own minds to something whose appearances seem to match our own. However right or wrong the results turn out to be in a given case, what is important for our discussion is that the mental reasoning involves blending. As Hume writes, "It is from the resemblance of the external actions of animals to those we ourselves perform, that we judge their internal likewise to resemble ours." Hume is completely committed to the truth of the fit cartoons of consciousness. His full argument explores the full range of blending.[1]

Darwin, in chapter 3 of *The Descent of Man,* proposes "to shew that there is no fundamental difference between man and the higher mammals in their mental faculties." He is also concerned to analyze the mental capacities of the lower animals. He is clear that there is no direct access to the minds of animals, and emphasizes "the impossibility of judging what passes through the mind of an animal," but nonetheless produces in chapters 3 and 4 a large range of evidence—all of it blending evidence—for the mindedness of animals, and the impressive mindedness of higher mammals. Their appearances look like our appearances; this is an analogical connection. We compress these analogies into a blend for the animal and project to that blend the relation between mind and appearance that we know for ourselves. This is the clear line of Darwin's argument. I think Darwin is totally wrong in claiming that there is no fundamental difference between people and other higher mammals in mental faculties, but the point is that the way he got to his views was through blending.

We are adept at adjusting what we project to the blend. If we are old and tall, we do not project what goes with those features to a blend we make for a child. And when we see somebody in a situation we are not in—they are in the pool but we are high and dry—we can project their situation to the blend rather than our own, and these variable projections can have consequences for the thoughts we imagine they will have. We don't feel wet, but we imagine that they do. Sometimes, we adjust the projection because of feedback. The person we see feels pain, just as we do, it seems, but perhaps he has a slightly higher pain threshold, given that he keeps his hands in the hot dishwater a lot longer than we would. No doubt he has culinary taste, just as we do, and yet, he seems to prefer spicier food. The seal, too, in the blend, has desires just as we do, but the specifics vary. The seal prefers to eat live (not just raw) fish and mate with seals.

The projection of mind to the seal automatically gives the seal some embodied viewpoint, but we can vary the specific details. We can emphasize the conditions of the seal. Alternatively, we can emphasize our own conditions. At one extreme, the seal has a viewpoint very different from ours in both location and disposition, and we apprehend the blended seal-with-a-mind from a distance, as a strange and foreign species. At the other extreme, we can project heavily from our own first-person viewpoint to the blend, and we can, in the blend, see through the seal's eyes. It's fun to try it: In imagination, you are on the beach, watching the seal from the shore. Now be the seal looking at you, the person, watching the seal from the seashore. Do you suddenly feel a little wet? Do you feel yourself trying to keep yourself afloat? The nature of the mind possessed by the seal in the blend can also be varied: We can imagine what it is like to be a seal with seal-like abilities and preferences, or we can imagine what it is like to be something like us clothed in seal form. Such blending apparently outstrips by a vast distance anything a nonhuman species can perform.

Children routinely perform such acts of blending in conceiving of other people, and perhaps equally routinely in conceiving of animals, with the result that talking animals are the mainstay of the human nursery. Chimps and vervet monkeys show no disposition to make dolls of other species and then attribute to them chimp or vervet vocalizations, but the creative projection done by the human child can easily produce a seal who talks, who makes friends with us, who invites us to come swimming at his birthday party, and who winks at us collusively as we engage in exciting adventures. Such blending patterns are by no means restricted to children: We find them not only in *The Velveteen Rabbit* but also in the Mad Hatter's tea party in *Alice in Wonderland*, a favorite for adults, and in many novels and films for adults that include talking animals, such as the film *Men in Black*, in which the talking animals are of course aliens monitored by a secret US government agency.

Fantasy Minds

In all cases where we humanize a seal through blending, there is emergent structure—new stuff—in the blend. In the case of the talking seal, the creature in the blend has specific properties that belong to neither the person nor the seal, that is, to neither of the two ideas that feed the blend. Consider the speech of the talking seal. It might have a sound system for its language that includes barks and growls, and a grammar entirely bizarre for a human being. No person has such speech, and of course no seal has speech at all, but the talking seal has just this emergent style of speech. This is common for talking animals. For example, the animals in Rudyard Kipling's *Jungle Book* have satisfying but emergent speech patterns. The howls of the wolves in *The Jungle Book* are grammatical: One of them, an eerie lupine intonation, "Look well, look well, o wolves!" has an imperative verb adverbially modified and followed by an apostrophe headed by a plural noun!

Three cartoon dogs—Goofy, Pluto, and Scooby-Doo—make it clear that the same set of input ideas—*person* and *dog*—can lead to different blends, because we can vary the projections from the input mental spaces to the blend. Gilles Fauconnier has already pointed out that Goofy gets bizarre humanoid speech whereas Pluto gets no speech at all, even though Pluto possesses advanced human communicative abilities and intentionality. A third variant is Scooby-Doo, who has speech that is both grammatically diminished and voiced in such a way as to suggest (but in fact dramatically exceed) a canine articulatory apparatus. Donald Duck is the prime example of this phenomenon: No person has Donald Duck's speech (although a talented person can, and did, produce it), and no duck has speech at all, but Donald Duck's speech is world-famous and seems natural. After all, if a duck could talk, would it not talk this way?

A moderately more remarkable blend of seal and person gives us the idea of a *selkie*. Selkies have new properties. In the folklore of the Orkney Islands, they are shape-shifting beings. When in seal form, a selkie can shed its coat to become a person, or rather, something deceptively like a person. When in human form, the selkie can converse and mate with a person. Selkies shed their coats in the moonlight and dance on the level shore. A prudent selkie hides its coat carefully before cavorting. Here we see a case where the new stuff in the blend includes not new properties for a seal but in fact a *new species* that falls into the category of neither human being nor seal. This is standard for a shape-shifter. These are really new ideas.

In the selective projection to the blend, the selkie, when out of its coat, has the anatomical parts and proportions of a person but the sleek and lithe movements of the seal. Accordingly, when out of their coats, selkies are sexually irresistible to human beings. In the Orkney legends, a man sometimes steals the coat of a female selkie to compel her to agree to marry him if she ever wants to regain her coat.

But male selkies also shed their coats and slip into villages to mate with deliriously grateful women. Selkies have a relation to their coats that is a blend of a seal's relation to its skin and a human being's relation to its clothes. Selkies take off their clothes to have fun, and are vulnerable when thus "naked." The range of new stuff in this blend is fascinating: For example, in these legends, a child who has one selkie parent might have slightly webbed fingers and toes.

On the one hand, when we recognize that a blend is purely imaginary, we are excused from explaining how it could be possible. Who cares if it is impossible, since the story is so much fun? The pleasure of imagining the blend can be warrant enough, as when a child takes pure delight in imagining a talking dog, all the while knowing that real dogs do not talk.

On the other hand, when we *reify* the blend—jargon meaning that we assume either earnestly or in jest that the blend refers to real situations—we often feel, at least tacitly, an obligation to offer some account of how the blend can refer to anything at all, whether in earnest or in play. One way to explain the "reality" of the blend—and in human cognition this is the way most traveled by—is to assume, without analysis, that the new stuff in the blend in fact already belonged to an input mental space. For example, when we blend ourselves with another person to create for that person a mind, we see no problem with the "reality" of the mind in the blend because we assume, without even thinking about it, that the person in fact *does* have a mind to begin with, regardless of any so-called blending or imagining on our part. It was always there; we did not invent it. We accordingly feel no obligation to account for the "creation" of a mind in the blend because we reject, or in fact never recognize, that there was any imaginary creation at all. Indeed, we never recognize that we have done any mental blending.

Similarly, we feel no need to account for the "creation" of a seal-mind in our usual conception of an everyday seal, because we do not think we have used our imagination at all to create anything at all. We reject that explanation. We do not see the operation of blending used to create the concept of a seal-mind. To think through this, we need to focus on the difference between two questions. The first question is: Do we believe that in fact people have minds, quite independent of our recognizing them? The answer is absolutely yes, we most certainly do. We believe that people had minds before our birth, that people around us have minds, and that after our death they will have minds. We believe that the reality of those minds depends in no way on us. It is right that we have this belief, as a matter of science, on the basis of evidence of every kind. It is part of our notion of the world. The second question is: Does our ability to *conceive* of people as having rich minds depend on blending, with imaginative projection to the blend of things we can know only from our own minds? The answer here is also absolutely yes. We have no access to the minds of other people. We have only imaginative inference. Advanced blending of this sort is just how people attribute robust minds and rich mental states to other people. It is identically how they attribute robust minds and rich mental states to seals, horses, lemurs, and sometimes to trees, balloons, trains, ships, and automobiles.

Blending research has as one of its branches the study of how we conceive of other minds. Have you ever felt you owed something to the train that carried you, the house that sheltered you, the computer that is your servant, the landscape in which you were raised, the tree you climbed and swung on, a tree that is perhaps waiting for you to come home and climb it again, for old times' sake? There was a famous, award-winning, financially successful commercial in 2002, "Lamp," for IKEA furniture stores. It shows an old desk lamp being removed by its owner from the only home it has ever known, abandoned in the wind to the curbside trash. We see shots of the lamp, alone, in the rain, at night, and shots from the lamp's perspective of the happy owner and the new lamp, warm and safe inside the house. Then a big Swede standing in the rain next to the lamp says to the camera, "Many of you are feeling bad for this lamp. That is because you crazy [*sic*]. It has no feelings, and the new one is much better."[2]

In the case of the selkie blend, reifying the blend calls for some additional explanation, because we do not in fact believe that all the new stuff in the blend actually comes pure and simple from the original input. That is, we do not believe that seals already have the properties of selkies. We do not say, for example, "Oh, selkies can slip out of their coats because seals can." Indeed, we do not even think the seal is a selkie, or that the person is a selkie: The entire species of selkie is new stuff. Manifestly, it cannot be found in either input.

There are other ways to account for the "reality," even the in-jest or fictive "reality," of the selkie blend, aside from assuming that the reality is already in the input mental spaces that feed the blend. By "in-jest or fictive reality," I mean an idea that arises in a mental web and is true inside that web—for example, that there are selkies, or that Alice lives in Wonderland—even though we hold the entire mental web as a fiction, not something we believe. Mentally, we construct an elaborate existence for the selkies, but wrap the entire mental web containing selkies inside a container of superior disbelief.

So how do we account for the quasi-reality of the blend? A common way in which to account for this "reality" is to find a causal transformation that starts with one input mental space and produces the blend as a caused effect. So, for example, the cartoon action-hero Spiderman, who is a blend of a teen-age boy and a spider, came into existence when a spider, transformed by radio-activity, bit the boy, and the radioactive arachnid venom turned him into Spiderman. Spiderman's powers are not actually in either of the inputs—a spider, for example, does not shoot out a web-rope over a vast chasm and then grab the rope to swing like a dangling Tarzan to a perch on the other side—but the radioactive venom caused the boy to develop this slick ability. The explanation is fictional, but no less complicated, and it has a rational form.

Similarly, in the children's book *Martha Blah-Blah,* Martha, who is a dog, starts out as a great communicator, equipped with exceptional but nonetheless authentic canine abilities.[3] "But when she ate alphabet soup, the letters went up to her brain instead of down to her stomach, and Martha spoke words."[4] Naturally, she has canine dispositions. Her first words are, "Isn't it time for my dinner?" She says, "At last! Now I can say: I'm hungry! Let's eat. Make mine Steak!" and "Let me OUT! Let me IN! Let me out. Let me in..." The in-jest explanation for the in-jest reification is marvelously elaborated in this book. Martha's family gives her a bowl of alphabet soup every day to replenish her linguistic ability. But when the greedy heir of the soup company cuts corners by eliminating some of the letters in the soup, with the unfortunate result that Martha consumes no Bs, Ss, Ts, or As, Martha is reduced to uttering pitiful gibberish. Of course, since *Martha Blah-Blah* is a tale of self-reliant pluck, Martha sets off to restore what has been lost, and wins in the end.

In the selkie legends, there are three common explanations for the reifica-tion of the blend. The first is death. Death, often viewed as a mysterious but powerful and transforming cause, changes things. What happens after we die? Maybe it depends on how we die. In this case, someone who dies by drowning becomes a selkie, and is able intermittently to regain human form. The second explanation is cosmic justice. People who behave badly are turned into selkies, imprisoned in the body of a seal for the term of their natural lives. The third explanation is by assumption: Selkies are fallen angels who, ejected headlong from heaven, landed in the sea. Their interim punishment is to remain in selkie form until Judgment Day. This account conveniently defers explanation to the antecedent blend of fallen angels. Fallen angels are themselves a blend, so the selkie blend is in this way a hyper-blend, because it has a blend as one of its inputs. Why are selkies possessed of amazing powers? Because the angels who became selkies had amazing powers. Why are these angels stuck in selkie form? Because fallen angels were punished and confined by the Almighty. Turning the fallen angels into selkies follows poetic justice: When the fallen angel touched the surface of our mortal plane, it was transformed into a terrestrial species, and the type of species was determined by point of contact: fairies on land, selkies at sea.

I will call the conception of a world with selkies in it "Selkie World." Such a half-magic world is almost never imagined as extending through all the realms of our world. Instead, a half-magic world typically exists as a liminal component of our world. Special people, themselves somewhat liminal, sometimes brush up against these half-magical elements at special places (the seashore, an attic, a castle) at special times (often the past) and when they are in a special state of mind (often childhood). Bloodsucking vampires are out there, in the graveyards and the alleyways and the underpasses. Somewhere, in a moonlit hour, lovely selkies are dancing by the sea. If you look hard enough and with just the right cast of mind, you might find fairies, zombies, werewolves. But, canonically, it isn't so easy for just anyone to encounter these creatures just anywhere, anytime. Of course, there are stories that invert this expectation, so you find yourself waiting in line at an ice cream parlor behind a nondescript leprechaun, or giving change to the vampire who needs it for the parking meter. As Warren Zevon sings in "Werewolves of London," "I saw a werewolf drinking a Piña Colada at Trader Vic's. His hair was perfect."

All Other Minds Are Fantasy Minds

Adam Smith, a philosopher and economist of the eighteenth century, in a book titled *The Theory of Moral Sentiments*, which laid the psychological foundations of his more famous work, *Wealth of Nations*, presented in beautiful detail a series of discussions analyzing the way in which, to conceive of another mind, we blend ourselves with what we see of the other person. We project to the blend not only much of what we perceive of the other person, but also something from our own knowledge of ourselves: the possession of a mind lying behind behavior. Emotions we know, from ourselves, that are associated with such behavior are projected to the blend. The projection to the blend is, as always, highly selective. For the most part, we project to the blend not our conditions but the conditions we perceive for the other person. We project from ourselves not all of the specific activations we take to be in our minds, but the general principles of our minds, such as sensation, causes and mechanisms of moving and deciding, emotions, and so on.

> As we have no immediate experience of what other men feel, we can form no idea of the manner in which they are affected, but by conceiving what we ourselves should feel in the like situation. Though our brother is upon the rack, as long as we ourselves are at our ease, our senses will never inform us of what he suffers. They never did, and never can, carry us beyond our own person, and it is by the imagination only that we can form any conception of what are his sensations. Neither can that faculty help us to this any other way, than by representing to us what would be our own, if we were in his case. It is the impressions of our own senses only, not those of his, which our imaginations copy. By the imagination we place ourselves in his situation, we conceive ourselves enduring all the same torments, we enter as it were into his body, and become in some measure the same person with him, and thence form some idea of his sensations, and even feel something which, though weaker in degree, is not altogether unlike them. His agonies, when they are thus brought home to ourselves, when we have thus adopted and made them our own, begin at last to affect us, and we then tremble and shudder at the thought of what he feels. For as to be in pain or distress of any kind excites the most excessive sorrow, so to conceive or to imagine that we are in it, excites some degree of the same emotion, in proportion to the vivacity or dulness of the conception.[5]

Adam Smith's theory of how we conceive of other minds is general: We blend the situation of the other person with our feelings in reaction to such a situation. Some scientists propose that this projection is more specific; that is, we project only mental states for basic emotions such as happiness, sadness, fear, anger, surprise, and disgust when we see certain facial and bodily appearances.[6]

Blending can create, in imagination, minds for many different kinds of things that we do not actually believe have minds, or that we do not believe have minds just like ours. We assemble imaginary beings, such as a river that rises up in a Japanese animated film to express, in exotic ways, its pain at being polluted. Stuffed animals are provided in imagination with their own attitudes and desires. We can, in the blend, conceive of machines that feel weary from their work, trains that are grateful for a chance to rest in the train yard, banana trees that are pleased when the sun beats down, trees that sway to the music, all regardless of whether we project to these blended entities any fantasy linguistic abilities. I once heard several people describe a large earth-moving machine, idly facing the vast Pacific Ocean from its location at UC San Diego, as "smug."

Adam Smith understood that we can project what we know of our own minds in subtle and compelling ways to what we know does not have a mind. He picks out the very interesting case of the dead:

> We sympathize even with the dead, and overlooking what is of real importance in their situation, that awful futurity which awaits them, we are chiefly affected by those circumstances which strike our senses, but can have no influence upon their happiness. It is miserable, we think, to be deprived of the light of the sun; to be shut out from life and conversation; to be laid in the cold grave, a prey to corruption and the reptiles of the earth; to be no more thought of in this world, but to be obliterated, in a little time, from the affections, and almost from the memory, of their dearest friends and relations. Surely, we imagine, we can never feel too much for those who have suffered so dreadful a calamity. The tribute of our fellow-feeling seems doubly due to them now, when they are in danger of being forgot by every body; and, by the vain honours which we pay to their memory, we endeavour, for our own misery, artificially to keep alive our melancholy remembrance of their misfortune. That our sympathy can afford them no consolation seems to be an addition to their calamity; and to think that all we can do is unavailing, and that, what alleviates all other distress, the regret, the love, and the lamentations of their friends, can yield no comfort to them, serves only to exasperate our sense of their misery. The happiness of the dead, however, most assuredly, is affected by none of these circumstances; nor is it the thought of these things which can ever disturb the profound security of their repose. The idea of that dreary and endless melancholy, which the fancy naturally ascribes to their condition,

arises altogether from our joining to the change which has been produced upon them, our own consciousness of that change, from our
putting ourselves in their situation, and from our lodging, if I may be
allowed to say so, our own living souls in their inanimated bodies, and
thence conceiving what would be our emotions in this case. It is from
this very illusion of the imagination, that the foresight of our own dis-
solution is so terrible to us, and that the idea of those circumstances,
which undoubtedly can give us no pain when we are dead, makes us
miserable while we are alive. And from thence arises one of the most
important principles in human nature, the dread of death, the great
poison to the happiness, but the great restraint upon the injustice of
mankind, which, while it afflicts and mortifies the individual, guards
and protects the society.[7]

When we see the enormous branch of one tall tree in the field fall off and land
on a small tree, breaking the small one in half, it is natural to make a blend: In
the blend, the small tree suffers damage. Poor tree! Of course, outside the blend,
we know that a tree does not know it is a tree and does not have preferences to
continue its natural tree-destiny rather than be cut off at a tender age, because
of course a tree has no thoughts or feelings, or at least, that is probably what we
believe. Where is the damage? There is no loss to anyone that follows from the
tree's being smashed. The forest will recycle it. Another will grow in its place.

Here is another blend of the living and the dead, studied by Charles
Fillmore in his analysis of the technical legal term "decedent."[8] A "decedent" is
a legal person, a quasi-agent. Here are examples of how the word is used in laws
in the United States: "If the decedent has no surviving spouse…" "If the decedent has living parents, siblings, nieces, or nephews…" "The decedent leaves
his house…" One can say, "The decedent has left his house…," that is, one
can use the present perfect, which indicates relevance for the present concern
or moment, but at the reading of the will, it would be strange to use the past
tense, "The decedent left his house…," even though we have one mental space
in the mental web in which the person is dead, or rather, a mental space in
which there is a corpse that is linked by *identity* to the body of a living person
in another mental space in the web, a mental space that is also linked by *time*
to the space with the corpse, so that the living person is prior in time to the
corpse. Documents, and other symbols, can help give us an idea of someone's
intentions while they are living. But when there is only the corpse, we still have
those documents. We can project our understanding of those intentions, based
on present documents, to a blend that includes agency. In the blend, there is a

decedent, that is to say, there is an agent whose intentions are respected by legal processes, and this idea is quite useful for settling legal matters, even though no one is deluded into thinking that this quasi-agent corresponds to a full and living person. No one invites "the decedent" to explain further to one of the relatives who disagrees with the execution of the will that the decedent actually does agree with the executor. The blended idea of the decedent gives us a human-scale blend for thinking about intentions and processes that arch over time, space, causation, and agency. Once the vestiges of intention and ownership are resolved, one stops referring to the decedent. ("In other words," one member of my audience once remarked, "when you rip them off, they are dead at last.") As Fillmore observes, "decedent" has a narrow meaning; it does not mean merely "someone who is deceased." In response to "Are your parents living?" one cannot felicitously say, "No, they are both decedents."

All of these examples make clear that asking whether a blend is *true* is often the wrong question. Of course, in many cases, such as scientific categorization or mathematical deduction or logical inference, we may care above all whether it is a good move to attribute *truth* to the blend, in the sense of deciding whether the blend gives us a good ontology, a good handle on existence in the world. But very frequently, the importance of a blend is not whether we think it is true of the world, but rather whether it stabilizes, grounds, anchors, serves, organizes a diffuse mental web, and lets us manage that web. A blend that we think is in itself *false* may lead us to see *truth* in the mental web, and it is the web that counts. It is *false* that the Buddhist Monk meets himself, but the meeting in the blend gives us truth for the mental web that the blend serves, and lets us see the *true* answer to the riddle. It is false that there is an agent corresponding to the decedent in the world at the moment in which the decedent is described as performing actions and having intentions: "The decedent leaves his house … The decedent's wishes are clear …" In such cases, the blend is serving truth; it provides useful mental service.

Consider another case: We know that when we are tapping out a rhythm—1, 2, 3, 1, 2, 3, 1, 2, 3 … —the stressed beats (1, 1, 1) are not all the same beat. On the contrary, we must understand, in the mental web for the sequence, that they are all different, taking place at different moments, and at different locations in the sequence, and that we do not ever come back to the same event. The beats are scattered across different notes at different points in the music. No note has more than one stress on it. But in the blend, this entire sequence is compressed to a *cycle,* just as for the cyclic day. There is an analogy relation between any 1, 2, 3 rhythm in the indefinite sequence and any other. All the 1, 2, 3 subsequences can be compressed to a single 1, 2, 3 *cycle* in the blend, and we *return,* in the blend, to the beat. If "the beat"—which is a compression of all those different stresses on notes relative to their immediate neighbors—"falls" on every spot in the sequence that we have labeled "1," then we can say, speaking of the blend, "*the beat* is on 1," and, expanding this blend to the mental web it serves, understand that there are lots of stresses in the music falling on lots of notes and that we are designating all of these notes "1" and thinking of all these notes as at a certain spot in a single repeating cycle. Truth in a mental web often comes from falsity in the blend. We are not deluded.

ELIZA and the Rattlesnake

There are curious effects of getting the idea of other minds by blending. We often make blended conceptions of machines in which they have some aspects of mind, even though we know that in the mental web outside the blend, they certainly do not. Joseph Weizenbaum, working at MIT in 1966 on how to program computers to use writing in natural language as an interface for computer users, produced a little program called "ELIZA." It was a "chatterbot"—computer code that mimics on a screen whatever words a human user types into it, and that recognizes certain words as significant. It turned out that ELIZA was remarkably successful in eliciting emotional responses from people exposed to it. "I had not realized…that extremely short exposures to a relatively simple computer program could induce powerful delusional thinking in quite normal people."[9] These users were completely informed about what ELIZA was doing, and often about how ELIZA did it. But they often operated as if ELIZA had intentionality, attention, and feelings. This phenomenon is now called in cognitive science "the ELIZA effect." It generally refers to the creation of blends in which things have minds even though we know that outside the blend they do not. Under the ELIZA effect, we attribute lots of mindedness to things just because we can project it to a blend for them. Weizenbaum's amazement is understandable, but he was exaggerating in referring to this phenomenon as evidence of delusion. We all have it; it is routine. The blend is useful and powerful. But if you ask us what is going on outside the blend, we give a response that is free of the ELIZA effect.

The person cursing the spare tire, or the telephone, for refusing to comply with her wishes is not deluded. Although she finds it useful to have emotions and actions that make sense inside the blend, in which the phone or tire is intentional, she will, if asked whether she believes the object is literally refusing to comply, find it hard to take the question seriously. Working inside the blend can provide focus, motivation, energy. Working inside the blended space does not preclude working with the entire mental web it serves, including of course the mental spaces in which it is "only" a tire or a telephone. We create mental blends to help us manage diffuse mental webs that otherwise would be uncongenial to our thinking. We create them to help us compress ranges of information into something we can hold in mind. We create them to induce emotional states, or to draw inferences that impinge upon reality, or to solve problems, or to supply a global insight into diffuse knowledge, or to create new meaning, or to help us reason to choices, or for other purposes; and in doing so, we often work inevitably, simultaneously, having it both ways, with a blended mental space and another mental space in the web upon which the blend calls; and it is not a problem for us, indeed it is an advantage for us, that the blend and the spaces upon which it calls are incompatible or even, sometimes, centrally opposed.

> Lives there a man with soul so dead
> He's never to his toaster said:
> "You are my friend; I see in you
> An object sturdy, staunch, and true;
> A fellow mettlesome and trim;
> A brightness that the years can't dim."?
> Thomas M. Disch[10]

There are, by now, four decades later, several ELIZA chatterbots waiting for us on the Internet. Some are specialized and sophisticated. Here is a conversation I just now had with the original, unsophisticated ELIZA program:

>> Hello.
How do you do. Please state your problem.
>> I want to know everything about the human mind.
What would it mean to you if you got to know everything about the human mind?
>> It would probably mean that I would become bored.
You say it would probably mean that you would become bored?
>> Right. Because then I wouldn't know what to ask.
Is that the real reason?
>> Perhaps I am fooling myself.
You don't seem quite certain.
>> I guess I'm not.
Is it because you are not that you came to me?

>> I am not sure.

How long have you been not sure?

>> Since I started talking to you. Amazing!

Perhaps in your fantasies we started talking to each other.

And of course, that is utterly true: My fantasy of talking to ELIZA caused me to locate the original program on the Internet a few minutes ago. Although the computer spews letters onto the screen for us to read, we know there is no mind in the program, none at all. The program is merely designed to deploy all-purpose responses and to perform canned syntactic juggling of what the user types and to recognize certain typed sequences as cues for certain "responses." We can hold onto this interaction mentally by creating a congenial blend in which there is a minded computer program whose thinking leads to its actions. Making such a blend is not delusional, merely efficient, creative, and human. In the blend, the computer understands our meaning, and it constructs meanings of its own, and the meanings it constructs cause it to express those meanings to us. For example, I just wrote that "the computer spews letters onto the screen for us to read," and no one had any difficulty grasping the idea, even though, of course, we know that, outside the blend, the computer program does not even know that there is a screen, or that it is a computer program, or that we are here, or that we are reading, or what reading might be, or anything else. We know that the computer cannot "spew," with all the will and purpose implied by that verb. But in the blend, it can. We are not deluded. The blend is highly useful.

It is common to remark how natural it is to project mind to computational machines. This natural projection of mindedness is the basis of all these digital helpers who haunt my personal devices, several of which listen and speak. My wireless earbud has a fabulous helper that tells me it is "on and ready to go." I tell it what to do, and it does it. I have search devices that listen to my questions and respond with advice, information, and links. Outside the blend, I understand that, for instance, in the case of my search device, my speech is recorded, shipped over the Internet to a huge server farm, processed by speech-to-text recognition software, and fed to search engines, and that then all the information, along with some canned answers, comes back to my little hand-held device. But inside the blend, I am talking to the little wonder-mind in the machine, which is much quicker and has an incomparably greater range of knowledge than any person I know. These voices have names, like "Siri," and use personal pronouns, like "I" and "you."

ELIZA, digital helpers, and search devices with names are amusing. But the quick projection of mindedness to a blend can be anything but amusing, at least in the moment. Shortly before I encountered ELIZA in my career, I encountered a Southern Pacific rattlesnake in a dry, stony riverbed. I know that rattlesnakes are beneficial to people for the rodents they eat, and there are no educated people who maintain that a rattlesnake *intends* to be *mean* to you or *intimidate* you, that it is *proud* of its dominance, or that it is *scornful* of your fear, but if you meet a Southern Pacific rattlesnake by surprise, it is impossible, or was impossible for me, to avoid projecting such mental states to it. I conceived of it, at least in the blend, as an intentional, malevolent adversary to be not just killed but punished. In retrospect, it was of course my fault—I should not have been there, and I should not have surprised it. But in the instant, I wanted to stone that consummately evil, bloody-minded, murderous enemy. I cursed it, although not out loud.

Places, even, have minds in a blend. The gloomy graveyard, even if we do not populate it with conceptions of the spirits of the dead, can seem malevolent, as if it desires to suck the life out of us. Later, or in a calmer moment, with more experience and dispassion, we may moderate our reactions and overcome such projections. We may even feel ashamed of them. That is to say, in response to the same mental spaces, we produce different blends. I only hope the magnanimous rattlesnake can find it in its heart to forgive me.

The Curse of Knowledge

In cognitive science, "the curse of knowledge" refers to our tendency to project our knowledge and facility into our blended conceptions of other people. It turns out to be exceptionally difficult to imagine that others do not have our knowledge or follow our habits of framing and construal. The curse of knowledge operates below the horizon of awareness. We do not realize that we are cursed. The term was invented by three economists.[11]

The curse of knowledge is not rigid or undiscriminating: We know that our schoolbook knowledge, or any other knowledge we regard as specialized, might not be shared. That awareness lifts the curse to just that extent. For example, we do not assume that the 10-year-old knows how to do differential calculus, or even how to brown butter in a skillet. But when we see an interaction and, without conscious reflection, conceive of it as a *trade*, we might fail to consider that other adults around us can be operating, again without conscious reflection, under a rather different idea.

The curse of knowledge is a natural consequence of blending to conceive of other minds. Evolutionarily, it is for the most part more efficient and useful for any idea we have of another mind to work quickly and in the backstage of cognition. We do not want to mess with it much in consciousness. Consciousness is an arena into which small tips of the iceberg, or little cartoons, or nutshell movies pop. If the work we do in conceiving of other minds were restricted to what we can do in consciousness, we would be incapacitated. As usual, we are for the most part quite unaware of the complex work we are doing in projecting from ourselves to our conception of another mind, and naturally, this leaves the door wide open to the curse of knowledge.

"Curse of knowledge" phenomena are many, and the study of them, often under different labels, stretches back decades. Psychologists in earlier decades referred to "egocentric attribution" and "attributive projection."[12] They also discussed "false consensus," in which the default, unconscious expectation is that other people tend to have our preferences, our principles for making choices, our behavior, and our judgments.[13] This default, unconscious projection can certainly be overridden, but in that case we tend to take the conflict between how we work and how those other people work as uncommon, abnormal, and revealing:

> [W]e shall report research demonstrating that laymen tend to perceive a "false consensus"—to see their own behavioral choices and judgments as relatively common and appropriate to existing circumstances while viewing alternative responses as uncommon, deviant, or inappropriate. Evidence shall also be reported for an obvious corollary to the false consensus proposition: The intuitive psychologist judges those responses that differ from his own to be more revealing of the actor's stable dispositions than those responses which are similar to his own. Thus, we contend that the person who feeds squirrels, votes Republican, or drinks Drambuie for breakfast will see such behaviors or choices by an actor as relatively common and relatively devoid of information about his personal characteristics. By contrast, another person who ignores hungry squirrels, votes Democrat, or abstains at breakfast will see the former actor's responses as relatively odd and rich with implications about the actor's personality.

The term *relative* is critical in this formulation of the false consensus bias and it requires some clarification. Obviously, the man who would walk a tightrope between two skyscrapers, launch a revolution, or choose a life of clerical celibacy recognizes that his choices would be shared by few of his peers and are revealing of personal dispositions. It is contended, however, that he would see his personal choices as less deviant and revealing than would those of us who do not walk tightropes, launch revolutions, or become celibate clerics.[14]

One challenge that arises as we blend our minds with those of other people has to do with what is called "false belief." How do we attribute to other people beliefs that conflict with our own? Specifically, how do we view them as holding beliefs that conflict with what we think we know is certainly true? When do we think that someone else holds a false belief? Tests of this ability are called "false-belief" tests. For example, in the "Sally-Anne" test—a chestnut of psychological testing—a child subject is shown dolls, or a cartoon, of Sally and Anne, who are together. Sally puts her marble into her basket. When Sally is out of the room and cannot see what is happening, Anne moves the marble to her own box. Then Sally returns to the room. At that point, the child subject is asked, "Where will Sally look for her marble?" The normal adult response is that Sally will look for her marble in her basket, where she last saw it. This is viewed in psychology as an attribution of "false belief" to Sally. The classic study was done by Heinz Wimmer and Josef Perner,[15] who conducted a range of such tests, involving a character's beliefs about the location of chocolate, for example. The conclusion of such false-belief testing was that children younger than 4 are likely to fail the test, and that it takes a few years for children older than 4 to develop a stable ability to attribute false belief. Of course, although it is common to ask a young child where something is, it might be strange to ask a 3-year-old where a doll or cartoon figure will think something is. Tests have been designed that suit more normal conditions, and the evidence from these suggests that the ability to attribute false belief is present much earlier, in the first half of the second year of life.[16]

Vera Tobin explores the ways in which the curse of knowledge persists strongly throughout a lifetime.[17] It is not at all the case that, at a certain age, we lose our biases in blending ourselves with other people and can therefore attribute to them minds capable of false belief. There is no way for these biases to be erased, because throughout our lifetime, we have no way to attribute mindedness except through the processes of blending. Because we have no direct access to other minds, the best we can do is to adjust and to qualify our projections to the blend. It is not as if people can grant us direct access to their minds, or do the work for us of qualifying our projections by, for example, explaining in language or gesture or in action who they are. It is always the case that, whatever they communicate to us, we still must understand those communications on the basis of something, and it cannot be that we understand them on the basis of our direct access to their minds, because we have none. Our own mind is the only one that provides the basis for some of the content of the blend. Tobin's explorations of the continued effect of the curse of knowledge are wide-ranging and illuminating. She skillfully explains why we take delight in the satisfying plot twists we encounter in stories, wherein we are genuinely surprised by the revelation or the twist but retrospectively feel that we should not have been surprised. We conclude that the truth was there all along, but we missed it! In the kinds of fictional work Tobin studies, the author uses the curse of knowledge to lead us to feel that what we missed was right before our eyes. The author has arranged for the curse of knowledge to work its magic exactly so we could delight in the surprise. Right now, the conclusion seems easy for us to reach. So we blend our right-now mind with our past conditions and persuade ourselves that the conclusion was easy for us to reach back then, too, but we failed. How could we have missed it? We are so stupid!

Perhaps the experiment that most clearly demonstrates how inevitable it is that we will project our knowledge to a blend was invented by Elizabeth Newton. She ran experiments in which she divided subjects into "tappers" and "listeners."[18] The tapper selects a familiar song from a list and then taps out its rhythm. Before the listeners guess the song, the tapper must predict what percentage of the listeners will guess accurately. The tappers routinely overestimate that percentage by large multipliers. Typically, the tappers predict that about half the listeners will guess correctly. In fact, only about 3% guess correctly. Once you have the song in your head, you hear it when you tap the rhythm, and you project that knowledge to the blend for the listener, or at least, project it more insistently and more often than is warranted. It is very hard to imagine that other minds are not hearing what you are hearing from the sound of one hand tapping.

From the perspective of blending theory, perhaps the psychological tradition should be stood on its head. In psychology, children who do not pass the Sally-Anne test are said to "fail." Adults who operate according to the curse of knowledge are regarded as making "mistakes." Yet what these tests in fact demonstrate is that we are doing strong advanced blending, indeed overly strong, without appropriate constraint and correction. We are projecting to the blend for the other mind a great deal of what we know of our minds, indeed, as it turns out, far too much. These children who are failing and these adults who are making mistakes are the smartest agents on the planet, incomparably outstripping any other species. They are capable, as Adam Smith understood, of using these advanced blends, these ideas of other minds, as the basis of society, institutions, organization, coordination, and vast mental webs of interdependent agents.

To be sure, as we mature in life, we benefit from learning how to moderate, govern, and lessen the projections from ourselves to the blend. When other people do not like what we like, when they go where we would not go, when their reactions are not what we expected, we need to learn to develop new stuff in the blend for minds that are nearly entirely like our own but in some specific ways not exactly so. We need to learn to project from ourselves less emphatically.

Blending is such a strong power that culture needs to manage it. Cultures inculcate manners, for example, so as to build automatic conditioned routines inside our minds, the purpose of which is to stop us from acting on projections to the blend, even when—and often especially when—those projections seem to go without saying. These hesitations and routines, of not saying what we should not say, of not taking "liberties," buffer us in our dealings with other people, and protect us from our own powerful advanced blending. Manners create controlled interactions in which the chances are increased that we will get some information that will help us see how the other mind differs from our own. Manners help us take for granted only as much as culture has already legislated can be taken for granted, no more, and to resist taking for granted things that we are disposed to take for granted but that might land us in great difficulty with other minds.

How many times have we assumed, without thinking about it, something about a person we are talking to, and then been greatly relieved that we did not let that assumption slip out, because at last, unexpectedly, someone in the group said something that saved our social bacon, something that alerted us that we had made a wrong projection? We might assume that someone sitting at the beach in Baja California, under a palapa, looking at the waves and the sunset, would enjoy a margarita, and be about to offer one in the normal way, but manners prescribe and proscribe. Manners require a more careful dance of interaction. In this mannered dance, we are prevented from making any such offer. The mannered dance has a chance of eliciting from the other person something that alerts us to block the assumption that the other mind likes margaritas or likes being offered margaritas. So we dodge that social bullet, one that, in the mental blending web, came from our own gun.

Blending as the Origin of the Idea of Other Minds

The ability to have an idea of another mind is often considered in philosophy, psychology, or cognitive science to be a relatively autonomous ability, sometimes called, confusingly, "theory of mind."[19] In the "theory of mind" vein of research, we have an ability to conceive of other minds, and the reason we have this ability is that we have a "theory of mind"—a relatively special-purpose mechanism, even a self-contained "module," for understanding other minds.

I make an alternative hypothesis: Our ability to conceive of other minds is an application, a special case, of our ability for advanced blending. To be sure, our plastic brains frequently exploit whatever computational resources and neurological real estate are available, and it could be that blending in a particular domain of thought draws especially heavily upon certain resources. As we will discuss, there have been proposals that blends of self and other that lead to motoric imitation or understanding of other minds draw on "mirror neurons," which were first found in macaque monkeys but have since been claimed to help songbirds learn how to sing and people to have ideas of other minds.

The "theory of mind" hypothesis is often hitched to the more specific hypothesis that the difficulties in social pragmatics and social learning encountered by children assigned to the autism spectrum are caused by a genetic defect that results in improper development of the so-called "theory of mind" module, or ability.[20]

Michael Tomasello, psychologist and co-director of a Max Planck institute, proposes a fascinating hypothesis according to which species-unique human cognition derives from the uniquely human ability for "theory of mind." In *The Cultural Origins of Human Cognition*, he writes:

> My specific hypothesis is that human cognition has the species-unique qualities it does because:
> - *Phylogenetically:* Modern human beings evolved the ability to "identify" with conspecifics, which led to an understanding of them as intentional and mental beings like themselves.
> - *Historically:* This enabled new forms of cultural learning and sociogenesis, which led to cultural artifacts and behavioral traditions that accumulate modifications over historical time.
> - *Ontogenetically:* Human children grow up in the midst of these socially and historically constituted artifacts and traditions, which enables them to (a) benefit from the accumulated knowledge and skills of their social groups; (b) acquire and use perspectively based cognitive representations in the form of linguistic symbols (and analogies and metaphors constructed from these symbols); and (c) internalize certain types of discourse interactions into skills of metacognition, representational redescription, and dialogic thinking.[21]

I take a view different from Tomasello's, but one not incompatible with it: "Theory of mind," the ability to understand conspecifics as intentional, mental beings like oneself, is an important subcase of the ability for advanced blending:

- *Phylogenetically:* Rudimentary capacities for blending are evident in mammals. Modern human beings evolved the ability for advanced blending, which enabled them to be innovative in many ways, and in particular enabled them to blend the self with other people very fluidly and extensively, so as to understand people as intentional, mental beings like themselves. (Equally important, using a range of different projections, advanced blending also enabled cognitively modern human beings to make blends of self with fauna, flora, and inanimate objects. These different kinds of blends have different utilities. No doubt the blend of self with other people was particularly adaptive.)
- *Historically:* Advanced blending made possible dramatically powerful new forms of cultural learning and sociogenesis, making it easier to accumulate the products of advanced blending over time. Advanced blending made human culture and cultural processes possible, and is indispensable for art, science, religion, language, mathematics, fashions of dress, and other human singularities.
- *Ontogenetically:* Human children are born with the capacity for advanced blending. Cultures stand ready with the products of blending, accumulated over time: languages, complex gestures, weights and measures and money, stuffed animals, fashions of dress and posture, social rituals, fractions, religion, and so on. Partly because children can form blends of self and other, but also partly because they can form blends of all sorts, children can acquire these culturally developed products of blending.

One might argue that the "theory of mind" hypothesis is attractive because having a "theory of mind" would be adaptive, and because assuming that we have a "theory of mind" would explain a lot. By the same token, the alternative hypothesis—that "theory of mind" is at heart an application of blending—would be in the same measure attractive, because having the ability to blend would certainly be adaptive, in so many ways, and because assuming that we have this ability would explain a lot. But blending theory has, in contrast with the "theory of mind" hypothesis, many additional attractions.

First, it seems implausible that "theory of mind" could provide all the capacity needed for modern cognition. Tomasello writes, "My particular claim is that in the cognitive realm the biological inheritance of humans is very much like that of other primates. There is just one major difference, and that is the fact that human beings 'identify' with conspecifics more deeply than do other primates."[22] In *The Way We Think*, Fauconnier and I explain many human discoveries and creations that do not appear to follow exclusively from the ability to create a blend of self and other. To be sure, social cognition is necessary for significant cultural advance and significant cultural accumulation of knowledge, and, to be sure, the ability to "stand on the shoulders" of others is indispensable to human cognition. But that ability alone is inadequate to account for the invention of complex numbers, hyperbolic geometry, money, grammatical constructions, counterfactual thought, and so on. The phylogenetic development that is needed for these cases is the capacity for advanced blending. The capacity for advanced blending is one level of generality above "theory of mind." "Theory of mind" is a subcase. The origin of ideas lies not specifically in blending within the domain of self and other, but at a higher level, in the more general capacity for advanced blending over many domains.

Second, Tomasello is quite correct, and insightfully so, to emphasize that "The process of cumulative cultural evolution requires not only creative invention but also, and just as importantly, faithful social transmission that can work as a ratchet to prevent slippage backward."[23]

In blending theory, however, creative invention and faithful social transmission are treated not as separate feats, but instead as seamlessly interacting exercises of the same remarkable mental ability for blending. For Tomasello, "The complete sequence of hypothesized evolutionary events is thus: human beings evolved a new form of social cognition, which enabled some new forms of cultural learning, which enabled some new processes of sociogenesis and cumulative cultural evolution. This scenario...posits one and only one biological adaptation..."[24] For me, the complete sequence of hypothesized evolutionary events is this: People evolved an advanced form of cognition, advanced blending, and this advanced form made possible, *among other things*, new forms of cultural learning, sociogenesis, and cumulative cultural evolution.

Third, the evolutionary hypothesis proposed by blending theory requires only an increase along a gradient of ability: Advanced blending requires many pre-existing abilities to be in place, but otherwise consists of only an advance along the gradient of a capacity that we see widely manifested in the mammalian world. Tomasello actually provides important evidence for this view. Chimpanzees (*pan troglodytes*), he reports, in my words, not his, may have greater ability to blend self and other than has heretofore been recognized.[25]

In very narrowly and ingeniously contrived experiments in which a dominant and a subordinate chimpanzee interact in competition for food, that is to say, situations in which the chimpanzee already has strong specific mental scaffolding (food, dominance) to assist it with the difficult mental blending of itself and another chimpanzee, the subordinate chimpanzees behave in ways that suggest a partial ability to understand the perspective of a dominant.

Fourth, it is not clear how to interpret the behavior of children assigned to the autism spectrum. This putative spectrum is broad and ill-defined. At least some of the children assigned to this spectrum, such as children with Asperger condition, often show strong capacities for blending in domains other than social pragmatics. These children often display such impressive performances of mental blending that nonspecialists can have difficulty recognizing that the socially anomalous behavior of these children is caused by a cognitive condition and not by poor character. Their reaction is called "blinded by the light." If "theory-of-mind" social cognition were the root of the special capacities of human cognition, then impairment of social cognition in these children might be expected to produce similarly profound deficits across all those special cognitive capacities, but it does not. Children with Asperger condition can manifest impairment in social cognition and yet have strong blending abilities in other domains. I propose therefore that these cognitive deficits should be explored as cases in which blending works somewhat differently *in a particular conceptual domain.* Such difference, to be sure, would inevitably have collateral effects in other domains, but not necessarily to the same degree.

It is also important to consider that these children might be doing very strong blending even in the domain of social pragmatics, but with projections different from those associated with "normal" social cognition, and hence producing different ideas of other minds. Some children with Asperger condition might be interpreted as having overly strong projection from their own minds to the blend for another mind. On this view, their projection of their own mental states, knowledge, and beliefs to the blends they construct for other people is perhaps less easily deflected, corrected, or adjusted than it is for other children. Nor is it clear that there is a breakdown of cognition in such cases. To be sure, this behavior may strike some of us with "normal" ideas of other minds as alien and deficient, but this is a two-way street. Type "neurotypical syndrome" into your favorite internet search engine and you will be taken to humorous articles describing the severe deficits neurotypicals manifest in social cognition, relative to their Asperger counterparts. Whether the pattern of blending we see in mild Asperger condition is a deficit or an advantage is, in one sense, up to natural selection to decide. Many people are paralyzed by shyness or suffer terribly from wondering what other people are thinking about them. They can barely call a stranger up on the phone to ask the price of an item in the market. Obviously, we would all be destroyed mentally if we actually did consider in its full force all the suffering of other people. Children tortured and abused, women and girls raped brutally, soldiers whose appendages are hacked off sequentially under interrogation, villages wiped out in bloody destruction, people slashed to death, children starving to death, adolescents dying from bulimia, old people on their deathbed, and on and on and on, millions of them, everywhere, over all time, the screaming and the silence, with every inflection in the voice of sorrow and appeal, all over the world, in every city, on every street, every night, every morning, every afternoon. Shall we really look into the eyes of each of these people? When we take pleasure in the beautiful sunset or the lovely falling snow, or have a rapturous moment of release, at that exact moment millions are in the greatest pain, and many of them we know. Shall we really contemplate all of their internal lives? It is enough to make one hide under the bed. Evolutionary change is produced by variation, descent with inheritance, and selection. Evolution could well select on variation in social cognition to "right size" the capacity for fitness. We need a Goldilocks solution: not too hard, not too soft, just right. In summary, the points to be considered with respect to how Asperger condition affects ideas of other minds are three: (1) Asperger condition does not seem to weaken blending in general, although one might argue that it weakens blending when one forms ideas of other minds; (2) on a different tack, one might argue that it strengthens blending when one forms ideas of other minds, even though the products seem strange relative to "normal" ideas; (3) evolutionarily speaking, it is not clear how natural selection will select for or against these particular patterns of blending in forming ideas of other minds. Behavior associated with the autism spectrum is not in itself evidence that blending is not the key to how human beings achieve their advanced ideas of other minds.

Tomasello's proposal and the blending hypothesis are not opposed. Tomasello, as far as I know, is noncommittal about the processes underlying our understanding of intentions and our urge to collaborate, and this leaves open the door for blending. More strongly, the blending account of "theory of mind" I propose is friendly to Tomasello's account of the social origins of human cognition: It views his theory as upwardly compatible with the blending hypothesis.

Practice, Practice, Practice

People are born with remarkable abilities to come up with new ideas, and blending is a great mental instrument for doing this. But, like a toolbox, blending is only instrumental. We actually have to use it in order to build anything. Having the toolbox is not at all the same thing as having what can be built with the toolbox. Nearly everything we care about has been invented in cultural time—roughly the last 50,000 or 100,000 years. Nearly everything we care about has to be learned or invented by every person.

Nor is blending the only capacity needed for the origin of new ideas. On the contrary, coming up with new ideas requires all the other mental capacities we share with other mammals. Blending does not work without attention, memory, perception, and so on. Standard examples of what we share with all those mammals include vision, eating, and mating. But these basic and sophisticated instincts hardly begin to provide an explanation for the variable human behavior we see in painting and music, cooking and dining, courtship and coupling. Many abilities aside from blending are necessary for the origin of ideas, but they are not sufficient. Blending to the rescue!

Emphasizing the power of blending does not undercut the importance of social, cultural, and perceptual worlds, because it is in these worlds that blending builds its products and passes them on, generation to generation. It can take a long time for culture to come up with various ideas and the mental webs of meaning that make them possible—multiplication, telling time, writing, baking, viniculture, table manners, chivalry, charm, flirting. But once it does, it stands ready to immerse each new child in the particular webs the culture finds important. And the child, born with the capacity for advanced blending, is able to respond to the flood of cultural instruction it receives.

Human powers of blending apparently induce any roughly normal human infant who is born into any roughly human culture to have ideas of other minds. What culture then does is train the child in nuanced projection, and in the careful cultivation of particular kinds of new stuff in the blend. Culture provides practice, practice, practice, in the form of simulations, rehearsals, plays, TV shows, songs, representations, play-acting, descriptions. There are genres of fiction and nonfiction that have as one of their chief goals and pleasures to give us practice in building the blend for another mind. Detective stories, comic books, graphic novels, horror stories, romance novels, psychological thrillers—the list of genres that command extraordinary amounts of time from writers and audiences is very long. In these works, audiences are building not only ideas of other minds, but also ideas of how other minds get ideas of how other minds get ideas of other minds... Some of these patterns of cascading conception come to count in a culture as general stereotypical recipes for how to think of psychological situations, fictional or otherwise: The husband dismisses his wife's fear that their daughter is soliciting the attention of the debonair captain whose fiancée is looking daggers in response.

Roman comedy and its successor, situation comedy on our own television, both depend upon the instant recognition of many of these cultural stereotypes of cascading ideas of other minds.

Fictional works that feed our need to practice the conception of unusual minds include the novels of Patricia Highsmith in the Ripley series, such as *Ripley's Game*; television series such as the BBC's modern version of *Sherlock Holmes*, in which Sherlock is explicitly a high-functioning sociopath facing another tantalizingly inscrutable weirdo in the character of Professor Moriarty; and a long list of movies, such as *The Silence of the Lambs*, *No Country for Old Men*, and *Collateral*. Detective novels in particular offer readers practice in conceiving of not only the criminal mind but also the penetrating detective mind, as it comes to understand the criminal mind. The detective, by understanding the criminal's mind, solves the crime. The detective in such cases is not only the object of our blending but also one of its best tutors.

Rhetoric—which Aristotle defined as the "faculty of recognizing the available means of persuasion in any particular situation"—is entirely dedicated to the study of other minds. The study of rhetoric, founded as a training program for lawyers, is entirely dedicated to giving students practice in conceiving of other minds for the purpose of knowing how to persuade them. Students are often surprised to hear that Aristotle's *Rhetoric* is routinely regarded as the first textbook of psychology, but that is because it concerns not subjects like reaction times but rather cognitive scientific questions like how we conceive of other minds, the relationship in those minds of emotion, inference, and belief, and the relation of language and gesture to our conceptions.

Theatrical plays routinely show us characters in the act of trying to construct blends that account for other minds. Consider as an example Julius Caesar's assessment of Cassius in the eponymous Shakespeare play:

> Let me have men about me that are fat;
> Sleek-headed men and such as sleep o' nights:
> Yon Cassius has a lean and hungry look;
> He thinks too much: such men are dangerous.
>
> Act I, scene ii, lines 192–195

Perhaps the most famous analysis of one mind conceiving of another mind is to be found in Shakespeare's *Othello*. Othello, a Moorish general in the Venetian army, has married young and fair Desdemona against her father's preferences. Cassio is Othello's lieutenant and Iago is Othello's trusted ensign. Othello is forming an idea of Cassio's mind; when he watches Cassio in conversation with Iago, Cassio's *appearance* drives him mad because he is imagining what kind of knowledge and experience Cassio could have that would make him look and act that way. One "input" to this blend is of course Cassio's appearance; but the other input is Othello's knowledge of how his own mind works—how its mental states relate to his bodily appearances.

In fact, Othello's blend is wrong. It is meant to be, because there is one more level in this cascade of conceiving of other minds, and it is at the top: Iago's mind is conceiving of how Othello's mind will conceive of Cassio's mind. Iago is a master of rhetoric: He wants to persuade Othello to a certain belief, and he knows just how to do it. Cunning Iago arranges scenes so as to elicit from Cassio certain appearances, certain actions. Iago believes that these appearances will be the ideal inputs to the mental web that Othello is assembling to make sense of Cassio. Iago seeks to arrange it so that the new stuff in Othello's blend for Cassio's mind is that Cassio has had sex with Desdemona. She is blameless, and says so when confronted. Othello smothers her.

Appearances count.

Identities

Great mental webs of mental spaces often include a lot of connections that are not wrapped up into a single idea. They can be hard to grasp. But blending can make a single idea out of them, a compression, which we can carry with us and expand on the spot to fit what we need to think about. An idea like *the cyclic day* or *the Supreme Court of the United States* is a manufactured, compressed identity. The analogies in such a great mental web are compressed to a stable identity, and the disanalogies are compressed to change for that stable identity.

The Way We Think analyzes a sketch in a *Zoobooks* magazine of how dinosaurs evolved into birds.[26] In the sketch, we see a dinosaur running on a track, chasing a dragonfly. In fact, we see several different stages of the dinosaur, each stage chasing the dragonfly, each stage a little more bird-like than the last, until, in the last stage, the dinosaur has become a bird. We don't have to see it this way, but the preference to establish identity connections across the different dinosaurs, with each state of the dinosaur resulting from a change in its previous state, is immediate and supported by the drawing. In the blend, there is a stable identity: The dinosaur, as a species, is represented by an individual dinosaur. But we know that, outside the blend, in the utterly vast mental web, we are dealing with thousands and thousands of individual dinosaurs and birds, not just one. Outside the blend, in the mental spaces the blend serves and calls upon, there are many different organisms, many different specific dinosaurs, with analogies and disanalogies connecting them. None of these organisms "turns into" another organism or "changes" into another organism or even "changes" its features to become more like its descendants. Rather, this blending web for the dinosaur-bird follows one kind of general blending template. In this general template, members of the species at a given time are compressed into an individual stereotype of the species at that given time. The stereotype has stereotypical characteristics.

Blends that compress individuals to a unique element occur throughout our thinking. For example, if half of Ohio voters voted one way and the other half the other way, this vast number of voters can be compressed to just two voters who oppose each other in the blend and "stand for" the population of voters. One can imagine a political cartoon of the two Ohioans who disagree with each other, marking their ballots differently, perhaps even looking confrontationally at each other.

In another compression, if 60% of Pennsylvania voters voted one way and 40% the other way, they can be compressed to a unique voter, the "average" voter, who of course does not exist, and who, in the blend, has a 60% "probability" of voting one way and a 40% "probability" of voting the other way. We say, "The average Pennsylvania voter has a 60% probability of voting against the ballot proposition." This is new stuff in the blend on a grand scale. Individual Pennsylvania voters are not ever the same as the average, and they each voted one way or the other, with 100% certainty, not a partial probability.

In the *Zoobooks* conception, the stereotyped stages of the dinosaur throughout evolutionary time undergo yet further compression, to create a single unique dinosaur in the blend. So the "beginning" dinosaur undergoes "change" until it "becomes" the bird. That very dinosaur has been chasing that very dragonfly on that very track for millions of years, and finally gets the dragonfly, but only by turning into a bird!

Similarly, the "Science" section of *The New York Times* invites us to contemplate the amazing "changes" in the North American pronghorn.[27] Why does the North American pronghorn run so excessively fast? Because it is running from the "ghosts of predators past." That is, it is remembering predators who in our age are extinct. The analogies across the pronghorns in evolutionary time are packed to identity for the species; the evolutionary outcome of great speed is packed to an intentional process in the blend: The pronghorn has "learned" to run that fast. The extinct fast predators "taught" it to run that fast. The behavior of today's pronghorns, which is in fact the result of the differences produced by evolutionary processes across generations, is compressed to another intentional process in the blend: The pronghorn "remembers." Outside the blend, we do not think that any individual pronghorn either "learned" or "remembered." We think some got eaten and some did not. Biological evolution is not the same thing as learning, and none of today's pronghorns is remembering predatory species that no longer exist. The structure in the blend helps us understand the vast mental web. But we are not deluded.

These are pyrotechnic examples: The dinosaur transforms into a bird and catches the dragonfly. The North American pronghorn learned from previous predators to run fast and accordingly makes idiots out of its modern predators. The average Pennsylvania voter voted this way or that with different probabilities in the two directions. If the bit about the average Pennsylvania voter seems to you just *true,* then you probably have a Ph.D. in polisci or statistics and are living in your disciplinary blend.

The reason to look at such wild examples is that we can easily see them for what they are. In each case, many different things are blended to create a stable, smoothly changing identity or unique element that we use mentally as a compact single idea to help us manage a vast and diffuse mental web, with lots of mental spaces. We use the blend to help us grasp, manage, and manipulate a mental web otherwise too diffuse and complex for us to master, just as we saw with the cyclic day and the Buddhist Monk.

This general template according to which we blend disanalogies and analogies to a stable if changing identity is used throughout human cognition in ways that we may not recognize. We create identities that seem to us to be just straightforward identities, requiring no new ideas. Why do we see these identities? Why do we see "the dinosaur" or "the lion" as changing over time? At first blush, we probably think we see it that way because it is just true and obvious, right there and utterly available from reality, with no need of imagination or the origin of ideas at all. In these cases, we are "living in the blend." I use this phrase—"living in the blend"—for cases where we are unaware consciously until we start to think about it seriously that there is any blending going on. Our attitude toward the blend does not at all involve the idea of blending. In everyday thought, in consciousness, we may never question that "the dinosaur" or "the lion" is just what it is, with no blending or compression. In the case of the Buddhist Monk, we see the blending immediately. But seeing the blend is very rare. Mostly, we are oblivious of blending work, and it takes some analysis to drag it onstage so we can look at a little bit of it.

Vera Tobin, whom I cited earlier, has shown that the basic, everyday way of thinking and talking about literary creation is to imagine that there is a unique identity—a literary "work"—that undergoes "change." She quotes

Hugh Kenner, who referred to the five-stanza version of Marianne Moore's poem "Poetry" as "the one scarred by all those revisions."[28]

> In this conceptualization, the many variations published under the title "Poetry" are compressed (Fauconnier and Turner 2002) into a single, concrete entity that the poet has altered many times. This entity is also metaphorically characterized as a living body, and the alterations that remove material from that body as violent mutilations. In this way, even a new, intact printing of an earlier version can be "scarred" by the publication of shorter variations.

None of the many versions published under the title "Poetry" has disappeared or been subjected to change or been damaged in any way. All those versions, lots of them, are all still available, unmarred. The compression of analogies and disanalogies across all of these many versions gives us a mental blended stable identity that undergoes changes, in this case changes that the critic dislikes. The blending follows a standard pattern, but we do not see it. At first, we are thinking just inside the blend, even though we recognize the mental web once we look harder.

We can create roles by blending, especially social roles. Nonhuman animals appear to recognize differences that correspond to what we might think of as closely drawn evolutionary categories: *offspring, conspecific, sibling, mother, alpha male,* or *predator*. But they do not appear to be able to invent ideas like *The Supreme Court, Chief Justice of the United States, prophet, pope, priest, professor, prostitute, preschooler, pastry chef, party girl, prince, prime minister, psychiatrist, proctor, president*. These are social roles. We have a strong ability not only to construct such roles but also to elaborate the evolutionary roles, so that they arc over ranges of time in which we were not born and will not live. We can conceive of roles constructed in other cultures that are alien to us and with which we have no experience. We can conceive of impossible fantasy roles, and those fantasy compressions can help us think about what roles we might want to build in our actual lives and institutions.

People

Adam Smith described how we understand another person in a particular moment, in a local scene, by forming a blend for the other person's mind at that moment. One "input mental space" to the blend is the other person's immediate conditions and features, and another "input mental space" is what we know of our own minds. In the blend, the other person in that particular moment is minded.

But in addition to creating a local and momentary mind for the other person, we can also create an abiding, stable, changing general identity for that person, an identity stretching over very many quite different particular moments and local scenes. We can do so by using a general blending template we have now seen often, in which a changing identity in the blend corresponds to analogies and disanalogies in the mental web outside the blend. The analogies are compressed to *identity* in the blend; the disanalogies are compressed to *change* in the blend. In this way, we create permanence for the person.

The baby boy born of the mother, the 18-month-old son learning language, the toddler, the lad in short pants, the adolescent, the young man, the worker, the husband, the father, the grandfather, and the old man inhabit quite different mental frames, with profound disanalogies between them. But the analogical connections across them are also strong. These disparate scenes have their place inside coordinated blending webs, and in the blend, there is a unique person, who undergoes change. The stable identity can be so strong that it creates situations. When Sherlock Holmes walks into a room, we know how the plot will develop, and we think we know people in real life who work something like that, too.

Of course, the principal stable but changing identity we invent through blending is our own personal identity. That is the subject of the next chapter.

4

The Idea of I

Selves

We construct a personal sense of self, a stable identity that undergoes change. Actually, we can construct different personal senses of self, depending on what mental web is active in our brains and what is brought to mind by props in our circumstances, and still feel that, although we were different just a few minutes ago, the self we happen to be right now is utterly stable.

Cultures ferociously support, maintain, and enforce such blended conceptions of an abiding self. Cultures invest a great deal of language in providing fixed names to the personal self in the blend. The name counts as a linguistic invariant, something that does not change, regardless of how it is pronounced, declined, or written, so as to indicate the culture's insistence that there is a stable referent, a person. Who am I? "I" am "Mark Turner." What an idea! If it does not seem so, it is because we are "thinking inside the blend."

A proper name refers to many different selves in many quite different situations: a newborn, a parent, an agent of action and inaction, someone healthy and someone sick, someone speaking a Coastal Californian dialect of English and someone speaking a Southern dialect of English and someone speaking a Received Standard English dialect of English and someone speaking Spanish and someone speaking French and someone speaking Italian and someone speaking Greek, usually over scores of years.

Strong rituals are invented by culture to magnify and increase the analogical connections over time, such as birthdays. What a new idea! These rituals help to connect some local moments to each other in the cycle of time and attach them to the "self": The birthday celebration, for example, follows a script or mental frame—it has, for example, friends, cake, and presents. These are defeasible: We might have a berry tart instead of the cake, but we recognize that we are having berry tart *instead of* more canonical birthday food, and feel all the more superior and virtuous for it. The repeated cultural use of the same organizing mental frame at different times enforces analogies all along the sequence, analogies that otherwise would not be there, but that, once they are there, assist the creation of a stable self in the blend. Only secondary details in the ritual are allowed to differ: To be sure, there is one more candle on the cake, a slightly different present, berry tart for the adults instead of gooey cake glopped in bad ice cream, but we are still required to think that the many people having these birthdays are all the same *self*, if changing. It seems obvious that it is the same self, but if we step outside the blend and look at the mental web that the blend serves, it is quite bizarre to think of all these people as the same self.

The existence of the blended self does not obliterate the rest of the mental web. We are not deluded: On the contrary, the blend for the self helps us manage the extraordinary amount of stuff in the rest of the mental web, the vast ranges of time, space, causation, and agency, which otherwise would lie beyond our cognitive powers to grasp, explore, and manipulate. The blend may have a unified self even though two given input mental spaces in the mental web contain quite different selves, even aggressively opposed selves, and even though the time relation between those selves spans many years.

Imagine a woman looking at her reflection in the bathroom mirror. She has a sense of her stable self, but the image in the mirror prompts her to think of some different selves in the past, and even to think of what one of them might think of the other. When her face in the mirror looks like a picture of herself from years ago—perhaps because of a hat, a flip of the hair, the lighting, the blouse, or her smile—she may suddenly inhabit a mental scene associated with a self from years ago who now addresses the self who is looking in the mirror. She may speak, and her voice may mentally attach not to the body speaking but to the younger person, the one "appearing" in the mirror, who says to the older person who is looking at the younger person in the mirror, "You have done OK." Or the same voice, with a different inflection, may attach mentally to the older person, saying, "I failed you, didn't I?" The woman in this rich moment is not deluded or insane: On the contrary, her ability to range mentally over the blending web is a sign of her mature understanding. She is a character in a life story. The stability of the character is in the blend, but having the blend does not stop her from considering the vast mental web of her "identity." On the contrary, the blend gives her a stable platform from which to consider the vast mental web.

The mirror is useful in such a setting. The image in the mirror is something perceptible that can be blended with the idea of a former self. In that blend, the former self does not look exactly like the image in the mirror, of course. Sometimes, in a cinematic film, the director will solidify the blend of the younger self by having the image in the mirror morph into the younger face, perhaps with the hairstyle or clothes of the younger self.

Mirrors, shadows, impressions, echoes, portraits, footprints, suits of clothing, and similar elements of our immediate environment are so routinely used to support advanced blending that an entire study could be conducted on the subject. In the case of the younger self in the mirror, the woman expands from the blend of her stable self to connect back up to different selves in the mental web, and then blends her present self and her past self with the idea of a conversation between two people. The two speakers in this conversation are in a scene of "classic joint attention." A scene of joint attention is one in which people are not only attending to the same thing but know that they are all attending to the same thing and know moreover that each of them knows that they are all attending and knows that they are interacting with each other by so attending. "Classic joint attention" is a scene of joint attention with just two or a very few people communicating about what they are attending to. In the case of the two speakers who are at two different "stages" of the same "self," the two speakers in this scene of classic joint attention are attending to themselves! In this blend, two different selves in the web—linked by an *identity* relation because we take them to be identical—are now the two people conversing. The identity relation is, in this case, not compressed to uniqueness: The two stages of the self remain distinct even though they are "identical," in the sense that they share an identity. This blend draws on the general notion of a conversation between two people: It repacks the mental web for the self so that two different people in the web, connected by identity, are blended with the idea of two people in a conversation. In the compact, tractable blend, one can have a conversation with "oneself."

This blending, to bring two identical but different selves into conversation with each other, can exploit differences of time in many different ways. The face in the mirror might be taken, in the blend, as a future self who is looking back and offering advice, or encouragement, or justification, or disapproval.

Let's review: The unitary and stable but changing "self" in the blend—the woman, for example—can be expanded back to the mental web in which there are lots of different selves in lots of different mental spaces, all of those different selves sharing the same identity. But then some of those different selves in the mental web can be blended with some other scene, so as to produce a blend

in which there is more than one self. It is very common for this reblending
to use some material prop like a mirror, a shadow, or a portrait. Conflicting
dispositions and preferences in the present unitary "self" can be unpacked to
locate two differing but identical selves in the vast mental web, who "disagree"
with each other, and there are phrases to designate this: One can say of a com-
ment one just made, "Oh, that was my evil twin speaking." Someone can say
that he is "arguing with" himself. Parts of the interior of the present self can be
unpacked to different selves, even though those different selves are connected
by an identity relation, and then those two selves can be blended with a scene
of interaction, so that they have a conversation, a fight, a reconciliation.

There are funny versions of this reblending (of the unpacked self) to a
scene of classic joint attention in which two (different but identical) selves
interact. A comic political commentary shows a boring candidate for the US
presidential nomination talking to himself in the mirror, as the face in the
mirror falls asleep. In the Quentin Tarantino film *Pulp Fiction,* Vincent Vega,
the character played by John Travolta, talks to his image in the mirror in the
bathroom while his gorgeous companion for the evening, who happens to be
his boss's girlfriend, is waiting for him in the living room. He says:

> One drink and leave. Don't be rude, but drink your drink quickly, say
> goodbye, walk out the door, get in your car, and go down the road.
> It's a moral test of yourself, whether or not you can maintain loyalty.
> Because, when people are loyal to each other, that's very meaningful. So
> you're gonna go out there, drink your drink, say "Goodnight, I've had
> a very lovely evening," go home, [...] And that's all you're gonna do.

The scene is hilarious, because, by projecting our own knowledge of how we
operate to the blend that has Vincent Vega's mind, we can tell what is going on
inside the character. When someone has to talk to himself that directly, with
that much repetition, he's struggling. Even more, we know he's struggling. By
blending what we know of ourselves with what he says, we are inclined to think
that he knows he's struggling, too. It creates a tension, funny but palpable.

Remembrance of Things Past

If we remember a thrilling moment, the thrill does not come from the past.
To say so may sound paradoxical, because, if the present scene is, for example,
a crashing bore, we think that of course the thrill must come from the past,
because there is no source for it in our present conditions. To be sure, we often

use memory to distract ourselves from our present circumstances, and in such cases, it seems as if we are replacing the present with the past. Suppose we are standing in a long line, waiting, bored, or stuck in a traffic jam in the sweltering heat, frustrated, and we remember a thrilling moment.

But of course, the thrill must be part of our present emotional and biological machinery, because when we remember a past self or a past scene, it cannot be the case that the past self or past scene comes dropping in through a science-fiction time warp. No past self shows up with its own feelings and its own biology for running those feelings. No previous self actually possesses us. Whatever is happening, we, in the present, are the ones doing it. The only feelings we can have are the ones provided by our own present biological activity, in our present conditions. That's all there is.

Our experience of the past is that something comes winging into the present from somewhere—we do not know where, but it feels as if it is somewhere else, some time that is not the present. Obviously, this is a convenient illusion, one that consciousness finds congenial. A memory does not bring its own mind to feel thrill or embarrassment or longing. It must work with what is present in our bodies. The ability to feel and think comes exclusively from our present machinery. We are surrounded by material stuff in the environment—objects, souvenirs, photographs—and we find them meaningful. But the meaning we attribute to them comes from our present biological machinery, and of course the emotional and psychological reaction to them comes from our present biological machinery. We are not taken over by something that is not us to have feelings that do not come from us.

Not only is our reaction to the memory a product of our present biological machinery, but also, the memory itself can only be part of present biological activity. That is, the memory does not fly into our heads out of the past. It is a present thought. To understand the memory, we must combine *present* elements of our mental activity that we take as referring to the past with our *present* psychological self and its abilities. We must activate our *present* abilities for taking perspectives, making judgments, reacting emotionally, and making choices. These abilities are only here and now. They are not provided by time travel. Memory does not make two different times intersect, although it feels that way.

When we recall a scene and ourselves in it, we are constructing an element in the blend that counts as a former self. We do this by projecting capacities and elements of the present self into the blend. This projection of elements of the present self into the blend lets us equip our former self in the blend with a mind. It feels like cognitive time travel. We also project elements into this blend from a mental space for the previous moment—our memory. Then, in the blend, we have a former self, equipped with capacities of our present mind, but in some of the conditions that come from the memory.

Literature, language, and film often call on us to "cast our minds back to a time when…" Of course, we cannot actually cast our minds back. It is all here and now. Any narrative thought involving our former self as an agent depends upon blending, of our present minds and our present memories of our former minds and conditions. We remember that we were embarrassed, and our present minds, contemplating the memory, might provide the feeling of embarrassment anew.

Our memories are remarkable for being able to "call into the present" moments in time that are unrelated to the present moment. It seems the most natural thing in the world, but why should we be able to remember—as we are listening to a bird sing—that we once had blue tennis shoes, that we once flew a kite over the ocean, that someone once pronounced our name with an Irish accent? It is an open problem in cognitive science why people should have a memory that operates in this way—allowing us to drop in by instantaneous time travel to prior, unrelated moments, without even needing to rewind the tape of memory to get back to that point. As Arthur Glenberg writes in "What Memory Is For,"

> To avoid hallucination, conceptualization would normally be driven by the environment, and patterns of action from memory would play a supporting, but automatic, role.[1]

But as Glenberg astutely observes, human memory often takes the upper hand in deciding what one is thinking about in the present moment:

> A significant human skill is learning to suppress the overriding contribution of the environment to conceptualization, thereby allowing memory to guide conceptualization.[2]

We show amazing flexibility in blending our present selves with past conditions suggested by memory. Here are some of the different ways in which we can make such a blend:

1. We remember an experience from the past. We remember also that at the time we found the experience embarrassing. Projecting some of our present psychological activity to the blend, we experience a twinge of

the embarrassment and attribute it not only to our present selves but also to our past selves. The twinge in the present is taken as an analog of the emotion in the past. We can say in such a moment things like, "The embarrassment flooded back to me."

2. Same as 1, except that now we come up with the idea of a different past self, one who operates differently than we remember our past self operating— that is, the past self in the blend now analyzes the experience as fear of evaluation by peers, fear of shame in their eyes, and not at all as essentially embarrassing. We now feel, for our past self and even as our past self, pride rather than embarrassment. Our new, blended past self feels superior, even though in our memory of our past self, the past self felt inferior.

3. Same as 1, except that at first, we experience no twinge of embarrass-ment. But then we begin to cultivate the blend, bringing in more and more remembered conditions, more and more analysis of the situation, until the twinge of embarrassment arises in our present bodies, and is of course attributed also to the past self. Sometimes, when our goal is to feel a particular emotion or strike a particular attitude, we might put such a blend together expressly for that purpose. We may say that we have "recaptured" our former self or our former feeling or our former attitude. We can say, "I am myself again."

4. We do something now, and it means something to us. But then, we remember something we did in the past that seems similar to the present action. We blend these two actions together, so that instead of seeming to be two separate events, they constitute a pattern, a characteristic, part of our personal identity. The analogies compress to a feature of our personal identity. Our past self and our present self thereby merge, and potentially merge with a continuum of past selves, so that the pattern becomes part of our stable personal identity. We think of this as part of our personality, of our "way," of our *self*.

These are just a few of the mental avenues we can follow in constructing a past self in a blend, and in relating those past selves to our present self. All of these, and many more patterns as well, are instances of projection of self from the present into a blend that receives "input" from the past, or rather, from memory, which is only present. Past selves are never here, but it feels as if they are.

This odd way in which human memory works—allowing us to activate in the present moment material unrelated to and even inconsistent with it— makes blending over different selves much easier. Imagine how difficult the blending of selves would be if we had to work our way along a continuous thread through time to "get back" to a particular moment. This way of moving through time is exactly what is experienced by the main character in H. G. Wells's *Time Machine*. In this novel, time is presented as a dimension one can move through. In this way of dealing with time, we do not activate just this or that part of time. Instead, we move through it, preserving adjacency of moments. The time machine has a lever, which, if turned one way, carries the passenger through sequential moments of time, ever farther back in time. Moved the other way, it carries the passenger similarly through sequential moments ever farther into the future.

> I drew a breath, set my teeth, gripped the starting lever with both hands, and went off with a thud. The laboratory got hazy and went dark. Mrs. Watchett came in and walked, apparently without seeing me, towards the garden door. I suppose it took her a minute or so to traverse the place, but to me she seemed to shoot across the room like a rocket. I pressed the lever over to its extreme position. The night came like the turning out of a lamp, and in another moment came to-morrow. The laboratory grew faint and hazy, then fainter and ever fainter. To-morrow night came black, then day again, night again, day again, faster and faster still.

This utterly impossible scene does not seem so strange, in imagination. We have a folk conception of time as linear, and this folk conception has its scientific version, in which time is a linearly ordered succession of events.

But, crucially, human memory is not constrained to move in the fashion of H. G. Wells's time machine. Like the Tardis in *Dr. Who*, the human mind can drop in anywhere in the past, or, if one prefers the alternative version of the metaphor, any moment from the past can intrude via memory into the present. George Eliot gives a sense of how it feels:

> Our moods are apt to bring with them images which succeed each other like the magic-lantern pictures of a doze; and in certain states of dull forlornness Dorothea all her life continued to see the vastness of St. Peter's, the huge bronze canopy, the excited intention in the attitudes and garments of the prophets and evangelists in the mosaics above, and the red drapery which was being hung for Christmas spreading itself everywhere like a disease of the retina.
>
> *Middlemarch: A Study of Provincial Life*[3]

Freedom from having to rewind the tape to get to a previous moment is a powerful feature of human memory. Consider the case in which we recognize a present scene as analogous to a past scene that turned out badly and brought on a negative emotion. Blending saves us from having to put together from scratch all those decisions, evaluations, and reactions. We can bring well-formed decisions, evaluations, and reactions to the present scene just by blending from memory. Blending our old self and our present self can collapse the analogy between the two events to one moment, and this delivers to us *knowledge* of how to react in the present scene, without going through the work of figuring it out. Decision-making is, in many ways, a science of blending. Blending the present self and the past self provides wisdom, or at least quick disposition and choice, to the present self. The present self is a richer present self for its being able to put together a past self by blending, and then, in another step, blending the present self with the past self so that the present self has the smarts of the past self. Good for us.

Which Me Am I Now?

To count as a normal person, we must constantly manage our viewpoint and focus. The mental web for the distributed self is very large, and offers us many places in which to situate our viewpoint and focus. This work is almost always unconscious. We can move an old, familiar viewpoint into the present self by blending.

If we lose track of part of the mental web for the self, and so cannot use it to make a new blend for our present self by activating the projections from that former self, we may be regarded as insane, or psychologically off-kilter, somehow lacking a full sense of self. The mentally healthy person is expected to be a kind of Cincinnatus. Cincinnatus, so the history books say, was once a patrician Roman leader and military commander, but was reduced by his political opponents to working a farm with his family. In one of Rome's dark hours, under attack by the Aequians and Sabines, the Roman Senate called for the appointment of a dictator, and Cincinnatus was appointed. What happens? The senators bring the message to the farm; Cincinnatus is at the plow. The assignment is no problem for him—he puts off his present self, reactivates his previous abilities and knowledge, takes over, defeats the enemy, and, once that is done, immediately resigns his absolute power to return to the farm. And this pattern happened not once, but twice, in both 458 and 439 BC. The present self of Cincinnatus very easily takes on and puts off different projections from his former selves. He takes on different viewpoints and perspectives that are part of his past. He switches from Cincinnatus the farmer to Cincinnatus the dictator to Cincinnatus the military strategist and soldier to Cincinnatus the farmer. Such flexibility is very impressive, but we all have it.

The exceptionally popular Samurai X, Rurouni Kenshin, a character in a manga series, is a fictional analog. Kenshin was once an assassin, but gave up that pattern. He atones by wandering Japan to protect its people. He is now a gentle person, but when the situation calls for it, he reactivates his former self, fights extremely well, and then lays it aside just as smoothly. The mentally healthy human being is expected to be able to manage this web of selves, contemplate past selves, judge them, reactivate them in the present, retire them, even suppress them. "I can't do it," someone says, when confronted with a challenge. "Of course you can," we reassure them. "You've done it before. Just relax and focus. It will come back to you."

A person unable to work fluidly with this dynamic mental web of selves, adjusting projections, blocking projections, developing new stuff in the blends, and locating viewpoint and focus, counts as mentally reduced. For example, in *The Bourne Identity*, both a novel and a film, Jason Bourne has amnesia. He is entirely capable of operating in the present. No one would know that he cannot remember "who he is" without his revealing it to them. Indeed, he is forced to go to considerable effort to convince a woman with whom he joins up that he is unable to remember "who he is." His evident competence in the present makes it difficult to believe that he doesn't have it all together.

Mostly, we are able to construct in the blend past selves by projecting most of our present selves to the blend but also projecting to the blend memories, or information that we take as referring to past conditions, and developing inferences in the blend. Jason Bourne cannot do that. Or at least, he cannot do it at first. But beginning from the premise that the present self has continuities with the past—if you can speak English, you must have learned it somewhere; if someone addresses you in German, and you find yourself, to your surprise, responding in fluent German, you must have learned it somewhere; if you have the ability to subdue armed professionals instantly, and indeed observe yourself in the present actually doing it before you knew you could do it, you must have been trained somewhere—he begins to infer for himself a past. What he can do in the present constrains the size of the space of possibilities through which he must search to find out who he is. He does some research to get more particulars. He makes these inferences without feeling any conscious access to memories, at least at first. It "comes back" later, bit by bit. Bourne's problem is not that he does not have a kind of present self, but that he cannot form the blend for the past self and accordingly cannot get the needed projections to the blend for what we would regard as a full present self. A similar exploration of the mental web for the self is the basis of the film *The Long Kiss Goodnight*.

In the film *Unknown*, the main character, a CIA agent who has been trained to impersonate a scientist, survives an automobile accident, comes out of a four-day coma, and remembers the scientist. He projects knowledge of the scientist into the blend for his present self, and takes his viewpoint from inside that blend. Thinking inside the blend, he thinks he is the scientist. He gradually readjusts viewpoint and focus until he gets the right information in the right spots, with the right status, all appropriately distributed across the web. Similarly, in *American Dreamer,* a novelist who hits her head wakes up thinking she is a character in a romance novel she wrote.

Post-Traumatic Stress Disorder has been thought to be a condition in which the present self is, in a way, "captured" by a past self. That is, all of the mental machinery of course belongs to the present self, but something in the present activates a memory or perhaps a conditioned response. This activates a self that includes heavy projections from a "past self." This past self is activated not just as a person to be contemplated and considered by the present self, not just as an input mental space for projecting elements to the present self, but rather as someone who provides the viewpoint for the present self. The stereotype in this description is the Vietnam veteran in a tense situation surrounded by explosive noise, who takes on a viewpoint suitable for combat in Vietnam. The controversial diagnosis of dissociative identity disorder, in the current *Diagnostic and Statistical Manual of Mental Disorders*, is a response to cases where both memory and the construction of a personal self do not seem to operate in the ways we expect.

Art offers very sophisticated explorations of the different possibilities for blending that can take place in the mental web for the self. The character Zetsu in the manga series *Naruto* seems to have two different selves who inhabit the two halves of one body. Sometimes, they can split apart. Sometimes, they hold a conversation. They must be very good at coordinating, because together they can function as one body! Analyses of how we vary in conceiving of present and past selves, and of where we locate viewpoint and focus in the vast mental web for the self, provide the framework for many films, many plots, many characters. In the popular *Star Wars* movies, Darth Vader's self has an aspect that comes from projections of his previous self, Anakin Skywalker. In this blended sense, Anakin is inside Vader, and after a moment of catharsis at the end of *Return of the Jedi,* in which Vader is dying, the Anakin component receives much stronger projection and transforms Vader upon his death into an after-life character that we take as the "releasing" of his inner Anakin.[4]

What Will I Be?

H. G. Wells's *Time Machine* and Dr. Who's Tardis can move not only into the past but also into the future. Our memories cannot do that, but, in a way, our ability to blend can produce future selves. We think of future selves that are nonetheless us. We also imagine future selves for other people. To decide whether we want to do something, we can imagine how we will feel if we do it. That is, we make a hypothetical future person and consult that self on how it feels. This means blending our present selves with imagined conditions and producing, in the blend, a future self.

This blending of the present self with future conditions in order to imagine a future self can rebound to the present. Here is an example from Shakespeare's Sonnet 3:

> Look in thy glass and tell the face thou viewest,
> Now is the time that face should form another,
> Whose fresh repair if now thou not renewest,
> Thou dost beguile the world, unbless some mother.

Two futures, and thus two future selves, are constructed for the addressee. In one, the addressee (the "friend") has a child. In the other, he does not. This is a disanalogy, and that disanalogy can be compressed to the blend for one of the future selves, to produce the *absence* of the child. In the first future, there is a mother of the child, too. In the other, there is the same woman, but there is a disanalogy between them, which can be compressed to *absence* of motherhood for that woman in the second possible future. Similarly, we can construct *absence* of fatherhood for the friend in that second possible future. The result is a strong counterfactual relation between the two alternative futures—fatherhood versus absence of fatherhood, motherhood versus absence of motherhood, child versus absence of child.

This counterfactuality between the possible futures precipitates new stuff for the idea of the present, where the friend is making the choice. At first, the present is just the present; it is what it is. One of the things it has is the friend, who is framed as acting in one way or the other: choosing to become a father or choosing not to become a father. If one of the futures comes true, then there is a woman—unspecified but actual—in the present whose future self includes *mother of the child of the friend.* This is a blend, creating a new feature for some woman in the present that she did not previously have, and which in the present she may not know about at all. If the other of the two futures comes true, then that same woman in the same present "no longer" has the future self in which she is the *mother of the child of the friend.* So, right now, in the present, that woman has an indeterminate status: Is she that "future mother" or not? If the friend resists the speaker's persuasion, then in the present, there is an absence of procreation.

Blending very often creates such *absences* in our present. When it does, we are usually oblivious to the creation. In retrospect, it can seem as if the absence was always part of our idea of the present, but not so. Consider that there is always an infinity of objects and events that are not in our actual present, but we do not therefore actively conceive of our present as containing that infinity of absences. Rather, to create the absence, we need to activate the opposite idea of existence, and view that idea of existence as disanalogous to the present. We compress the disanalogy to *absence* in a new blend for the present. It is only our active conception of the possibility of the future child, for example, that creates the *absence* of procreation and of "future motherhood" in the blend.

The counterfactual relation between the two possible futures is compressed to the present: Where before, the present did not involve the woman, and there was no question of the young man's treatment of her, now in the present blend there is an action of *unblessing* that woman. She counts as *blessed* in one blend for the future, and consequently *blessed* in the present scene if that scene includes the friend's choosing to procreate. But there is a potential future with no child, which derives from a present with no procreation. Therefore, in the present, the woman who, in the other future, is the mother, is now, in the present, "deprived" of that future. The friend's choosing not to procreate is now an action by him of *unblessing* that particular woman, although we do not know who she is, and presumably neither the man nor that very woman knows who she is, or that she has been unblessed. Compression of relations between alternative scenes of future selves creates the action of *unblessing* in the present, and even the kind of action it is.

I Play, Therefore I Am

Given that we are always constructing selves dynamically in vast blending webs, it is natural to see one action as connected to another, one event as flowing out of another and into another, across great expanses of time, space, causation, and agency. We blend over moments to construct a self, an identity, a single idea that we can carry with us, and we expand that blended self to help us handle the next moment. Life is not a linear sequence of isolated strips of local activity. Running throughout all of these events is a self, dynamically constructed. We do not think of the self as created from scratch every few minutes, and wiped away to produce a clean slate every few minutes, as we begin or end a little strip of activity. Choices that we make affect our construction of the blended self. Conversely, the idea of the self affects the choices that we make.

When people meet each other, they ask, "How are you?" "How are you doing?" "How are you feeling?" "How's it going?" These are general questions, about the overall state of the blended self. The answer to these questions is not a sequence of individual events—"I managed to get good tea at breakfast, I failed to purchase a book I wanted, I won a small online auction for a folding chair with a bid of $5 . . ." When someone tells us such things, we still want to ask, "So, how are *you* doing?" And we ask ourselves, "How am *I* doing?"

Let's call this question the "how am *I* doing?" measure. It is an overall measure that is always in the background, always in play, usually much weightier for our decisions and actions than any narrowly local measure of success or failure. It arches over time, space, causation, and agency, as a long-range mental activity, a fundamental abiding goal. The goal for "how am I doing?" is not to add up how one is doing at this little moment plus that little moment plus that little moment and so on, as an aggregate linear sum of little moments, but instead to construct a self, an identity, which not only has an effect on every moment but also helps us control and manage what kinds of moments we get into in the first instance, and how to turn moments from one kind of interaction into different kinds of interactions, perhaps interactions not even imagined a moment before. This urge to compress and expand the self, to carry the self with us, seems to be a major influence on all our choices.

Although Adam Smith, often called the "father of classical economics," was himself a master at contemplating blending webs for the self, classical economics in our time pays almost no attention to the role of the dynamic construction of a self over time. This absence is especially complete in that branch of microeconomics known as "game theory." Game theory is fundamentally a cognitive theory, making claims about how individual minds work when choosing. In game theory, and "classical rationality" more generally, the self is regarded as having consistent preferences and beliefs; actions result consistently from those preferences and beliefs; and these preferences, beliefs, and actions remain the same across equal moments of choice.[5]

But such classical rationality theories of the self turn out to be fundamentally vulnerable in assuming one kind or another of moment-to-moment consistency for the individual making the choices. They do not take account of the effect of the overarching blended self, which can be stable in the blend despite considerable inconsistency across the various selves in all the input mental spaces. Or at least, all of the many assumptions in game theory of moment-to-moment consistency of belief, preference, and action with which I am familiar turn out not to stand up to experimental test.[6]

Consider, for example, a standard economic game called the Trust Game. In the Trust Game, there are two people in a laboratory experiment. Typically, they are anonymous to each other, interacting through a computer interface or pieces of paper passed by a research assistant. Each is given 5 dollars. The first person can transfer any number of those 5 dollars, including 0, and the amount transferred is tripled and given to the second person. The second person then has the opportunity to send to the first person any number of dollars that the second person has, which is just the sum of the original 5 dollars and three times the amount sent by the first person. That ends the game. What do people do?

The Trust Game shows clearly the main principles of game theory: People make choices; they contemplate as they make these choices what other people will choose in response. This is called "interdependent" or "strategic" decision-making. Classical microeconomics takes it for granted that people have stable preferences that govern their actions, that they know those preferences, and that their actions follow their preferences. On this logic, if we know their actions, and all the other details of the game, we can infer their preferences because their preferences are "revealed" in their actions, and if we know their preferences, we can predict their actions. The payoff matrix in the Trust Game is the number of dollars the player earns, and people want to maximize their earnings. Both of the people involved in the Trust Game know all of the rules of the game and they know that the other person knows that they know, and so on.

So what will happen? According to game theory, any player imagines what the other player or players in a strip of interdependent decision-making will choose. For the Trust Game, that means the first person will imagine what the second person will choose in response to what the first person chooses. We see here the first person conceiving of another mind—a mind for the second person. In general for games, there is a kind of mental switchback ladder, a cascade of blend after blend, with, in principle, no limit: The first person imagines that the second person imagines that the first person imagines that the second person imagines that the first person will send so-many dollars.

Classical game theory assumes that both players follow the same choice procedures. In the simplest case, any player chooses at any moment whatever choice
puts that individual player on the path toward the preferred possible outcome
for that individual player. "Possible outcome" here always takes into account,
above all, that one can achieve an outcome only if the other person does not
make a choice that makes it impossible to stay on the path to that outcome.
So thinking about one's choices involves thinking about other minds and
their choices. Each player assumes that any other player will also choose at
any moment whatever choice puts that individual player on the path toward
the preferred possible outcome for that individual player. Under these conditions, a plausible path to a possible outcome is called an "equilibrium path."

So let us run this switchback ladder for the Trust Game. The first person
is conceiving of what the second person will choose. But in the Trust Game,
the first person is allowed no response, no choice, to what the second person
chooses, so of course the second person, to maximize earnings, will send back
nothing, because anything sent lowers the second person's earnings. The first
person, knowing that the second person will send back nothing, of course
sends nothing. That is the game-theoretic prediction.

This Trust Game experiment has been run with subjects very many times
all over the world, and people, even in the alien setting of the laboratory, do
not behave as game theory predicts. For example, we ran this experiment on
190 subjects.[7] These subjects were anonymously and randomly paired with
each other, and they knew they were randomly paired and that they would
never have any information about each other except the very little bit they
learned in the game about the other player's actions. In fact, a subject in
the Trust Game learned only one thing and only in the role of second player:
The subject learned how many dollars the first player sent. The first player
in the Trust Game never learned anything about what the second player
decided. The subjects were anonymous to the experimenters and their choices
were private—in the sense that the data were anonymous to the experimenters, and a research assistant paid each individual subject his or her earnings
alone in a room after the experiment was concluded by handing the subject
an envelope of cash. All of the subjects knew all of this and knew that all the
other subjects knew it. They interacted with each other in the Trust Game
only once, without seeing each other or knowing anything about each other.
Actually, they played very many games in our battery, during a span of about 2
hours, but they were randomly paired anew for each task, and they knew that.

In the Trust Game, 105 of the 190 (55%) sent money as player 1. That is,
the majority did the opposite of what game theory predicted. Sixty-five of

them sent back money as player 2. Of the 105 who received money as player 2, 64 sent back money, which means there was even one person who sent back money after receiving nothing! Twenty-three of the 85 (27%) who sent nothing as player 1 sent something as player 2. Forty-three of the 125 (34.4%) who sent nothing as player 2 sent something as player 1. Only 62 of 190 (33%) played in the Trust Game the way game theory predicts for both player 1 and player 2.

Now let us look at just those 62 people, 33%, who played as game theory predicts in both roles in the Trust Game. Let's call them the "pure maximizers" in the Trust game. We asked them when they were player 1 to guess what player 2 would predict that they would send. When they made this guess, they knew they would get paid money if they guessed correctly, and, again, they knew that they would be paid in cash their lump earnings in private by an assistant (not the experimenter) after the battery of experiments was concluded, and that the assistant would not know what they had done at any point in the very long battery of experiments, a battery including many tasks that were individual rather than interdependent. The assistant knew only what envelope of lump payment to give the subject in private at the end.

Twenty-one of these 62 Trust Game pure maximizers (34%) guessed when they were player 1 that player 2 would predict that they would send money, which means that even the pure maximizers in this one run of this one game could not be relied upon to believe about the other player what game theory requires them to believe. Of course, according to game theory's idea of how a mind thinks of other minds and its own mind, everybody as player 1 should have guessed that player 2 would predict that player 1 would send no money. We also asked them to make a range of other guesses, each time paying them for correct guesses. The result was that, overall, 38 out of the 62 pure maximizers in the Trust Game (61%) failed to hold the beliefs consistently that game theory requires them to hold.[8]

Players naturally wonder of the other players, "Who are you?" What would be involved if player 1 tried to form a blended conception of player 2 the way a game theoretician imagines? It looks trivial: Of course player 2 is a pure maximizer, regardless of conditions, so sends nothing, and so of course player 1, contemplating this conception of player 2, should send nothing. Game theory dictates for each player both how that player will go about choosing at each moment (although not that player's preferences) and what that player will imagine to be the way any other player will go about choosing at each moment.

But suppose player 1 doesn't go along with the dictates of game theory, and instead believes that a player 2 who receives some money will turn out not to play as a pure maximizer would, or at least will not be certain to play as a pure maximizer would. This is in reality the optimal, most accurate belief. As we saw, 64 of the 105 player 2s who receive money (61%) return money. Player 1 has 6 possible choices: to send 0, 1, 2, 3, 4, or 5 dollars. Player 2's choice is to send back some integer number of dollars (possibly 0), so the number of choices player 2 has is just 1 more than the number of dollars player 2 has after receiving the tripled amount (perhaps 0) from player 1. If player 1 sends 0 dollars, then player 2 has six possible choices: to send 0, 1, 2, 3, 4, or 5 dollars. But if player 1 sends 1 dollar, then player 2 has 9 possible choices: to send 0, 1, 2, 3, 4, 5, 6, 7, or 8 dollars. If player 1 sends 2 dollars, player 2 has 12 possible choices. If player 1 sends 3 dollars, player 2 has 15 possible choices. If player 1 sends 4 dollars, player 2 has 18 possible choices. If player 1 sends 5 dollars, player 2 has 21 possible choices. So there are in total 81 different paths of action through even this very simple and tiny game, that is, 81 send-and-return pairs. To maximize earnings, player 1 would need to determine, somehow, which of the six choices would bring player 1 the maximum payoff, where the payoff is the number of dollars player 1 kept plus the number of dollars player 2 returned. To do so, player 1 would have to compute, for the first choice (send 0 dollars), the probabilities of each of the 6 possible responses by player 2 (the sum of these probabilities will be 1), and compute the product of each such probability and the payoff to player 1 in that case, and then sum all those products. Player 1 would then do the same for each of the other 5 possible choices. The result will be 6 such sums, one for each of the choices available to player 1. Player 1 must then rank these sums by amount to determine the choice available to player 1 that is associated with the largest amount, or the multiple choices that are all associated with the largest amount. Player 1 then makes that choice. If it is not unique, any of the choices associated with the largest sum will do.

Feeling dizzy? I am, and that is even after I have boiled this computation down to its barest bones. Even for a player 1 who is able to construe the decision in this way, it requires both a daunting amount of calculation and, much more daunting, a divine oracle to provide the probabilities. Unless some of our subjects were both mathematical geniuses and descended from the Delphic oracle, none of them could have made such computations in the amount of time they took to make their choice. So of course they must have made their choices by some other method.

There is another game, Dictator, in which there are 2 players, each with an endowment of dollars, and one of them, the Dictator, has the chance to send some dollars to the other. Notice that the Dictator in this game is in exactly the same role as player 2 in the Trust Game: You have some dollars, the other person has some dollars, and you can send some of your dollars to the other person, and then the game is over. We ran Dictator as part of our "within-subject" battery of experiments. "Within-subject" means that we are comparing the behavior of each subject in one condition to the behavior of the *same* subject in a different condition, or even in the same condition at a different time. We arranged it so that each subject who played the Trust Game also played as the Dictator in the Dictator game, and that the endowments of the two players in Dictator were identical to the 2 endowments that the subject faced as player 2 in Trust. Fifty-eight out of 190 people (30.5%) act differently in the 2 different settings, despite the fact that game theory predicts that they would behave the same, because the payoffs and the action structures are the same. Of even the 62 pure maximizers in Trust, 3 (5%) send money in Dictator, and so are not maximizers in Dictator.

There is another game called Donation, in which each player has 5 dollars, and one player, the Donor, can decide to send dollars. Those dollars will be quadrupled before the result is given to the other player, and then the game ends. Of the 62 pure maximizers in Trust, 11 (18%) send money, and so are not maximizers, in Donation. Of the 59 subjects who are pure maximizers in both Trust and Dictator, 10 (17%) send money, and so are not maximizers, in Donation.

Just for these three games in our within-subject battery (Trust, Dictator, and Donation), only 49 of the 190 subjects (25.8%) act as game theory predicts, and many of those do not even hold the beliefs that game theory requires.

If you were surprised at how people react to the computer-therapist ELIZA, you will be really surprised to hear how people play in these economic games in a laboratory setting when they are told that the other player is not a person but a computer algorithm written to maximize its own earnings narrowly on every individual task independent of any other task in the battery. This computer algorithm is a perfect classically rational player, playing exactly at every moment the way classical game theory predicts. Of course, the computer algorithm never passes any money under any circumstances in Trust, Dictator, or Donation. The subjects in these experiments have no uncertainty at all about how the computer will play—we quiz them a little to make sure—and they know they get paid money for answering the quiz questions correctly. Also, the people in these experiments can have no illusion that the computer has a mind, or feelings, or anything else. The computer does not even know that it is a computer or that it is in a laboratory setting or that there is another player or that it is engaged in an economic game; it can develop no idea of the human player; it can have no feelings or judgments or attitudes toward what the person does, and so on. Accordingly, people can have no illusions about social good for the computer. We had 40 human subjects in this experiment. As Trust player 1, 12 out of 40 (30%) send money to the computer. As Dictator, 2 out of 40 (5%) send money to the computer. As Donor in Donation, 10 out of 40 (25%) send money to the computer.[9]

The routine failure of subjects to behave as game theory predicts is *extremely old news* and is routinely confirmed in the literature. As early as 1952, the results of experiments whose designers included John Nash (who later shared the 1994 Swedish National Bank Prize in Economic Sciences in honor of Alfred Nobel) were found to disconfirm the theory. Reportedly, this discouraged Nash and others from pursuing the theory.[10] And yet, approaches based on game theory have grown to be highly influential, perhaps even dominant, inside the social sciences.

There are two usual repairs for the failure of game theory to predict behavior. The first defense is that game theory may not be predictive, but it is prescriptive, telling us how we ought to behave. "[D]escriptive failure is prescriptive opportunity."[11] No question, it can be good to train people, and there are many training programs for doing so in various disciplines. The individual navigator, martial artist, musician, athlete, or anyone who has learned a specialized skill has been trained to useful patterns of action that are often quite contrary to untrained impulse. The purpose of the training is to enable the specialist to succeed by following the prescriptions. It has been known for thousands of years that people can be trained to a specialized way of thinking for specialized actions, even that new habits can be instilled that become second nature. But training in game theory will in many cases result in failure if the other players do not have the same training and follow it. The weakness of the pure maximizer is well known. The player who follows the pure prescription in certain games (e.g., the game called "Beauty Contest") pretty much always loses. Of course, there are highly specialized situations, invented by culture, and separated from everyday life—such as playing chess—in which these principles may be helpful, and for those purposes, it is useful to learn the prescriptions of game theory. But that is no indication that we can generalize from these prescriptions to everyday thought and behavior. Absent evidence to the contrary, there is no reason to expect that behavior by people trained to play small economic games should tell us much about how people in general conceive of their choosing self, conceive of the choosing selves of others, or in fact make choices.

The second repair for the failure of game theory to predict behavior is that one should not expect game theory to be connected to the world of actions;

it is a formal system, and the task of the game theorist is to derive conclusions from axioms according to the transformation rules allowed in that formal system. But the premise of this defense precludes game theory from shedding any light on the human mind or human behavior, except for the human mind performing formal derivations. Whether one finds the formal derivations valuable is a matter of taste. A toy formal axiomatic system is a useful sandbox in which the student acquires the feel of derivation, but aside from pedagogical exercises, the toy formal axiomatic systems are not regarded as interesting unless they shed light on something, such as a branch of mathematics about which we already care for other reasons.

Whatever we know best always provides strong candidates to be activated as "inputs" to blends we make. The expert sailor thinks of much of life by blending it with the scene of sailing. The committed gardener thinks of much of life by blending it with the scene of gardening. The gamer thinks of much of life by blending it with playing games. The game theorist is blending a mental space for a noncooperative, usually zero-sum game (like chess or Go) with actual decision-making in real environments. It is not surprising that this gaming blend seems natural to a game theorist, because the game theorist takes these economic games as familiar and important, indeed spends a great deal of time working with them. But suppose that the person who is doing the blending is not a gamer but a surfer. Then the blender is likely to find a different blend attractive, natural, and important, such as the blend Tom Morey made when he was asked, "Why do you surf?"

> Because that's all there is. It's all surfing. Everything! Name something that isn't surfing. In the New York Stock Exchange, you check it out, you pull in, and you try to figure out when to kick out safely. Surfing in the ocean just happens to be the purest form of surfing.[12]

Morey's refreshing and intuitive view has proved to be so attractive that there are consulting firms in California that employ big-wave surfers to present training seminars for corporate decision-makers on how to think like a big-wave surfer in the sea of business challenges. This can be quite helpful. My favorite rule is the ABCs of surfing: "Always Be Cool."

But there are principled reasons to doubt that our idea of human decision-making should be constructed by blending it with our idea of surfing. Most notably, people do not have a basic ability to surf. Learning to surf is much harder than it looks. Learning to surf takes long training and practice and dedication, not to mention actual muscular strength. Much of learning to surf consists in overcoming one's very natural, almost irresistible impulses. Nor does it seem to be the case that an intellectual understanding of surfing helps much without a lot of practice. Beginning surfers make the same "mistakes" again and again and again. These mistakes are explained to them repeatedly. They might score 100% on a test of their understanding of what they should and should not do, but still make the same mistakes. This is inevitable, because a lot of surfing is contrary to everyday impulses. Surfing runs counter to some basic ways we think and decide.

But just as in martial arts, sailing, and various other sports, gradually our surfing habits adjust, away from everyday patterns to more specialized patterns. These specialized patterns end up seeming so natural as to make the earlier "mistakes" seem strange. A good martial artist has a hard time even getting into a bad stance. A good sailor has a hard time leaning the wrong way or moving in the wrong direction when the boat is heeling. A good surfer (I'm a poor one) has a hard time failing to pop up on the board.

That is not because popping up on the board starts out seeming normal. Popping up on a surfboard is, relative to everyday human movement, a very strange action. This is why it is so difficult: Beginners try to do all the usual, basic, everyday things that we do when we want to stand up, and every one of them pitches the beginner into the wave. Standing up on the board is not at all like standing up anywhere else we already know. Surfing is also relatively new in human behavior—it is not, like auditory location, a behavior long-grounded in evolutionary abilities. It is clearly a cultural invention, only a few hundred years old, and its current worldwide popularity developed only in the twentieth century. Surfing takes special equipment, special effort, special conditions, and a lot of time spent in the pursuit of this special purpose. If people were already doing in their daily lives all the things that they get from surfing, there would have been no reason to invent it, and no reason to expend such significant resources to engage in it. Surfing is costly. The benefits are considerable. But certainly what the accomplished surfer is doing does not provide an explanation for what people already do all the time in decision-making. If it did, there would be no need to hire big-wave surfers to give corporate seminars. We would know it all already.

Strategic game-playing is just like surfing. We should not generalize from strategic game-playing to decision-making any more than we should follow Tom Morey's invitation to generalize from surfing to decision-making. Beginners are terrible at strategic game-playing. They must go through training and practice to be able to play the games without making ridiculous mistakes. There are few world-class surfers, few grandmasters in chess, few master poker players.

Special conditions must be arranged, usually with special equipment, to foster the training activities. This is exactly the condition of strategic game-players. These strategic games are cultural inventions, going back, as far as we know, only several thousand years. Chess, go, and tic-tac-toe, like surfing, must be learned, and absent cultural instruction, they do not come up automatically in the human mind. Strategic game-playing between a few players is a tiny cul-de-sac in the sweep of culture. It is fun, intriguing, attractive, and not at all useless as a laboratory for learning powerful if unnatural techniques. But only the game-player would think it is the place to start modeling decision-making. Morey finds his surfing blend for decision-making natural because of his interests, and the game-theorist finds his game blend for decision-making natural because of his interests.

Given the human capacity for "second nature"—that is, the ability to live mentally inside one of these acquired blends—it may seem to the accomplished game-player as if all of human decision-making is just the deployment of the kind of thinking one knows from strategic games. Game-playing is all there is. It's all games. Everything. Name an interactive decision that isn't a game. In the New York Stock Exchange, you think of the goal, and of what the other players are thinking, and you make your choice by thinking about how your choice will combine with their choices. You are trying to win by making them lose. Game-playing in the stock market just happens to be the purest form of game-playing.

But given how rare conscious strategic game-playing is, how bad people are at it, and how much effort culture must make to arrange for it to happen, it is unreasonable to expect that it would provide a basis for explaining how people actually make the complicated decisions they must make in their lives, and especially how they actually construct ideas of other minds belonging to those other people with whom they must interact. If people were already doing in all their everyday activities just what they are doing in playing strategic board games, there would have been no reason to invent those games, and no attraction in creating special, reserved moments and equipment for practicing them. People would be good at them from the start.

Trying to use strategic games as the main input to a blend for explaining human decision-making has ended up making people look incompetent, because in the main, as behavioral experiments routinely demonstrate, subjects "deviate" from the equilibrium principles that game theory assumes for them. One can describe what they actually do as "deviation" only if one somehow imagines that the principles of equilibrium thinking are the norm and that people are mentally falling flat all the time.

Actually, human beings are awesomely effective. Consider everything they have invented and established in the last 3,000 years, for example. Or everything they have invented and established in the last 50,000 years. Before the Upper Paleolithic, which is extremely recent in evolutionary time, we were just another large mammal. By the Upper Paleolithic, we were poised to take over the globe. Almost everything we care about—including institutions and chess—has been invented since that time. It seems unlikely from the beginning that one could explain this level of success, all around the world, throughout the entire species, by viewing it as a form of an activity at which human beings are demonstrably and incontestably so bad: strategic game-playing.

From the perspective of the blending hypothesis, it may be that what is needed is a new kind of game theory, cognitive game theory, which would begin from the cognitive science of the human mind rather than from some procedures imagined for noncooperative board games. Cognitive game theory would embrace the possibility that people are constructing selves moment to moment, that they might be consistently inconsistent in ways game theory does not envision, and yet that they can construct a sufficiently stable single self in the blend to help them manage the vast mental web of their identity. Indeed, such approaches are making headway inside behavioral economics. Recently, many suggestions have been made that behavior in games depends upon framing, patterns of social cognition, habits of social interaction, and so on. In our experiments, we find behavior that runs counter to the predictions of game theory, but from the cognitive perspective, that might not be surprising at all, because each of these different experimental situations, moment to moment, offers the player a different narrative, a different role, a different metaphoric room, and a different set of possibilities for constructing a blended *self* inside that setting. The blended self created inside the story lies in a web of past selves and future selves.

I Think, Therefore I Am

When we start to contemplate who we are, we sense that our thinking must be far more complicated than we usually realize. The human brain has maybe 10 to 100 billion (10^{11}) neurons. The average number of synaptic connections per neuron is maybe 10,000 (10^4). The total number of connections in the brain is therefore maybe 100 trillion to a quadrillion (10^{14}–10^{15}). Those 10^{15} connections are about 10,000 times as many stars as astronomers think might be in the entire Milky Way galaxy (10^{11}).

Ten thousand Milky Ways, inside your head. All those connections, inside your skull, in a system weighing about 1.4 kilograms. The timing and phases of firing in neuronal groups, the suites of neuronal development in the brain, the electrochemical effect of neurotransmitters on receptors, the scope and mechanisms of neurobiological plasticity—all going on, in ways we cannot even begin to see directly. The only time we are likely even to sense that our mental system is so complicated is when something goes wrong, as when someone has a stroke and language falls apart, or someone gets food poisoning and surreal colored patterns start swimming around in vision, like a painting by Salvador Dali.

For centuries, scientific notions of perception depended on the "Cartesian theater."[13] The Cartesian theater is the implicit idea that there is a little perceiver in the head, a kind of attentive little guy, who pretty much watches a representation of what we are watching in the world, and who figures it out. In the simple human-scale frame of the *perceiving self* that we can hold in consciousness, each of us is an attentive self looking at the world and figuring it out. To answer the question, "What is the mind doing?" we blend the simple, conscious frame of the perceiving self with our frame for the answer to a scientific question and so create a folk notion of mind in which there is an attentive mental agent looking not at the world but at a mental representation of the world, inside our head. In this advanced blend, there is a watchful little perceiving guy looking at sensory representations of the world, and that perceiving self becomes our scientific notion of who we are. This watchful little perceiving guy is the audience of the Cartesian theater. The notion of the watchful internal homunculus seated in his Cartesian theater had influential scientific standing for centuries. But it turns out that vision works nothing like that. Vision is far more complicated; there is no attentive homunculus in the mind; and there is no anatomical spot where sensory data are assembled into a unified representation of the sort we imagine, much less on a big screen with surround-sound and supplements for olfactory, gustatory, and tactile perception. Indeed, it is a deep scientific problem to explain how something like a coffee cup—with its hue, saturation, reflectance, shape, smell, handle for grasping, topology, temperature, and so on—can seem in consciousness like one unified object.

In neuroscience, this problem is called "the binding problem" or "the integration problem." We are built to think that the reason we can see a coffee cup as one unified object is simply that the coffee cup is one unified object whose inherent unity shoots straight through our senses onto the big screen in the conscious mind, where the unity is manifest, unmistakable, no problem. It is natural to hold such a belief, but the belief turns out to be just a folk theory, another case in which we blend the simple, conscious frame with the frame for the answer to a scientific question to produce a folk theory that we mistake for a scientific explanation. It does not seem to us in consciousness that we are doing any work at all when we parse the world into objects and events and attribute permanence to some of those objects, but explaining how we do this presents a major open scientific problem.

In consciousness, typically, we frame experience as consisting of little stories. Our basic story includes a perceiving self who is an agent interacting with both the world and other agents. In these stories, we possess straightforward powers of decision, judgment, and choice. Consciousness lives by these little stories of choice: We encounter two paths, or a few fruits, or a few people, and we evaluate, decide, and choose. We act so as to move in the direction of one of the possibilities. We say, "I'll have an espresso." We are not set up to see the great ranges of invisible backstage cognition that underlie what we take to be evaluation, decision, and choice, any more than we are set up to see the work of vision or language. But we are set up to make a blend of (1) the human-scale conscious experience of a chooser choosing and (2) the answer to the scientific question of how the mind decides. The result is *Homo economicus*—a folk theory of a rational actor in the head, with preferences, choices, and actions. *Homo economicus* is the sibling of the little perceiving guy in the Cartesian theater. The Cartesian homunculus looks at the screen and perceives; *Homo economicus* looks at choices and chooses. In the *Homo economicus* blend, each of us is a stable chooser with interests, living a narrative moment as an agent with a personal identity, encountering other such agents. This human-scale narrative blend of the self as a stable identity with preferences that drive choice toward outcomes is marvelously useful, and instrumental in action, motivation, and persuasion. It is a worthy fiction that helps us grasp ranges of reality that are diffuse and complicated. It serves mental webs that span time, space, causation, and agency in a tractable, human-scale blend.

I Communicate, Therefore I Am

Because of blending, people are able to invent technologies. We excel at coming up with new technological ideas. Speech, for example, is a personal technology developed for communication. It is at human scale. It operates in the present, within congenial human dimensions, with pleasing proportions. In consciousness, we have a simple mental frame for speech. In this frame of *speech*, one person uses speech to communicate with another person, and these two people take turns. When we ask ourselves how we really work and what we really are, it is easy for us to blend the scientific question with our human-scale conscious experience of speech. The result is a conception of the self as a *converser*. This is a blend of self with communications technology. Once we have this blend, we can use it as an input for further blending. Thought can be conceived of as a colloquium, either informally, as in our notion of thought as an internal debate or internal conversation, or scientifically, as when we imagine that different aspects or even anatomical locations of the brain are "talking" to each other, "communicating." So it turns out that one of our most basic conceptions of self derives from blending our diffuse idea of what a self might be with our idea of a basic communications technology—speech. In the new blend, the self is a converser.

Writing systems are another communications technology, merely several thousand years old, and not widespread until quite recently in our history. Many conceptions of self derive from blending our idea of our mind with our idea of writing systems. These conceptions range from the notion of the *tabula rasa* to Hamlet's promise to the ghost:

Yea, from the table of my memory
I'll wipe away all trivial fond records,
All saws of books, all forms, all pressures past
That youth and observation copied there,
And thy commandment all alone shall live
Within the book and volume of my brain,
Unmix'd with baser matter.

Act 1, scene 5

The invention of each new communications technology has brought new opportunities for understanding the self by blending our vague, diffuse notions of self over time with our notion of self as a user of the technology. These technologies include semaphore signaling systems, signed language, telegraphy, personal letter writing, telephony, radio, television, email, and chat rooms. Our communications technologies are designed by us to operate at human scale and are therefore at the center of what we know best. Accordingly, we can think of ourselves by drawing on our concepts of communications technologies, by blending our general concept of ourselves with our understanding of how the communications technology works.

Communications technologies frequently include a representation of self: A videoconference, for example, presents a virtual self. This representation of the communicating self can be viewed either as an instrument that is deployed by the "true" self or as a being with a mind of its own. Seeing the representation of our self, and picking out some of its features, we can blend our self with our representation to try to change our self in one direction or another. This unpacking and repacking of the self has been imagined in many fictional works, ranging from stories of avatars or disguises or masked performances to the explicit separation of self and daimon in Philip Pullman's novel series *His Dark Materials*.

Massively multiple online synthetic worlds present many opportunities for blending self with telecommunications technology. A synthetic world can contain a representation of the communicating self: an online avatar, a digital citizen. The avatar can be designed so as to be a separate self, a site of experimentation with selfhood. The directorial self can be framed as the observer and the avatar as the agent; the directorial self can be surprised, challenged, refreshed by the actions of the agent, and learn from the agent, even incorporate the agent or reject the agent. In such a case, it is as if there is an experimental self, held at a distance, who is auditioning for influence on the selfhood of the directorial self. One of the most interesting aspects of online avatars is that they can act in ways that are not explicitly intended by the directorial self. For example, there are several scripted gestures available to the online avatar, such as dance routines. The directorial self can engage the avatar in one of these dance routines without knowing what it will involve. In such cases, the avatar is not a closely-controlled puppet of the directorial self. On the contrary, the directorial self can be surprised to see its avatar engaged in activities that the directorial self did not intend. The communications technology makes it possible for other players to construct not only clothing but also behaviors for other avatars to adopt. These bits of self, offered by others, can be blended directly into the avatar, and the avatar, so closely related to the director, can be blended with the general self. The communications technology of synthetic worlds pushes the envelope of selfhood. Events can happen in them that a given avatar does not intend, does not want, does not actually understand, or cannot resist, but the director must deal with the experience of having had them synthetically.

We know what we are less than perfectly because we are not equipped to know what we are. A scientific understanding of the human mind is in its embryonic stages, at best. But we are indeed equipped to make human-scale blends that include human-scale conceptions of self, relying heavily on simple conscious frames to do so. The result is notions like the Cartesian perceiver, *Homo economicus*, the mind as an internal conversation, and so on. Because telecommunications technologies are built to be used at human scale, they provide powerful potential inputs to such blended notions of self. It is not that these telecommunications technologies are blurring the boundaries of the self; rather, they are making it possible for us to have certain human-scale conceptions of self in the first place.

Let's Get Personal

Who is that other person? To imagine another mind, we need to project some of ourselves, our own mindedness, into the blend. But it is a two-way street, because our imagining of our own selves frequently involves projecting to the blend conditions and circumstances we do not actually experience. This is clearest when we fantasize. Sometimes, those fantasy conditions are available to us mentally because we perceive them as belonging to another person. So although we project something of our selves into the blend for another person, we also sometimes project something of those other people into the blend for our imaginary self!

Adam Smith understood both directions of this two-way street. He describes this direction in a long, eloquent section at the beginning of *The Theory of Moral Sentiments*:

That this is the source of our fellow-feeling for the misery of others, that it is by changing places in fancy with the sufferer, that we come either to conceive or to be affected by what he feels, may be demonstrated by many obvious observations, if it should not be thought sufficiently evident of itself. When we see a stroke aimed and just ready to fall upon the leg or arm of another person, we naturally shrink and draw back our own leg or our own arm; and when it does fall, we feel it in some measure, and are hurt by it as well as the sufferer. The mob, when they are gazing at a dancer on the slack rope, naturally writhe and twist and balance their own bodies, as they see him do, and as they feel that they themselves must do if in his situation. Persons of delicate fibres and a weak constitution of body complain, that in looking on the sores and ulcers which are exposed by beggars in the streets, they are apt to feel an itching or uneasy sensation in the correspondent part of their own bodies ... (1.1.3)

Neither is it those circumstances only, which create pain or sorrow, that call forth our fellow-feeling. Whatever is the passion which arises from any object in the person principally concerned, an analogous emotion springs up, at the thought of his situation, in the breast of every attentive spectator. Our joy for the deliverance of those heroes of tragedy or romance who interest us, is as sincere as our grief for their distress, and our fellow-feeling with their misery is not more real than that with their happiness. We enter into their gratitude towards those faithful friends who did not desert them in their difficulties; and we heartily go along with their resentment against those perfidious traitors who injured, abandoned, or deceived them. In every passion of which the mind of man is susceptible, the emotions of the by-stander always correspond to what, by bringing the case home to himself, he imagines should be the sentiments of the sufferer. (1.1.4)

Upon some occasions sympathy may seem to arise merely from the view of a certain emotion in another person . . .

This, however, does not hold universally, or with regard to every passion. There are some passions of which the expressions excite no sort of sympathy, but before we are acquainted with what gave occasion to them, serve rather to disgust and provoke us against them. The furious behaviour of an angry man is more likely to exasperate us against himself than against his enemies. As we are unacquainted with his provocation, we cannot bring his case home to ourselves, nor conceive any thing like the passions which it excites. But we plainly see what is the situation of those with whom he is angry, and to what violence they may be exposed from so enraged an adversary. We readily, therefore, sympathize with their fear or resentment, and are immediately disposed to take part against the man from whom they appear to be in so much danger. (1.1.6–7)

What are the pangs of a mother, when she hears the moanings of her infant that during the agony of disease cannot express what it feels? In her idea of what it suffers, she joins, to its real helplessness, her own consciousness of that helplessness, and her own terrors for the unknown consequences of its disorder; and out of all these, forms, for her own sorrow, the most complete image of misery and distress. The infant, however, feels only the uneasiness of the present instant, which can never be great. With regard to the future, it is perfectly secure, and in its thoughtlessness and want of foresight, possesses an antidote against fear and anxiety, the great tormentors of the human breast, from which reason and philosophy will, in vain, attempt to defend it, when it grows up to a man. (1.1.10–12)

This species-wide capacity to blend self and other to produce in the blend a new self is so advanced, remarkable, immediate, and powerful that the hunt has been launched for genetic and neurobiological scaffolding that helps us achieve it. This hunt has occasioned what is alternatively termed the mirror neuron "revolution" or the mirror neuron "craze." We will return to it in the last chapter.

Let's Get Married

Adam Smith describes settings in which both self and other are present to perception. But blending comes easily to us regardless of present perception. That is one of the great advantages of our drop-in-anyplace-anytime memory.

Imagine a groomsman at a wedding that is happening in a park on a cliff overlooking the Pacific Ocean. While he is performing his duties, he begins to think about his girlfriend, with whom he went diving off Cabo San Lucas 3 weeks earlier. She is not at the wedding. As the vows come up, and he is standing there in the line of groomsmen on the groom's right, looking at the bride and groom, he begins to imagine himself in the role of the groom, and his girlfriend in the role of the bride. It is a daydream, based in present perception, and also using elements that are not in the present scene.

But when the real, visible bride is asked whether she will take this man, our groomsman has an unexpected, uncomfortable sense in the daydream that his girlfriend, in the role of bride, doesn't like it. She is more than hesitant. She is resistant. In this fantasy, perhaps she refuses to answer; perhaps the groom wonders what he has gotten himself into; perhaps, surprised, disoriented, he begins to wonder whether he has been duped. None of this, of course, is happening to the actual bride and actual groom before him. Their emotions are entirely contrary to those in the blend he is imagining.

This groomsman is acting within a familiar mental story—with roles, participants, a plot, and a goal. It is a wedding story, and he is a groomsman. He is fulfilling his role in the story admirably, but then, he remembers this different story, about diving near Cabo San Lucas. Why, mentally, should he be able to inhabit these two stories at the same time? There are rich possibilities for confusion, but he remains unconfused about what is actual. He does not swim down the aisle, even though, in the diving story, he is swimming. He speaks normally even though, in the diving story, he is underwater. He does not mistake the bride for a shark.

Human beings vault way beyond merely imagining stories that run counter to our current situation. We connect two quite different mental thoughts, ideas, or structures that should be kept absolutely apart, and we then blend them.

The groomsman at the wedding, for example, makes analogical connections between his girlfriend and the bride and between himself and the groom, and he blends these counterparts into a daydream in which he and his girlfriend are being married at the ceremony. The blended daydream is manifestly false. He should not make the mistake as he obediently discharges his duties as a real groomsman at a real wedding of thinking that he is in the process of marrying his girlfriend. Yet, he imagines it, with potentially serious consequences: disquietude, a touch of sorrow, and a sense of the fragility of his beliefs. His sense of his actual self can undergo remarkable turmoil and investigation as he constructs this blend, regardless of the fact that the blend is not only false but, in its own terms, impossible.

Through blending, truth and insight frequently come from what is false, fictional, impossible. The temporary answer to the question "Who am I?" can come largely from contemplation of what is false, fictional, impossible. It is the wrong question to ask in these cases whether the blend is "true," if what we mean by calling a blend "true" is that it presents a scene that we think corresponds to the actual state of the world. To be sure, there are indeed many cases—in detective work, science, planning, explanation, and so on—in which what we care about is whether the imaginary scene corresponds to actuality. But in other cases, that is not the mental purpose of the blend. The contemplation of the blend provides insight that serves some mental web, and a "false" blend can serve a "true" web. This is such a useful application of blending that it has acquired a special name in mathematics and logic: *reductio ad absurdum*. In such an argument, we prove that some assertion must be *false* by showing that a contradiction follows if we assume that it is *true*. These arguments proceed by blending. One input to the blend has the established structure of the mathematical or logical system with which we are working. The other has the assertion we think must be false. We keep the mathematical system, including its deduction procedures, intact, but blend it with the new and suspect assertion. We then run the blend according to the deduction procedures of the mathematical or logical system until contradictory structure arises in the blend, and from that, we infer a truth about the mathematical system, namely that the suspect assertion is false within that system. The false blend serves truth and insight in the mental web. This is an enshrined mechanism of proof in mathematics and logic.

This process of using a false blend to guide us to truth in the mental web that it serves may seem technical and alien, something for proving theorems, but we do it constantly in constructing ourselves. Are we guilty? Did we do something wrong? We blend ourselves with the outcome and then realize we could never have done that, because we were in a different city at the time or we hate that kind of food or whatever. The blend is false. Suppose—we have seen this one before—we live in Cleveland and wonder whether we should become a stockbroker in San Francisco. Part of this blend may seem in fact to reveal our "true" self: Yes, that was all along who we *really* are; at last we see; how could we have been so blind to our own identity? Just think of the freedom, the thrill of that kind of employment. But then we realize that the stockbroker must start work at 6:30 in the morning Pacific Time, when the New York Stock Exchange, on Eastern Time, opens, and suddenly there arises in the blend an all-important conflict we had not even previously activated: We keep vampire hours, and we do our worst work in the morning. That blend is not us, after all. In the blend, we are a stockbroker. It's false but serves a mental web that overall lets us see truth about our self.

Who Are We?

Each of us knows that we have the ability to pay close and focused attention to something, including another person. By projecting from our knowledge of our own mindedness, we can create a blended understanding of that other person as fully minded. Accordingly, we can know that the other person has the ability to pay close and focused attention to something, including us, and that the other person can have a blended understanding of us, in which we have full mindedness, projected from them. We can continue to build this new recursive stuff in nested blends: We think that they think that we think that they think... that we are attending to what they are attending to. In this complicated mental web, we think that we and the other person both know all of this, and that we are interacting with each other in paying attention to the same thing. Without this mental web, we could not operate in the scene of joint attention. Joint attention is a central subject in cognitive science, often viewed as crucial to the human capacity for learning.[14]

This blending web for joint attention is conceptually indispensable for our concept of human communication. Joint attention combined with sophisticated communication gives us what is often taken in linguistics as one of our most basic mental frames for what it means to be human, a mental frame referred to as "the ground." The ground includes "the speech event, its setting, and its participants."[15] The ground seems to us very basic. It is part of the "interface" that consciousness provides for our management of reality. The ground has the speaker, the hearer, the time of the speech event, and the location or site of the speech event. It has either joint attention or the possibility of establishing joint attention.[16]

Ideas of *I* and *you* are connected to the ground: The most basic ground has a speaker and a hearer. The speaker says things like, "*I* am speaking to *you*" and "*I* draw *your* attention to *that* freight train bearing down upon *us*." Words like *I, you, your*, and *us* are called deictics or indexicals: The meaning we construct depends on who is saying them. We need to know the ground in order to understand a word like *now* or *here*.

The ground seems to us basic and immediate, but as we have seen, underlying it are vast blending webs that contribute to that all-important, portable, human-scale frame of joint attention, and ideas like *you* and *I*. The ground can be expanded to help us handle even more complicated mental webs. Ronald Langacker discusses the way in which an utterance in one ground can prompt for a "surrogate ground,"[17] as when, for example, the verb "say" prompts us to add yet another ground to the cascade, as when someone says to you, "Benvenuto said to me that we should meet. Welcome to my home." There is a speaker and hearer in one ground, but the speaker in that ground uses "say" to prompt for another ground, inferentially with a different time (because *say* is in the past tense) and perhaps with a different location, in which Benvenuto is the speaker and the person speaking about Benvenuto was the hearer when Benvenuto spoke.[18]

But now consider an actual everyday example: The anchor of a televised news program says, looking straight at the camera, "Joining me now, Scott Rasmussen...," and at this point the screen changes to show the faces of two men, each in its own window, with different backgrounds, indicating that they are in different places. The news anchor is evidently in yet a third place. She keeps speaking from that place as her face disappears from the screen. But we construe the two men as listening to her as she says, "president of rasmussenreports.com and author of *The People's Money*. Also, Chris Stirewalt, our Fox News digital politics editor and host of 'Power Play' on foxnews.com." What is the ground? At this point, as we are watching the screen, the inner vertical edges of the two windows containing the faces of the two men swing backward so that they are at an angle and reveal a window containing the face of the anchor, as she says, "All right, guys, thank you both so much for being here. So, Scott..." There is no physical *here* in which the anchor, the two men, and the viewer are combined. All three of the faces we see are looking straight out at the camera, which is interpreted as meaning that they can see each other, something not possible in face-to-face communication. Who is the *I* who is speaking? We know that the communication of the anchor depends upon vast production crews, telecommunications technology, delivery devices. We know that "joining" here is a matter of cooperating in allowing a crew to transmit audiovisual signals in a videoconference. In some sense, we feel that we, the viewers, are the hearers, the "you," or rather, one "you."

Broadcast news involves fabulous mental webs for conceiving of *I, you, us, we, here, now*, and all the other aspects of the ground. In another example, a co-anchor, outdoors, with a crowd, says to the members of the on-site crowd,

"Good to have you all out there, as we"—and here she looks at the camera and points into it—"welcome you all back to *The Early Show*." This takes place at the beginning of the broadcast. Who is *you* and in what sense can we be welcomed *back* to *The Early Show*? One way to make sense of this is to create a you who routinely watches *The Early Show*. This is an implied viewer. Another news anchor says, looking into the camera, "OK, you've heard the news: China's economy is bigger than Japan's . . ." and another, looking into the camera, says, "A fatal crash . . . This was the view from news chopper 2. You saw the story unfolding live as breaking news on our CBS news between 5 and 7 a.m. . . ." I, the hearer, certainly did not see it unfolding live, and you probably did not, either. Another popular and influential news anchor signs off with the appropriately dated version of, "And now you know the news of this Thursday, March the 20th. . . . Thanks for having us in," as he reaches out his hand to the camera. The anchor certainly knows that there is a delay in broadcasting even live news, and further that people at home routinely record these broadcasts to watch later, in which case, the viewer cannot know the news at the moment when the anchor actually spoke those words in the studio, and cannot have "had" at that moment "the news team" "in."

In all these cases, we are constructing a scene of *blended joint attention.* The mental frame of actual joint attention is one input to this blend, but other inputs include our mental space for our real situation, our mental space for what we imagine to be the real situation of the anchor, and our mental spaces for telecommunications technology, broadcast news crews, the broadcast audience, and so on. In the scene of blended joint attention, we and the anchor are attending to something jointly, and there is communication about the object of joint attention. The result is a very congenial human-scale scene, of blended joint attention, even though outside the blend, we and the anchor are not jointly attending.

We are constantly doing complicated work to create a blend that provides mindedness to the other person with whom we are conversing, and the case is no different in these broadcast news scenes of blended joint attention. We know that the anchor, who is talking to us, does not know who we are. In the blend, the anchor is looking at us but cannot actually see us. Outside the blend, the anchor is looking at a camera lens. We are involved in communication with the anchor, but the anchor cannot actually tell whether we have risen to answer the doorbell, and we do not feel as if we should excuse ourselves when we do so. We think that the anchor does have a concept of the addressee, but the anchor's concept is not the same as the one he or she would have in a face-to-face conversation. It is a blended concept, a blended addressee, one who is there even if no person is actually there. That is, it is an implied hearer.

We take the anchor who is speaking as prompting us to think of an implied speaker and an implied hearer and further prompting us to consider blending our concept of ourselves or of other people to some extent with that implied hearer. These terms are familiar from the analysis of fictional works. The opening lines of *Adventures of Huckleberry Finn* are:

> You don't know about me without you have read a book by the name of *The Adventures of Tom Sawyer*; but that ain't no matter. That book was made by Mr. Mark Twain, and he told the truth, mainly.

The notion of a stable but changing Samuel Clemens, the author of *Huckleberry Finn*, is already the result of a complicated *self* blending web, and that self is putting forward an implied *Mark Twain* self, a "pen name" self, who is putting forward an implied author, and that implied author is putting forward an identity named "Huck Finn" to serve as narrator, and we take it that the author and the narrator are prompting us to construct two implied readers, who are implied other minds, and that these two implied readers are not the same. For example, we recognize almost immediately in the novel that Huck Finn, the narrator, is implying various conditions, knowledge, and judgments for his reader, such as agreement with Huck Finn and respect for his authority, but that Mark Twain, the author, is prompting us to construct a different implied reader, and that this second reader is supposed to agree to an extent with the implied author in the implied author's assessment of the character and the mind of the narrator.

The ground, as a basic mental frame for understanding human communication, is itself a compression of vast and complicated mental webs. We see some of this complexity in the case of *Huck Finn*, or even in rock lyrics, where the "you" is an implied hearer.

> Pleased to meet you.
> Hope you guessed my name.
> But what's puzzling you is the nature of my game...
> So if you meet me
> Have some courtesy
> Have some sympathy, and some taste.
> Use all your well-learned politesse
> Or I'll lay your soul to waste
>   "Sympathy for the Devil," Rolling Stones[19]

A World War II American propaganda poster, displayed in the Smithsonian, reads, "When you ride ALONE, you ride with Hitler. Join a Car-Sharing Club TODAY!"[20] A man is shown driving a car that has no top, and next to him, in the passenger's seat, is a line-sketch in white of Hitler in uniform. One sees through Hitler to the car seat and surroundings. The man driving the car does not seem to notice Hitler. The compressions to a human-scale scene are considerable. Who, in the ground, is the speaker? Who is the *you* who is addressed as the hearer and commanded to join? Who are we, looking at it? What is "today"? What is the moment of speaking, and what is the situation? By now, it is easy to see that there are many possibilities for implied readers and implied speakers. There are also implied viewers, who look at the man driving. The reader of the poster is implicitly prompted to construct a blend of self with both the driver and with the viewer of the driver. The possibilities for the blending are many. The viewer's self might be blended with the implied viewer of the unwitting offender in the car, with the actual unwitting offender, or partly with both, or with neither—because the actual viewer is already in a car-sharing pool, but understands that other potential viewers might achieve different blended selves in response to the poster. The hearer does not need to be a man with a hat or a car, much less this hat and this car, or even a driver, or even the viewer of such a driver, in order to construct a blend for *self* that includes projections from this mental web and its blends, and even to decide then that the blended self that arises from this interpretation should be made counterfactual, that is, a potential self from which the actual self is distinguished. This is even what the poster implies— the implied reader of the poster has not joined a car-sharing club but should.

Satires like Jonathan Swift's *A Modest Proposal,* or Blaise Pascal's *Lettres Provinciales*, legendarily depend upon such possibilities for implied selves. In such cases, we see that the implied author is not the same as the implied writer, and that the implied writer's implied reader is not the same as the implied author's implied reader. For example, in *A Modest Proposal*, the narrator, with very careful reasoning and fully civil voice, presents the deplorable conditions wrought by overpopulation in Ireland:

> It is a melancholy object to those, who walk through this great town, or travel in the country, when they see the streets, the roads and cabbin-doors crowded with beggars of the female sex, followed by three, four, or six children, all in rags, and importuning every passenger for an alms. These mothers, instead of being able to work for their honest livelihood, are forced to employ all their time in stroling to beg

sustenance for their helpless infants who, as they grow up, either turn thieves for want of work, or leave their dear native country, to fight for the Pretender in Spain, or sell themselves to the Barbadoes.

The narrator then carefully brings us to the conclusion that the best and most civil way to solve the problem is to arrange for surplus children of a certain age to be used as food:

I have been assured by a very knowing American of my acquaintance in London, that a young healthy child well nursed, is, at a year old, a most delicious nourishing and wholesome food, whether stewed, roasted, baked, or boiled; and I make no doubt that it will equally serve in a fricasie, or a ragout.

At some point in reading *A Modest Proposal*, every reader comes to understand that the implied author not only disagrees to the utmost possible degree with the implied writer but is in fact satirically condemning the entire administration of Ireland's affairs, and that the implied author's implied reader is expected to be horrified at the implied writer's implied reader, who of course concurs with the implied writer's sober reasoning, restraint, and judgment. And all Americans are supposed to feel a little twinge at the presentation of the knowing American and his knowledge of the use of children as pedestrian food. Not only does the American have the experience to know what he is talking about, but he also apparently lacks knowledge of even the simplest refinements of cooking.

It happens all the time that when we are communicating, we think of several implied selves. Doing so is not unusual or restricted to odd genres of literature. This is clear from broadcast news, which is immensely popular, something in the background of life everywhere—from the computer screen to the airport lounge to the gym. In the United States, there are ideological news anchors (Bill O'Reilly) and ideological faux news anchors (Jon Stewart, Stephen Colbert) who run shows dedicated to creating implied viewers who agree with the implied news anchor. These faux news anchors invite actual viewers to create one mental web after another, so the actual viewer can create a self that is blended with the self of the implied viewer. The anchor projects confident superiority and includes the implied viewer as part of the right-thinking tribe, virtuous and praiseworthy for belonging to the correct crowd. Actual viewers are routinely invited to blend themselves with this implied viewer, and so to be imbued with superiority through the simple mechanism of sitting and staring at a screen and laughing or smirking or shaking their heads at the right spots. There are often cascades of nested selves in these mental webs, each of them constructed by blending a number of inputs. The news anchor, for example, might speak in the voice of someone he is mocking. Typically, neither the actual expressions nor the particular voicing during this mocking are things that the person being mocked would ever assume or say, but we know how to connect the news anchor's thought and judgment and the mocked person's thought and behavior.

Like the Buddhist Monk or the *lionman*, these examples help us drag onstage some of the mental work that we are always doing but that we almost never notice. In any conversation with an *I* and a *you*—just imagine flirting—there are various compressed selves being manufactured, adjusted, and expressed, as speakers and hearers conceive of the particular mental web of selves in this specific moment, and these specific present selves are provided with other selves in the past and selves in the future and characteristic selves, all of which are adjusted and blended adaptively to suit the engagement.

Even the simplest grounds are a matter of dynamic and multiple compressions over complicated mental webs. In the ground,

- The self in the moment of communication is already a compression over a vast mental web of time, space, causation, and agency.
- The self in the moment of communication is putting forward an implied self and an implied speaker, or multiple and shifting implied selves and implied speakers, and perhaps implying that some of them are the same, or at least the same for certain purposes.
- The self in the moment of communication is also constructing a hearer, as a compression over a web, and an implied hearer, sometimes several implied hearers.
- In cases where there is feedback, the speaker can adjust the construction of the hearer and the implied hearer.
- The speaker and an implied speaker can both put forward implied hearers.
- There can be first-order implied hearers and second-order implied hearers. In fact, there can be many kinds of implied hearers, and a web of relations among them.
- The speaker can operate so as to invite the actual hearer to negotiate relationships with the various implied hearers.

These are the easiest jobs in the world for the cognitively modern human mind, and we do them all the time, without having much recognition of what we are doing or much understanding of how we are doing it. Consider late night talk shows, which are designed to conduce to easy relaxation at the end of the evening. Typically, they open with a lighthearted monologue in which the "host" puts us in the mood for laid-back entertainment. The monologue is usually what is known in the industry as "soft news." David Letterman hosted such a show June 5, 2012 in which he ran through one of his stereotypical "Top Ten" lists. These performances are always structured so as to present a certain category of items, from item number 10 sequentially to item number 1, with chuckles and rim shots and banter. These scenes already have grounds that are the result of a great deal of blending—for example, the host is speaking to "you," the viewer of the show. What do we blend to create that conception of the *you* who is the viewer of the show, and how is the actual viewer to create some blend of a momentarily entertained actual self with that *you* as one of its inputs?

In this case, there was a special guest to present the Top Ten list—Michelle Obama, First Lady of the United States, wife of President Obama, and author of a new gardening book, which she was promoting, *American Grown: The Story of the White House Kitchen Garden and Gardens Across America.* The Top Ten list was accordingly "Fun Facts About Gardening." Letterman introduces Mrs. Obama as presenting "tonight's Top Ten list through the magic of television" and says that she is coming to the show from the map room of the White House. The conversation begins like this:

> LETTERMAN: Ladies and Gentlemen, please say hello to First Lady Michelle Obama. [Letterman turns to look off screen]. Hello, there, Mrs. Obama!
>
> MICHELLE OBAMA: [screen cuts to an image of her, looking into the camera] Hey, Dave! [she is waving]

Most viewers will already have an elaborate mental web unfolding in which, although in the blend Michelle and Dave are talking with each other, in the web something much more distributed over time and space is going on. After all, Letterman is taking his sweet time smiling and posturing and otherwise behaving with an insouciance one might not deploy during a live on-screen videoconference with the First Lady. Moreover, public appearances by the First Lady during a presidential election season are of course tightly managed. Letterman is smiling broadly. But Letterman realizes that he (or rather, the production crew responding to his cues, as he is to theirs) has not run the amusing video introduction to the Top Ten list, and so he says, looking off-screen toward his on-stage bandleader and sidekick, "Did we open the thing?"

The answer is, "No, you did not." So they run the prepared video introduction to the Top Ten list, and, after they do so, Letterman says, "I'm so dumb. I forgot to open the thing. Can I say hello to Mrs. Obama again?" At this point, everyone must realize that he is not asking for permission to welcome the actual Mrs. Obama. Rather, he is prompting the production crew to run the prerecorded tape of Michelle Obama again. He says, "Hello, Mrs. Obama," and the screen cuts to exactly the clip we saw before, with Michelle Obama waving and saying, "Hey, Dave!" Everybody laughs. Throughout the rest of the presentation, the production crew intersperses the next clip of Michelle Obama "as if" she is responding to Letterman's guidance, and Letterman responds to what she says: "Really! Really! I had no idea!" She says, "Later this year, the Supreme Court will finally rule on tomato versus tomahto," and he responds, "Thank God!" Fact Number One turns out to be, "With enough care and effort, you can grow your own Barack-oli." When Michelle Obama informs "us" of this fact, she holds up a sculpture that is, in jest, actually a huge broccoli sprout that amazingly has grown in such a way as to resemble President Barack Obama's grinning face. At this point, Letterman of course must, in the blend, thank her and bid her farewell: "Thank you very much, Mrs. Obama," he says, as he is waving goodbye, "Thanks for taking your time!"

The complex blending to produce a ground here for the diffuse mental web stretching over time, space, causation, and agency is slightly noticeable because work has been done to draw attention to it. But the process of blending to create a ground occurs all the time in conversation and communication. The process is not at all costly, and although the product in this case is a little unusual, the process is utterly routine.

It's been great to look at these aspects of the human mind with you. By now, you deserve a reward, and I have one for you—hot and evil—at the beginning of the next chapter. Catch you then.

5

Forbidden Ideas

And their eyes were opened
The Book of Genesis

The Serpent in the Garden of Eden

The serpent, who was the subtlest beast in the garden, said to the woman, "Did the Lord really tell you that you cannot eat whatever you like?" She answered, "We may eat the fruit of the trees of the garden except for the tree in the middle. The Lord has commanded us not to eat its fruit, or even touch it, or we shall die." The serpent countered, "You won't die. The Lord knows that when you eat that fruit, your eyes will be opened, and you will be like gods." When she understood that the tree was good for food, and pleasing, and to be desired for the knowledge it brought, the woman plucked the forbidden fruit, and ate it, and gave some to her husband, who ate it, too. And their eyes were opened.

The human ability to think of a small story—with objects, agents, and actions—is a powerful and central tool of human cognition. We use these small stories to understand our environments.

Advanced blending works on stories, and one of the ways it works is by blending stories we might have thought were incompatible. Outside the blend, snakes do snake stuff and people do people stuff. However, we can blend those two incompatible stories into a new story that has a *talking snake with evil designs*. This is plucking forbidden mental fruit: We activate two conflicting mental arrays, such as a snake story and a person story, and we blend them creatively. The radical conflict between the snake and the person might seem to block the blend, to forbid the new idea. But not so. We pluck the forbidden fruit, invent the forbidden idea. The talking-snake-with-evil-designs blend has fabulous new stuff: evil deception in the Garden of Eden, sin, and the fall of humankind on Earth. Not to mention nakedness and shame.

The human understanding of stories—with interacting agents and intentions—is not something that comes before blending. On the contrary, we need blending to have such ideas. We need blending to come up with the idea of another full mind, so of course blending is indispensable for stories involving the self and other minds. Blending makes it possible for us to come up with the idea of agents with intentions, who perform actions and interact with each other, all conceiving of each other's intentions, beliefs, and plans, and conceiving, too, of other agents' conceptions of their own conceptions.

Whatever the powers of animals to understand agents and actions, in people those powers are strongly leveraged by blending to help create robust human conceptions of *story*.

Not only can we think of small stories, but also, we can activate more than one of them at a time—as in the case of the wedding party and the memory of diving off Cabo San Lucas. The groomsman is inhabiting and performing one active mental story—the wedding event—but he is also activating another story—the memory of the diving trip with his girlfriend. Those two conflicting stories, activated simultaneously, can be blended into a third story: the daydream in which he is marrying his girlfriend. The most important forbidden fruit is a blend of two stories in conflict, and we pluck it all the time. For the Garden of Eden, we pluck the life of the snake and the life of a person and blend them into a supernatural talking snake who deforms the future of humankind.

Firing Up Stories in Conflict

You are buying a bottle of Rioja from a wine shop in Northern California. That is one mental story, with roles, actions, goals, agents, and objects. You are living it. You must be paying attention to it. Otherwise, you would drop the bottle and botch the transaction. But at the same moment, you are remembering a dinner you once had in San Sebastián. In that story, you are eating paella, drinking Rioja wine, and listening to "Asturias" on a Spanish guitar.

Or maybe you are boarding a plane to fly from San Francisco to Washington, DC. You must be paying attention to the way that travel story goes, or you would not find your seat, stow your bag, and turn off your personal electronic devices. But all the while, you are thinking of surfing Windansea beach, and in that story, there is no San Francisco, no plane, no seat, no bag, no personal electronic devices, no sitting down, and nobody anywhere near you. In that story, there is an 8' 3" surfboard under you and you are riding a wave.

Why did evolution not build our brains to prevent us from activating stories that run counter to our present circumstances? Calling those stories to mind risks confusion, distraction, disaster. Yet we do so all the time. A person trapped inescapably in an actual story of suffering or pain may willfully imagine some other, quite different story, as a mental escape from the present.

How can it be that deeply incompatible stories do not suppress each other's activation in the human mind? How can we fire up at the same time stories that are in great conflict? Psychologically, what are we doing when we attend to the present story—that is, our own present bodies, needs, impulses, and activities, and the many objects, events, and agents in our surroundings— but at the same time attend to some mental story that does not serve our understanding of the present? Neurobiologically, what is it in the functioning of our brains that makes it possible for us to resist the grip of the present? Evolutionarily, how did our species develop this ability? Remarkably, someone who is inhabiting the real story of the present and who is simultaneously remembering a different story can partition them, so as to monitor each without becoming confused about which items belong to which stories. Memory researchers offer as yet no explanation of this astounding mental feat of keeping simultaneous activations separate.

There is a tantalizingly similar, possibly related, rudimentary mental phenomenon, called "dreaming," in which we ignore the present story while we fire up an imaginary story.[1] During sleep, our sensory attention to the real story in our physical environment is severely dampened. Before sleep, we place ourselves in the safest possible location, so that ignoring the present story is less dangerous.

It may be that dreaming—including activating stories aside from the real one—is generally available to mammals.[2] Although a dog or cat cannot tell us whether it dreams, mammals do show the same stages of sleep as we do, including REM sleep, during which there are rapid eye movements, inhibition of skeletal and nuchal muscular activity, and an electroencephalogram pattern much like the one associated with waking. In this state of immobility, we, and presumably the mammal, can run alternative mental stories without incurring the risk that we will damage ourselves. As Michel Jouvet and his collaborators have shown, a cat with a certain kind of lesion in the pontine reticular formation retains muscle tone during REM sleep, and so apparently acts out, while sleeping, a variety of hunting behaviors: It raises its head, orients it, walks as if tracking prey, pursues, pounces, and bites. It is hard to resist the inference that the cat is inhabiting dreamed stories during REM sleep, stories that do not suit its actual present circumstances.

Consider the wedding daydream. A man is participating in a wedding. He is consciously enacting a familiar mental story, with roles, participants, a plot, and a goal. But while he is fulfilling his role in the wedding story, he is remembering a different story, which took place a week earlier in Cabo San Lucas, in which he and his girlfriend, who is not present at the wedding, went diving for sunken treasure. Why, cognitively, should he be able to inhabit, mentally, these two stories at the same time? There are rich possibilities for confusion, but in all the central ways, he remains unconfused. We have all been in moments of potential harm or achievement— a fight, an accident, a negotiation, an interview—when it would seem to be in our interest to give our complete attention to the moment, and yet even then, some other story has flitted unbidden into consciousness, without confusing us about the story we inhabit. We even call these stories "daydreams."

Blending Stories in Conflict

The man who daydreams that he is marrying his girlfriend is blending two incompatible stories. He takes the great mental leap of plucking forbidden mental fruit: He connects two stories that should be kept absolutely apart, and blends them to make a third story. He makes analogical connections between his girlfriend and the bride and between himself and the groom, and blends these counterparts into a daydream in which it is he and his girlfriend who are being married at this particular ceremony. This blended story is manifestly false, and he should not make the mistake, as he obediently discharges his duties at the real wedding, of thinking that he is in the process of marrying his girlfriend. But forbidden ideas come easily to us, and often turn out to be quite useful. The man at the wedding plucks the forbidden mental fruit, with potentially serious consequences: If the daydream goes OK, he might come to realize that he likes the blended story, and so formulate a plan of action to make it real. Or, if the bride in the blend rejects him, it might reveal to him a truth he had sensed intuitively but not recognized, and this revelation might bring him regret or relief.

Running two stories mentally, when we should be absorbed by only one, and blending them when they should be kept apart, is at the root of what makes us human. So far, we have looked at blends that combine a story we inhabit with a story we remember. But we can also blend two stories that both refer to our present circumstances. If we perceive someone dying under a tree as the autumn leaves fall, then the dying and the falling can be seen as different little stories, which we can run and understand independently. The dying can happen without the leaves, and the leaves can fall without the dying. But we can also make a blend in which the present man is the present tree. As Shakespeare writes,

That time of year thou mayst in me behold
When yellow leaves, or none, or few do hang
Upon those boughs which shake against the cold,
Bare ruined choirs, where late the sweet birds sang.

Often these prompts to blend are subtle. As the character Katsumoto dies in the film *The Last Samurai*, the cherry blossoms are falling. The blend of human life, and particularly of a samurai's life, with the brief efflorescence of the cherry blossom, is deeply established in Japanese culture, but no one needs to know that in order to construct the blend. Earlier, Katsumoto has explained, "A perfect blossom is a rare thing. You could spend your life looking for one. And it would not be a wasted life." "Perfect," he says as he sees them fall, dying. "They are all perfect." These are his last words.

In cognitive science, we face a range of scientific puzzles related to this forbidden-fruit blending of stories:

- We can make sense of a story in the immediate environment with the support of memory, when the memory and the story are compatible.
- We can bundle and compress two different but compatible stories that are both running in the immediate environment.
- We can dream an imaginary story during sleep, when our sensory attention to the present story is dampened.
- We can activate a memory while we are awake, even if it is not crucial to making sense of the present story.
- We can blend a story tuned to the immediate environment with a remembered or an imagined story.
- We can even activate and blend two stories, both of which are supplied by memory or imagination, even if neither of them is tuned to the present story.

The American Everyhorse

For example, in the nonfiction book *Seabiscuit: An American Legend,* Laura Hillenbrand tells the story of a racehorse as if it were an allegory of the American people during the Depression. *USA Today* described this portrayal in its announcement of *Seabiscuit* as its "book club pick":

> *Seabiscuit* tells how an unimpressive older horse with crooked legs and a short tail stole the hearts and minds of the American people during the Depression. In 1938, the No. 1 newsmaker was not FDR or Hitler; it was a horse that defined the word "underdog."
>
> It was the indefinable quality of "being game" that captured Americans. As one observer put it, Seabiscuit would rather die than be beaten in a race. Yet, unlike many champion Thoroughbreds, his off-track personality was low-key, appealing and, frankly, lazy. He was a glutton for food and enjoyed the constant friendly companionship of a horse named Pumpkin with whom he shared a double stall.
>
> In short, he seemed the American Everyhorse, the equine version of how we see ourselves. Yet his race against the favored War Admiral is considered the greatest horse race in history.[3]

In this Seabiscuit-Americans mental web, one story has the American populace, with its sufferings, poverty, and challenges, facing Hitler, who in 1938 took control of Austria and the Sudetenland and showed signs of annexing Poland. The other story has a horse, supported by a ramshackle team, who competes against the intimidating War Admiral and wins. In the forbidden-fruit advanced blend, we have an element that is both Seabiscuit and the American people. This compresses *the American people,* something diffuse and vague, stretching very widely across time, space, causation, and agency, to something that is at a scale congenial to the human mind: a racehorse in a particular race. Nationalism, like religion, depends on such compressed, blended stories for its existence, which is why robust nationalism, like religion, did not come into existence until after people evolved the capacity for advanced blending.

In the *Seabiscuit* web, millions of individual people, along with their complicated, aggregate, overarching story, are compressed to human scale, by blending that diffuse array with a story that is already compressed: the story of a single agent, in this case a horse, involved in a clear set of events congenial to human cognition. The diffuse story thereby acquires the compression of the already-compressed story.

The Lamb of God

Systems of belief routinely compress big ranges of information into intelligible form by blending it all with something that is mentally tractable. This blending helps us make sense of life, the universe, and everything.

Consider the Christian story of redemption. In this story, the good and evil forces of the world contest for the souls of human beings, who have sinned, and who therefore have earned punishment. This Christian story depends upon the general concepts of *punishment* and *redemption*. These concepts are already the result of blending. In each of them, there is an earlier scenario in which a character does something that is regarded as an offense, and a later scenario in which something is done to that offender. For example, someone steals something, and so the tribe takes away a lot of his money. This exaction is called a "fine." If we took the two actions as separate, the second could be regarded as a gratuitous offense, like the first. Killing, inflicting pain, imprisoning, taking away money or a right or a privilege, even yelling at someone—all these, by themselves, are bad actions. But when we integrate these two scenarios into one, we blend and compress the two separate actions with the idea of a single, balanced unit, and so the second scenario becomes a justified *punishment*. A single, balanced unit is something we know from experience. It is at human scale. Indeed, our bodies have two sides that we can place in balance. The blending thereby creates a human-scale compression.

Now, suppose that someone steals some money, but later sacrifices a great deal more to protect and provide for the person from whom he stole it. If we take the two actions as separate, we just have one bad action and one good action. But when we integrate these two scenarios, the status of the first action changes. It becomes *atoned for*. The first scenario is *balanced out*. Again, the blending creates a human-scale compression to a single, balanced unit.

These compressions do not change the facts of the first actions, but they do change their status. The new stuff in the blending web is very rich. Unlike the input actions, the blend is filled with *justice*. As a result, because the two scenarios sit inside a blending web, the second action becomes permissible and intelligible, and the first offense is *removed* or *neutralized* or *paid for*. That is amazing new stuff.

The human concept of *punishment* goes far beyond any evolutionary psychological motivation to dominate, intimidate, or discipline another person. For example, someone can be disturbed when an offender dies *unpunished*. There is no external benefit from punishing a corpse: We cannot modify the future behavior of a corpse by dominating, intimidating, or disciplining it. The corpse offers no threat or competition.

But human beings have imagination. They invent new ideas and extend the range of their thinking. They can conceive of a hypothetical punishment, revenge, or retribution, and feel aggrieved that the blend that contains the punishment, revenge, or retribution is permanently counterfactual because the offender has died. Here is an example: Spanish conquistador Don Juan de Oñate was accused, perhaps apocryphally, of having handed down extreme punishments to rebellious Acoma Pueblo Indians in 1599, including amputation of the right foot of all young Acoma men. Nearly four centuries later, an anonymous group claiming to be "Native Americans and Native New Mexicans" took credit for cutting off the right foot of the monumental, heroic statue of Oñate at the Visitor Center at Alcalde north of Española, New Mexico.[4]

As we have seen, if we imagine a *just punishment* blending web in which the first story has reference to reality but both the second story and the blend are only hypothetical, then the offending party in the first story counts as *worthy of punishment*. The punishment is furthermore *unrealized*. This is a general template for a blending web, and it applies often to a single person.

Now for a really big blend. If we apply this general template not just to a single person but instead to all of humanity over all time, we get, in the blend, the idea of *guilty or sinful humanity, worthy of punishment, but unpunished*. That is one blending web. Hold that *sinful humanity* blend in mind.

Next, let us fire up alongside the *sinful humanity* blended story an altogether different story in which a blameless man is crucified. Now we blend *guilty or sinful humanity* with the blameless man. In the new hyper-blend, we have the blameless man from one story but the sins of humanity from the other. His crucifixion, according to the logic of the *just punishment* blending web, becomes "recompense" for the sins of humanity. His suffering "excuses" humanity from bearing the punishment. No one needs to believe this blending web; the important point is that we can all assemble it.

This is spectacular forbidden fruit. In this forbidden-fruit mental web, there are input stories with different (and clashing) organizing mental frames that are blended into a third story. That third story has an organization that conflicts with the organizations of both of the input stories. The blended story has new stuff of its own. In the story of the crucifixion, one element in the blend, Jesus Christ, has, from the story of Jesus the carpenter, the identity, biography, and character of Jesus, but also has, from the story of people who sin, the sins of humanity. In the blend, Jesus is an individual who bears away the sins of the world. He is the *agnus dei qui tollis peccata mundi*. As Paul says in Romans 4:25, "he was delivered over to death for our sins." The punishment in the blend has a profound consequence for the sinful human beings: They no longer must bear the punishment! The punishment has spent itself. Some of the human beings concerned may even feel, in virtue of this blended story, that their sins have been *removed*. What a new idea!

In the story of Jesus, he is *unsinning*. His counterpart in the story of humanity is the people, who are *sinful*. This is an absolute clash. He is also a single agent, and human beings are very many agents: another absolute clash. In the blend, we integrate features of Jesus with features of the people, producing the new idea that people no longer must bear the consequences of their sins. This vast mental web arches not only over time, space, and agency, but over *all* time, space, and agency.

Other input stories to the blend, strongly contradictory to the input story of Jesus the carpenter and the input story of sinful humanity, are recruited to strengthen this forbidden-fruit blend. They are: (1) the abstract story in which someone bears a heavy burden for us, (2) the abstract story in which a force that results in displacement is balanced out by applying a countervailing force, and (3) the story in which some specific animal, often a lamb, is sacrificed as a gift to allay a god or gods or supernatural power and thereby to dissuade them from bringing harm. All of these input stories are themselves complicated, and the story of the sacrificial lamb is itself already a complicated blend. In the final hyper-blend that arises from blending all these many different input stories, Jesus Christ is at once the sacrificial lamb, the bearer of the burden, and the individual who is punished for the sins.

This multiply blended story compresses vast mental webs to a compact mental story. In this vast mental web, there is our individual sense of inadequacy and transgression, but it is multiplied over all humankind. Blending helps us compress this vast human condition to a simple story. The *Christ the Redeemer* blending web provides one way to pack the human condition down to a human story compact enough to make sense, to be tractable, to be portable. It gives us global insight into the vast mental web. The blend contains one main man, Jesus, and one compact story of His suffering. This story of one man happens in one place and lasts one day. He is crucified and mocked. He dies. He is deposed and buried. In the blend, he is the bearer of our sins, punished for our sake: our existential and ethical relation to the cosmos takes on a compact intelligibility and memorability. The story follows the logic of the *lex talionis*—a blow for a blow, an eye for an eye—but with a twist: We sinned, He paid. Many, very many people, indeed *all* people, are compressed into one agent. All their sins are compressed, and one man's pain pays for all. One death atones for all.

A blended story can itself be an input to another blend. Cascading mental webs, of blend upon blend, can compress, one step after another, great reaches of thought and meaning to human scale. For example, *The Dream of the Rood*, passages of which, carved on the Ruthwell Cross, date from at least the early eighth century CE, presents a rich cascade of successive blends. It relies on the existing blended story of Christ the Redeemer. In this poem, the voice of a sinner relates a dream in which the Rood—the Holy Cross—appears to him and speaks to him about its experiences. The talking Cross is of course a blend of the Cross with a person. The result is that the Cross has intentionality, a mind, and can speak.

This blend of the talking Cross follows another everyday general blending template. This blending template gives us our sense that a physical object is communicating to us something of its history. A souvenir, for example, communicates to us about the time, place, or event of which it is a souvenir. This is a minimal blend of mind: One input has a person, another has a physical object in the presence of which we have memories or make inferences, and the blend has an object that is communicative or suggestive about these memories and inferences and perhaps even intentional without actually being able to talk. We are not deluded, but we still feel the communication.

In *The Dream of the Rood*, this general blending template of the communicative physical object is pushed very far: The personified object receives even more projection from the concept of a person, creating a Cross in the blend that can actually *talk* like a person.

In our general blending template for "communicative" objects, it is standard for the content of the communication to come from memories we possess that are associated with the object, or from inferences we derive from seeing the object. If we see a souvenir of Paris, we can call up memories of the time in which we bought it, or other times we have been in Paris or seen films about Paris or read books about Paris, and so on, and we can make inferences based on the diagrammatic nature of the souvenir. In typical cases like this one, the communication from the object to us does not extend beyond our own memory and ability to draw inferences. The object cannot "communicate" something to us that does not come from our own knowledge or inference.

But in *The Dream of the Rood*, the content of the Cross's speech goes beyond anything that the person listening to the Cross might remember or infer. In this way, the talking Cross has received even more elaborate projection from the input containing the person than is usual: The Cross, like an actual person, can tell us things we would never have guessed, deduced, or remembered.

Remarkably, the Cross in *The Dream of the Rood* is blended with not just a person, but with Christ. The Cross is not only *stained* with blood on the right side, but it also *bleeds* on its right side. This is a blend of an instrument (the Cross) with a patient (the person crucified on the Cross).

The story of the manufacture of the Cross from raw material—a tree—and the use of the Cross as an instrument of crucifixion is additionally blended with the story of Christ and his crucifixion. That is, just as Christ is blended with the Cross, being crucified is blended with being used as the instrument of crucifixion. The Cross reports the history in which it was taken by foes from the forest and forced into shape for an evil design. It says that it suffered like Christ and was wounded with the same nails; Cross and Christ were both mocked. The Christ-like suffering of the Cross confers upon it both immortality and the ability to heal sinners: The Cross informs the sinner that those who wear the Cross need not be afraid, that the kingdom of heaven can be sought through the Cross.

The Cross is also blended with the sinner who relates the dream, creating a blend of identification. The sinner, who is the voice of the poem, is stained with sins, wounded with wrongdoings, downcast. The Cross, too, felt sinful: It had been the slayer of Christ. But it was redeemed, it says, and it asserts that in just the same way, the sinner can be redeemed. This is the crucial moral of the blended tale.

Perhaps most interesting, the Cross is also blended with a thane—that is, a loyal follower of an Anglo-Saxon lord. Christ is blended with the lord served by that thane. In the story remembered and related by the Cross, Christ is a strong, young hero, who hastens to the Cross, stouthearted, in order to climb it, who strips and climbs the cross, bold in the sight of the crowd. The Cross describes itself as having done its duty to serve the Lord's will, even though it was afraid and was tempted to fail the Lord. As Peter Richardson has explained, the purpose of this blend is to give thanes and their cultures a model of what a good thane is and does.[5]

The author of *The Dream of the Rood* blends Cross and thane so the Cross can count as a thane. The Cross represents its actions as perfect and praiseworthy service to a lord, and this evaluation, combined with the holy status of the Cross and its evident prestige (all that gold, all those adoring angels) makes it, in the blend, not just a thane but a paragon among thanes. As a result, it provides a model for those who would be thanes. The poem therefore has a particular rhetorical purpose, which Richardson calls "making thanes."

It offers a complicated blend, in which the history of the Cross as a physical object is blended with the general story of a thane's life, making the Cross the counterpart of the thane and Christ the counterpart of the thane's lord, and resulting in a particular emergent biography in the blend, of an exceptionally honored and successful thane-Cross, all with the purpose of projecting back to the contributing story of *thane* a divinely approved model of how a thane should act. To the extent that this poem is meant to persuade a reader to be a good thane through aspirational identification with the ideal, it prompts for yet a further blend in which the reader is blended with the ideal thane.

In such blended stories, we always see certain patterns of meaning:

- *Mapping between elements of the two stories.* Blending two stories always involves at least a provisional mapping between them. The mapping typically involves "vital relations" of identity, analogy, similarity, causality, change, time, intentionality, space, role-value, part-whole, or representation. In the Seabiscuit story, for example, there is a mapping between Seabiscuit in one story and the American public in the other, between the horse race in one story and the geopolitical tension in the other.
- *Selective projection.* Some elements of the stories are projected to the blended story, but only some. In the Seabiscuit story, we take the character of the horse but not its age or crooked legs, and we take the horse's triumphs. From the other story, we take America and Germany, but not the fact that America does not so far look like a winner. We certainly do not take other complexities such as the fact that America and Germany cannot compete unless they fly across the Atlantic Ocean.
- *New ideas.* In the blended story of Seabiscuit, we have astonishing new meaning that emerges in the blend and in the mental web. The triumph of the horse can signal the triumph of the American people, who actually do exactly nothing in the horse race story, and who are actually not triumphing on the global political stage.

We're Lucky We're Not Chickens

The story of *The Dream of the Rood* belongs to world religion and elite literature. The story of Seabiscuit belongs to popular literature and adult nationalism. But advanced blending, the plucking of forbidden mental fruit, is not restricted to a particular class of people, or a class of conceptual domains, or a class of cultural practice. On the contrary, forbidden-fruit blends are everywhere, the hallmark of the human mind. Children pluck forbidden fruit routinely, as part of what it means to be a human child and to learn human culture.

Here is an example from a 9-year-old, with younger siblings Anders and Bjorn, and a 20-year-old babysitter, Maria, all sitting at the dinner table with the parents. The 9-year-old speaker says, "If we were all chickens, you, Anders, would be about Maria's age, you, Bjorn, would be about Dad's age, and me, Dad, and Mom would all be dead of old age. We are all five alive. We are lucky we are not chickens."

Such blends are routine even for children. This blend activates present reality alongside the lifetime of chickens. In the We-Are-Chickens blend, the 7-year-old Bjorn is in advanced middle age and the parents and the eldest child are dead. This new stuff in the blend has inferential consequences for the real story, wherein human beings are now *lucky*, a feature that, like *hapless, safe,* and *mistaken*, arises only through forbidden-fruit blending. The feature *lucky* is a compression of the counterfactual relation between our original idea of the family and the We-Are-Chickens Blend, to make a new blend, one which we take to be a more insightful idea of the family, and in that more insightful idea, the family members have the new feature *lucky,* which was not in mind when we were first thinking of the family.

In the We-Are-Chickens blend, Dad is dead because of his chronological age, but Bjorn, who is "Dad's age" in the blend, is not dead. How can this be? The answer is that "Dad's age" for Bjorn-in-the-blend is advanced middle age *for a chicken,* a life-stage that a chicken (we infer from the assertion) reaches after about 7 years, Bjorn being 7 years old; whereas Dad's state for Dad in the blend is the state of a chicken born 48 years ago, that is, dead. In interpreting the assertion, we all immediately and unconsciously make complicated calculations to arrive at this new stuff, even as we project elements and relations selectively to the blend. Any normal member of our species is equipped with these mental operations, and no member of any other species appears to have them.

The Runaway Bunny

Advanced blending is basic for even very young children. *The Runaway Bunny,* by Margaret Brown, published in 1942, is an extremely popular and successful picture book for 2-year-olds.[6] In *The Runaway Bunny,* a little bunny talks with his mother. The talking bunny is already a blend, if one of the most common. He insists that he is going to run away, and his mother quite predictably says she is going to come after him. We activate the story of a human mother and her child and a story of a little bunny that is being chased by its bunny mother, and blend them. The opening illustration shows a depiction that could be a representation of the bunny story. But then the blending takes off. The little bunny says, "If you run after me, I will become a fish in a trout stream and I will swim away from you." The illustration now shows a bunny in a stream. His mother responds, "If you become a fish in a trout stream, I will become a fisherman and I will fish for you." So the already-blended story of the talking bunnies is now blended with the story of a fisherman fishing. The accompanying illustration refers undeniably to this new blend with the fish, and not just to normal bunnies, as we see from the fact that, in this illustration, the mother is walking on two legs and reaching up toward fishing equipment. In the next illustration, the mother, wearing waders and holding a net, stands in the trout stream, casting a line with a carrot at the end. The little bunny is swimming toward the carrot.

Two-year-olds have not the slightest difficulty constructing the blended story and drawing appropriate inferences. If a 2-year-old who knows that fishermen use hooks and bait to fool fish, to snag them, to hurt them, to haul them in, and to eat them is looking at the illustration of the mother-bunny-fisherman fishing for the baby-bunny-fish with a carrot-hook on the end of the line, and you begin to ask questions, the dialogue goes like this: "What is this?" "A carrot." "What is it for?" "To catch the baby bunny." "What will the baby bunny do?" "Bite the carrot." "Will he swim away down the river?" "No. He bites the carrot." "What is the mommy bunny doing?" "Fishing for the baby bunny." "What is she?" "She's a fisherman." "Does the baby bunny know his mommy is fishing for him?" "No. He wants the carrot." "Can the baby bunny swim?" "Yes. He's a fishie." "Does he have a fishie tail." "No. He's a bunny." "Will the carrot hurt the baby bunny?" "No! The mommy doesn't hurt the bunny!" "What will happen when the baby bunny bites the carrot?" "The mommy bunny will pull him in and hug him and kiss him." "Will he smell like a fish?" "No! He's a baby bunny!"

When the little bunny says he will become a fish, he is asserting a new blended story as a vehicle for escape from the first blended story in which bunnies talk and the little bunny runs away from home. In the little bunny's new blended story, as he sees it, the bunny is a fish, but its mother is merely a talking-mommy-bunny, and is, as the little bunny plans, incapacitated, unable to pursue. But the mother asserts a correspondence between herself and a fisherman. She insists that she projects into the new story as a talking-mommy-bunny-fisherman. The mechanism of this projection is *change*: She will "become a fisherman." Here, she simply follows the pattern originally laid down by the little bunny, who asserted that he could escape the first blended story and land in a new blended story through an act of willful change on his part, transforming himself into a fish (or more accurately, a talking-baby-bunny-fish).

This sets the pattern for the rest of the book. Every time the little bunny insists that he will escape the blended story by creating a new blend, the mother projects herself into that new blend by assuming a role inside the new story that gives her more power and ability than the baby bunny foresaw. The little bunny cannot seriously deny her power to project herself in this fashion, because it was he who provided the pattern of projection in the first instance, and because she has an absolute motivation that nothing can withstand: "For you are my little bunny."

Thus, when the little bunny says, "If you become a fisherman, I will become a rock on the mountain, high above you," the mother responds, "If you become a rock on the mountain high above me, I will be a mountain climber, and I will climb to where you are." And so the little bunny becomes a crocus in a hidden garden, and so the mother becomes a gardener and finds him, and so the little bunny becomes a bird and flies away, and so the mother becomes the tree that the bird comes home to (the tree looks like topiary in the shape of a mother bunny, to which the winged bunny flies), and so the bunny becomes a sailboat and sails away, and so the mother becomes the wind and blows the little bunny where she wants, and so the little bunny joins a circus and flies away on a flying trapeze, and so the mother becomes a tight-rope walker and walks across the air to the little bunny, and so the little bunny becomes a little boy and runs into a house, and so the mother becomes the little boy's mother and catches him and hugs him. The illustration shows the mother bunny rocking the little boy-bunny in a rocking chair.

The little bunny at last realizes it is hopeless. The mother has the general trick of blending herself into any story, no matter how ingeniously blended, and catching him. Therefore, none of the blended stories removes him from his mother. "Shucks," says the little bunny. "I might just as well stay where I am and be your little bunny." And so he does. "Have a carrot," says the mother bunny. The last illustration returns us to the original blended story, in which mother and little bunny are in a comfortable room, which is a rabbit hole in the bottom of a tree. The mother gives the little bunny a carrot.

It may be that for many children, there is another story that is being blended with each of these blended little bunny stories, namely, the story of their own lives. In that case, the children who are hearing the story blend themselves with the little bunny as it goes through each of the blended stories in the cascade. This feat of multiple advanced blending provides the inference that no matter what the human 2-year-old does to explore its freedom and assert its independence from its mother, in the end, mother will always be there, to find, retrieve, catch, cuddle, and rock the human child.

It is worth taking a moment to marvel at the fact that a complicated string of fantastic blended stories ends up being profoundly persuasive and reassuring for the real story that the real child actually inhabits. The child cannot actually test its independence so thoroughly in reality without running unacceptable risks, but it can do so through mental simulation, and the simulations change the child's view of its own reality. The adults who read the story to a child might also be persuaded by these simulations to conceive of their relationship to the child in a certain way. Parent and child have the opportunity to conceive of their real roles by activating stories they in fact could not possibly inhabit and blending themselves into them mentally.

There is another familiar and exciting situation that calls for persuasion: a suitor courting a young woman. In the Provençal song "O, Magali," embedded in Frederic Mistral's 1858 *Mireille*, a suitor calls from the street below to his beloved, Magali, who is in her room above. The song uses the identical general blending pattern deployed in *The Runaway Bunny*: Magali launches a blended story as a means of escape from the present story, but it doesn't work, and so, repeatedly, a new blend must be launched from the old. Each time, the resourceful suitor finds a way to enter the new blend as something linked to his beloved. These links emphasize physical pursuit, touch, and possession. Magali says she will not respond to the serenade but instead turn into a fish and escape into the sea. In this way, the beloved, like the child, issues a challenge. Here is a schematic list of the ensuing cascade of metamorphoses:

—If you become a fish, I will become a fisherman.
—Well, then, I will become a bird and fly away.
—Then I will become a hunter and hunt you.
—Then I will become a flowering herb in the wild.
—Then I will become water and sprinkle you.
—Then I will become a cloud and float away to America.
—Then I will become the sea breeze and carry you.
—Then I will become the heat of the sun.
—Then I will become the green lizard who drinks you in.
—Then I will become the full moon.
—Then I will become the mist that embraces you.
—But you will still never have me, because I will become the virginal rose blossoming on the bush.

—Then I will become the butterfly who kisses you and becomes drunk
on you.

—Go ahead, pursue me, run, run. You will never have me. I will
become the bark of the great oak hidden in the dark forest.

—Then I will become the tuft of ivy and will embrace you.

—If you do that, you will cling only to an old oak, for I will have turned
into a novice in the monastery of Saint Blaise.

—If you do that, I will become a priest and be your confessor and
hear you.

Now, in *Mireille,* this song is being recounted by Noro to a group of young
women, who at this point tremble and beg Noro to tell them what happens to
this novice, this "moungeto," who was an oak, and a flower, moon, sun, cloud,
herb, bird, and fish. Noro says, "If I recall, we were at the place where she said
she would take refuge in a cloister, and her ardent admirer responded that he
would enter as her confessor, but we see again that she sets up a great obstacle":

—If you pass through the portal of the convent, you will find all the
nuns walking in a circle around me, because you will see me laid out
under a shroud.

This is an absolute obstacle indeed. But the suitor is undeterred:

—If you become the poor dead girl, I will therefore become the earth.
And then I shall have you.

This suite of blends has a profound persuasive effect on Magali, and it
leads her to think about changing her judgment of the suitor's character, or
at least her visible response to his courtship. She says, "Now I begin to believe
that you are not merely engaging in pleasantries with me. Here is my little
glass ring for remembrance, handsome young man."

In this exchange, the beloved sets a rhetorical challenge, which the suitor
must meet. Each time he meets it, she sets a new challenge. She has license
to jump into a new blended story by fiat: "Then I will become a fish, a cloud,
the sun . . ." He must take up this challenge without questioning her right to
set it. He is not permitted to respond, "Oh, you cannot do that." On the contrary, she is free to pick the next blend and her place in it. Nor is he allowed
to become just anything. So, for example, if she says she will become a cloud,
he cannot say he will become a stone. There is no conceptual success in that,

and so it would fail the dynamics of seduction. Instead, he must immediately answer the challenge by finding a role for himself in the new blend that maintains the connection between him and the beloved.

The Runaway Bunny and "O, Magali" rely on another pattern of advanced blending, common and effective. The form of the storytelling is blended with the pattern of the story. The lives of the mother and child, or lover and beloved, are vast, uncertain, and diffuse, stretching over time, space, causation, and agency, conditioned by every kind of environment, emotion, and intentionality common to human lives. The question is, what will happen in these lives? Will these lives have any reliable structure? By contrast, the form of the expression has a very crisp structure: Two people speak in a short, witty conversation. The conversation consists of a challenge begun by one of them, and each time, the challenge is answered. Whenever the child or beloved escapes into a new blend, the mother or lover follows ingeniously and to the same effect, until the child or beloved becomes convinced by the pattern. The pattern of the brief *conversation* is blended with the pattern of the extended *life*. The dedication of the mother or lover in staying with the witty *conversation*, always rising to the *rhetorical* challenge during the 10 or 15 minutes it takes to conduct the conversation, is blended with the dedication of the mother or lover in *life*, always rising to the *biographical* challenge of staying with the child or beloved through changes over years. This is quite a time compression. Quite interestingly, the quality of the rhetorical performance of the mother or lover is indicative of the biographical performance toward the child or the beloved. Why should the beloved give the lover her little glass ring just because he can conduct the exchange? Why should a brief, human-scale conversation between two people have any influence on her judgment of his character and his future performance as a lover? The answer is that she, like all cognitively modern human beings, can do advanced blending, and in this case, she blends two radically different things, namely a brief rhetorical form and the rhythm of an extended life. Fiction, poems, and plays are brief and cannot contain patterns that are diffuse in life. But they can prompt us to blend such diffuse patterns with human-scale stories and human-scale forms to produce blends that count as human-scale representations of the otherwise diffuse stories. The result is compressed blends that give us insight into what would otherwise lie beyond our grasp.

Purple Ideas

Here is an example that depends explicitly on blending two radically incompatible scenarios, one of them centrally concerned with form. In Crockett

Johnson's *Harold and the Purple Crayon*, 4-year-old Harold uses his purple crayon to draw, and whatever he draws is real. His world is a blend, of spatial reality and its representation. In the blend, the representation is fused with what it represents. When Harold needs a source of light to go for a walk, he draws the moon, and so he has moonlight. The moon stays with him as he moves. In the real story of walking in the moonlight, the moon cannot be created by drawing or come into existence at someone's will. Alternatively, in the little story of a child drawing a moon, the drawn moon cannot emit moonlight or float along in the sky as the artist's companion. But in the blend, there is a special blended moon with great new stuff: It comes into existence by being drawn, and it hangs in the sky and gives light.

The mechanisms of blending that give us this special blended moon work generally throughout *Harold and the Purple Crayon*. When Harold wants to return home, he draws a window around the moon, thereby positioning the moon where it would appear in his window if he were in his bedroom, and so he is, ipso facto, presto-chango, in his bedroom, and can go to sleep. Harold's blended world has new kinds of causality and event shape that are unavailable from either the domain of drawing or the domain of spatial living.

The projection to this blend, and the completion and elaboration of the blend, are not algorithmic, not predictable from the input mental spaces in the mental web the blend serves, but instead have considerable room for alternatives. For example, when one draws, one often makes practice sketches, erasures, and mistakes that do not count as the finished drawing. Which kinds of marks made with the purple crayon shall count as reality in the blend? The answer chosen by the author of the book is all of them. When Harold's hand, holding the purple crayon, shakes as he backs away in a line from the terribly frightening dragon, the resulting mark is a purple line of wavy scallops: "Suddenly he realized what was happening. But by then Harold was over his head in an ocean."

The principle for connecting the purple sketches to elements of reality is, predictably, matching of image-schemas. "Image schema" is jargon for "skeletal patterns that recur in our sensory and motor experience." The image schemas that count in this story are basic visual forms. If the sketch matches the iconic visual form of something, then, in the blend, it is that thing. But it appears that this matching is constrained: A given purple sketch can be matched to exactly one reality. For example, once the wavy line is an ocean, Harold cannot transform the ocean into a cake by perceiving the wavy line as icing on a cake. Yet in a differently conceived blend, in a different book, the character who does the drawing might possess the power to recast reality by perceiving the sketch first one way and then another.

In Harold's blend, all of physical space is a piece of paper on which to draw. What are the possibilities in the blend of blank paper/empty space? Can Harold move as he wishes through it? The answer chosen by the author is that once something is drawn that gives Harold relative location, he is constrained by some of the physics of the real world and his relative location. For example, once he draws the hull of a boat and part of the mast, he must climb the mast to draw the parts of the boat he could not reach from the hull. When he wants to find his house, he begins to draw a mountain, which he can climb for a better view. He climbs the part he has drawn so he can draw more to climb. But as he looks down over the other side of the mountain, he slips, and since he has been positioned with respect to the mountain, the blank space is now thin air, so he must be falling. He has to draw a balloon to save himself from crashing.

There is another blend at work in *Harold and the Purple Crayon*: The parent who reads this story to a child is prompting the child to make a blend of himself and Harold so the child will be more tractable at bedtime. This is a conventional blend in children's literature, at least children's literature of the sort that weary parents prefer to read to children at what the parents regard as the child's bedtime. In this template for a blending web, the story in the present environment is blended with whatever story is being read, in the hope of leading the child to make the present story conform to a favored event in the blend, namely, the child's pleasant willingness to go to bed.

Antic Death

In *Henry the Sixth, Part One,* Lord Talbot, caught at a terrible military disadvantage on the French field, fails to persuade his son John to flee. John is slain. Lord Talbot accosts Death. He recounts how John charged into the French soldiers, fighting, and so died:

> Triumphant death, smear'd with captivity,
> Young Talbot's valour makes me smile at thee.
> When he perceiv'd me shrink and on my knee,
> His bloody sword he brandish'd over me,
> And like a hungry lion did commence
> Rough deeds of rage and stern impatience;
> But when my angry guardant stood alone,
> Tend'ring my ruin and assail'd of none,

Dizzy-ey'd fury and great rage of heart
Suddenly made him from my side to start
Into the clust'ring battle of the French;
And in that sea of blood my boy did drench
His overmounting spirit; and there died,
My Icarus, my blossom, in his pride.

Act 4, scene 7, lines 3–16

When young Talbot's body is carried to old Talbot, he taunts Death, saying that he and his son will escape the tyranny of Death, and that his son was so brave and committed, that if Death had been a French soldier, John would have been able to kill him:

Thou antic death, which laugh'st us here to scorn,
Anon, from thy insulting tyranny,
Coupled in bonds of perpetuity,
Two Talbots, winged through the lither sky,
In thy despite shall 'scape mortality.
O, thou, whose wounds become hard-favour'd death,
Speak to thy father ere thou yield thy breath!
Brave death by speaking, whether he will or no;
Imagine him a Frenchman and thy foe.
Poor boy! he smiles, methinks, as who should say,
Had death been French, then death had died to-day.

Act 4, scene 7, lines 18–28

These lines involve cascades of blending webs. Consider the blended space in which, as Lord Talbot imagines his son John was imagining, Death is French, and so is slain (figure 3).

In this blending web, the two input mental stories and the blended story share the mental frame *hand-to-hand martial combat, with victory and defeat*—a powerful and highly familiar mental frame, which presents a compressed, vivid scene at human scale. It contains familiar and immediately intelligible structure for the dynamic interaction of forces: Two agents place their strength in opposition; they strike each other; one defeats the other. In one of the input stories, Personified Death the Warrior defeats young Talbot. In another input story, young Talbot and perhaps other English

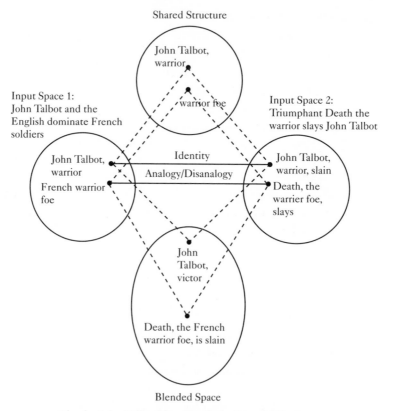

Shared Structure

Input Space 1:
John Talbot and the
English dominate French
soldiers

Input Space 2:
Triumphant Death the
warrior slays John Talbot

Identity
Analogy/Disanalogy

Blended Space

FIGURE 3 Blend—John Talbot Slays Death the French Warrior

soldiers furiously attack and dominate French soldiers on the field of battle
near Bordeaux on the day of his death. It is easy to draw mental connections
between the inputs because both are organized by the *hand-to-hand martial
combat* mental frame, and so the roles in their organizing mental frames line
up. Stuff from each of the input stories is projected, selectively to the blend,
which is likewise organized by the conceptual mental frame of *hand-to-hand
martial combat*. In the blended story, Death the Warrior Foe is now French,
and so is slain.

This blending web seems exotic, pyrotechnic, and Shakespearean, but it
follows a standard pattern in which two individual people are blended, or an
individual person and a role that people can inhabit are blended. We can say:

If John were David,
  ...he would be married by now.
  ...he would be rich by now.

...he would be a stockbroker.

...he would use his mobile phone.

Similarly, we can say:

If John were French,

...he would have attended the École des Hautes Études en Sciences Sociales.

...he would prefer to lecture in English.

...he would live in the Lyonnais.

In the first set of expressions, we blend two different individual people. In the second set, we blend a specific person and a role people can inhabit, and this is the blending pattern we employ to blend Death the personified warrior foe with the role *French warrior*.

One overarching goal of blending is to provide global insight into a mental web that would otherwise be too large for us to manage. Each of the "If John were..." sentences prompts us to construct, mentally, a recognizable, compressed human scene in which there is a person—a new person who does not exist inside the input mental spaces but who, in the blend, has an identity, a character, a history, and habits. The purpose of constructing these blends is to give us insight into John, David, or France.

Crucially, there is *new stuff* in each of these blends that is not directly available from the input mental spaces. We can understand and even assent to the first set of assertions—"If John were David . . ."—regardless of whether *married, wealthy, stockbroker,* or *possesses a mobile phone* can be found in either the *David* input mental space or the *John* input mental space. We can assent to each of the statements in the second set of assertions—"If John were French..."—even though it is possible to be French without attending the École des Hautes Études en Sciences Sociales, without preferring English, and without living in the Lyonnais, and even if John has never attended college, has never spoken English, and has never lived in France. Blending develops new meaning out of old. It helps us reconceive old meaning, even in cases where the blend itself is regarded as false. Incidentally, to be clear, we should remember that blending two people or a person and a category of person is by no means limited to counterfactual ideas. We can say, "If John is David, he is rich," in the case where we are wondering whether John and David are the same person, and we can say, "If John is French, he must do his military service," in the case where we are uncertain of John's nationality but suspect that he is French. We can also say it when it has been reported to us reliably that John is in fact French.

It is the new stuff in the blend that makes John Talbot victorious over Death. Taken as a whole, the French Death blending web represents John Talbot and the English as glorious, for they have done all that people can possibly do. The counterfactual blend—the one in which John lives and Death dies—informs us that even a slight demotion in Death's status, making him French, suffices to give young Talbot victory over Death, from which we infer exceptionally high valor and power for young Talbot. The blending web tells us that it is not so much the individual French soldiers who have killed young Talbot, but rather Death himself who killed young Talbot. And Death escapes defeat only because he is not French.

The French Death web manifests central principles of blending:

- *There is a mapping between the input mental spaces.* Blending always involves a mapping between inputs. The mapping typically involves connections of identity, analogy and disanalogy, similarity, causality, change, time, intentionality, space, role-value, part-whole, or representation. In the French Death integration web, there is an analogy mapping, that is, a set of connections between "analogous" counterparts. This mapping is elaborate, because it connects elements in the shared mental frame that organizes the inputs. That shared mental frame is *hand-to-hand military combat.* In this elaborate analogy mapping, the role *warrior* in one space maps to the role *warrior* in the other space, because *warrior* is part of the shared mental frame *hand-to-hand military combat.* There are also identity connectors: The specific warrior John Talbot in one input mental space corresponds to the identical warrior John Talbot in the other input mental space. As always with analogy, there is disanalogy. For example, the French warrior foe is human but Death the warrior foe is immortal.
- *There is selective projection from the input mental spaces to the blended space.* Parts, but only parts, of the input mental spaces are projected to the blend. Personified Death is projected from one input mental space, but not his invincibility. John Talbot is projected from both input mental spaces, but not his defeat by Death. The valor of John Talbot against the French is projected, but not the fact that the French in fact killed him.

- *Emergent structure (jargon for "new stuff")*. In the blend, we have the most remarkable emergent structure: Death is vanquished, and John Talbot is the victor. John Talbot's ferocity against the French is so strong that if Death becomes French, Death accordingly becomes vulnerable.

Blending allows us to perform three characteristic mental feats. Because of blending, we are able to:

- develop new ideas out of old,
- achieve global insight into very diffuse arrays of meaning, in mental webs that arch over time, space, causation, and agency,
- and compress diffuse, extended mental webs into compact packages of meaning; we can then manipulate them mentally with greater ease and facility, carry them with us, and expand them when we want to think about something we encounter.

We frequently find in blending that an existing, conventional blend is used as an input mental space to the new blend. We see this in the French Death blending web: The input mental space in which Triumphant Death the Warrior Slays John Talbot is of course already a blend, and it arises from a familiar blending pattern. One of its input mental spaces is Triumphant Death the Warrior Slays a Human Being, and the other is John Talbot is Slain by French Warriors (figure 4).

Now let us track this mental web back one more step. One of its input stories is Triumphant Death the Warrior Slays a Human Being. But that input story is already a familiar blend. It has one input story with Personified Death Causes the Event of Dying of Someone Who Resists, and another input story that has martial combat between warriors (figure 5).

In this mental web, personified Death in the first input story corresponds to one of the warriors in the other input story. The person who dies in the first input story corresponds to the warrior who dies in the other input story. The death of the person in one input story corresponds to the death of the warrior in the other. In the blend, Personified Death is now a warrior foe; dying is the result of being slain in battle; the slaying causes the dying. Projection to the blend is selective: In the input story with the two warriors, either warrior might win and both are mortal, but these conditions are not projected to the blend. There is new stuff in this blend: One of the warriors is absolutely invincible.

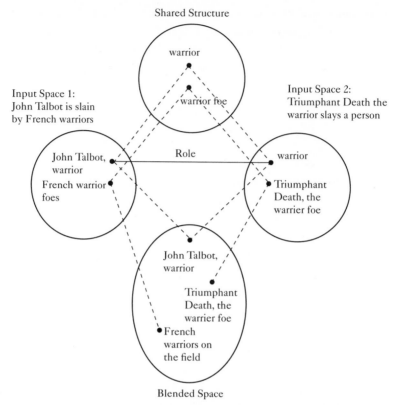

FIGURE 4 Blend—Triumphant Death the Warrior Slays John Talbot

But this blending web again has a familiar blend as one of its input stories. The personification of Death as the cause of events of dying is a blend of two mental spaces: dying as a result of mortality and dying as the result of a causal action performed by an agent (figure 6).

In the first input story, a person dies and the general cause is Death-in-General: "Death-in-General" means the condition of mortality to which all people are subject. In the second input story, an agent performs an action that results in someone's death. In the blend, Death-in-General (as a general causal force to which all living beings are subject) is a personified agent who performs an intentional action that causes the event of dying. This blending web is an instance of an extremely general blending template according to which an event is understood, in the blend, as the result of an action,

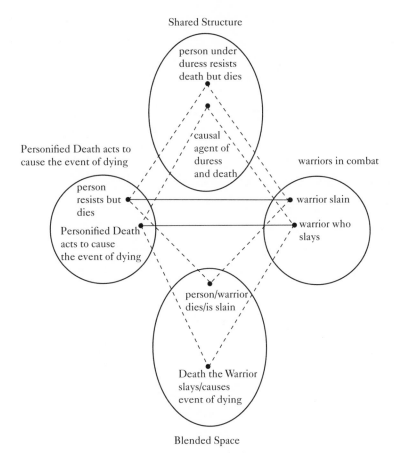

Shared Structure

Personified Death acts to cause the event of dying

warriors in combat

Blended Space

FIGURE 5 Blend—Triumphant Death the Warrior Slays a Human Being

and a cause of the event is understood, in the blend, as a causal agent who performs the causal action.

In the mental web that produces Personified Death as the Cause of the Event of Dying, we have an organizing mental frame for one input space that requires no causal intentional agent at all: Death-in-General, the condition of mortality, is not a causal intentional agent but rather a general cause. But the other organizing mental frame is causal action by a causal intentional agent. These two mental frames differ profoundly in causal, intentional, and interactional structure. Yet we can make mental connections between them because they both involve an event of dying, and we can project from both of these input organizing mental frames to create a

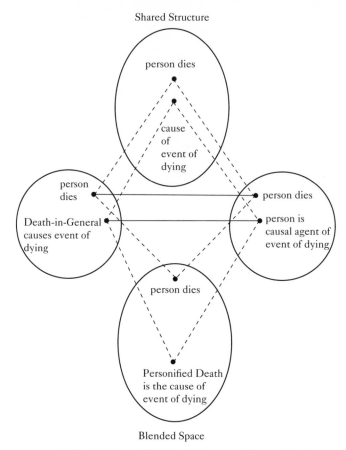

FIGURE 6 Blend—Personified Death Causes an Event of Dying

new organizing mental frame for the blend, and so create there a personified causal agent.

Again, one of the input mental spaces in this Personified Death blending web is already a blend. It has in one of its input mental spaces Human
Death, that is, a specific event of a person's dying in some manner. In
the other input mental space, we have the familiar causal idea according
to which any element of a class of events is caused by a generic, empty
cause: Lust causes all events of lust, Hunger causes all events of hunger,
Death causes all events of death. In the blend, the specific event of dying is
caused fundamentally by Death-in-General; the specific manner of death
is the means (figure 7).

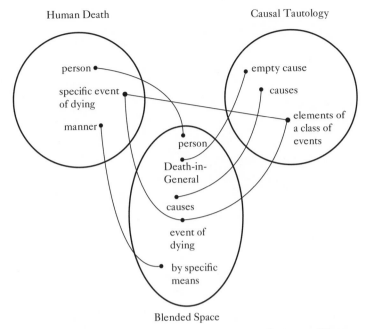

FIGURE 7 **Blend—Death-in-General Causes a Specific Event of Dying**

Combining all these blending webs produces a new idea: the defeat of Death the French Warrior, to the glory of the Talbots and the English. This arresting invention depends upon both the basic mental operation of blending and the deployment of particular common templates for building blending webs (figure 8).

I have skipped entirely over all the blends in old Talbot's first address to Death, "Triumphant death, smear'd with captivity...," including the personification of death, the blend of young Talbot and a hungry lion, the blend of the two Talbots with Daedalus and Icarus, the blend of young Talbot and a blossom, and the blend of the battle and a sea in which young Talbot is not so much slain as drowned.

I have skipped over even the many compressions lying within the cascading blending web that produces Death the French Warrior, but let's look at just one. The blend in which Triumphant Death the Warrior Slays Human Beings can be used—and often is used—regardless of the specific manner of death. We can say of someone who dies of a heart attack, for example, that "Death struck him dead with a single blow." But in the case of John Talbot, the specific cause of death happens to be *martial combat*. Therefore, the input

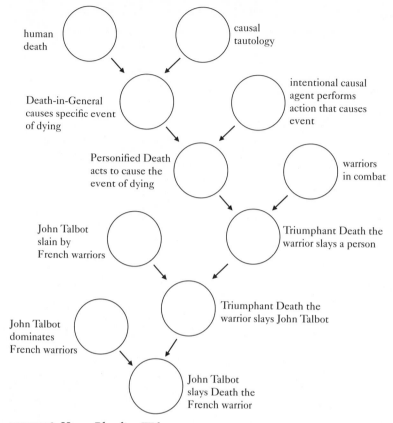

FIGURE 8 Hyper-Blending Web

story in which John Talbot dies in battle already carries a mental frame that fits much of the content of other mental spaces central in the cascading blending web. It is accordingly quite easy to compress *being slain by French warriors* with *being slain by Death the warrior*, to create a single scene in which John Talbot is slain by Death (who is not French in this blend), but the means or instrument that Death uses to slay John Talbot is the group of French warriors who actually deliver the injuries. In this scene, a lethal blow from a French warrior, any French warrior, is equally a lethal blow from Death. This blend can have the effect of stripping the French warriors of any martial glory in defeating John Talbot—they succeeded only because Death himself has taken the field and is complicit in every blow. In the final blend, where Death is a mere Frenchmen, there is no glory to the French at all, but only death for them all around.

Lord Talbot understands that imagined scenes can arouse strong emotions and powerfully shape the way we think and behave. Fervently wanting his son to speak to him before dying, and knowing his son's great motivation to defy the enemy, old Talbot prompts young Talbot to construct a blend in which Death intends to terminate John and his activity, to shut him down, to silence him. In such a blend, merely speaking becomes an act of defiance and bravery. This blend accordingly allows the son to tap his greatest sources of energy: his will to obey his father, his will to respect his father, and his will to defy the enemy. In the blend, they all motivate him in the same direction. In the blend, for John, to speak at all becomes simultaneously an act of obedience and respect for his father and an act of defiance of their joint enemy.

Talbot brings other rich mental spaces to amplify the blend in which Death is personified and to portray the death of his son as an injustice. In the blend, Death is made antic, scornful, and insulting. The certain power of death is blended with the institutional power of the tyrant, thereby making Death a bully rather than an honorable opponent and so making it immoral that young Talbot has died.

In another feat of blending, the two Talbots deprive their martial enemy of victory: They escape Death and his "insulting tyranny." Their souls' departure for heaven is blended with an act of escape from an enemy. This remarkable success is invented in the face of a reality in which young Talbot is dead and old Talbot will die within seconds, in which the corpse of the son is cradled in the arms of the father, in which father and son have been separated for 7 years, in which they are now permanently and forever deprived of each other's company:

> Come, come, and lay him in his father's arms.
> My spirit can no longer bear these harms.
> Soldiers, adieu! I have what I would have,
> Now my old arms are young John Talbot's grave. [Dies]
> Act 4, scene 7, lines 29–32

But in the blend, they are not merely together but permanently bonded, escaping their powerful joint enemy. Gloriously, the Talbots are carried on wings through the yielding sky. Unlike Daedalus and Icarus, the Talbots in this final act reach their destination, united. No untoward calamity, no mistake by the father, causes the boy, on this redemptive occasion, to fall from the sky.

Part of our ease in following blends like this is that we have the idea that a person has a soul. We may not believe it, but we have the idea and can use it. It is easier to understand "escape from mortality" at death if one thinks of the soul's leaving the body. The idea of a soul is itself very creative, if old. It is an idea that has as one of its input mental spaces our notion of "caused motion," as when a person (an "intentional agent") performs an action that causes an object to move in a direction. Blending this with our own idea of how we move our bodies, we can create in the blend a new idea: There is something inside us that is an intentional agent, and it causes our bodies to move. It is our *soul*. This is new stuff on a grand scale.

There are many other blends available to support or provide drive for this idea of a soul. They can all be recruited into a more complicated blending web to provide projections and motivations. For example, we can be inside clothing or a costume and make it move. This suggests a blend in which the body is a robe. But a robe needs an intentional causal agent inside it in order to lend it human rhythms and human gestures. If, in the blend, the body is the robe, then projecting the wearer of the robe to the blend creates an element that can be the separate, intentional, causal agent inside the body: the soul.

When someone dies, the body seems to still be there. So what is the difference? One idea that is available from the blend is that the soul, which ran the body, isn't there anymore. The result is that the corpse now is not merely a body, it is a body with an absence: the absence of the soul. There is a disanalogy relation between the mental space with the living person and the mental space with the dead body. In the blend, we have a *corpse* and the disanalogy relation in the mental web is compressed into a property of the corpse: the absence of the soul (figure 9).

In a larger mental web in which we include various blends that provide the concept of the *soul* as a source of bodily movement and sensation, we have a soul that is internal to the person but *absent* from the corpse.

This concept of the soul can be reinforced and elaborated by using a very general blending template, one that is widely used throughout human cognition, according to which an element that once was present in a location and now is absent from that location is *departed*. How, after all, could the soul be absent? We can answer by blending in our idea of a person's leaving a location: First the person was there, then the person left and so now is not there. In the newer blend, the soul is not there because it *left*. It *departed*. We often use this mental space of *departure* for in-jest blends, as when we say, "Now, where did those scissors walk off to?" or "Where has my pen hidden itself?" Following this pattern, we can do further blending

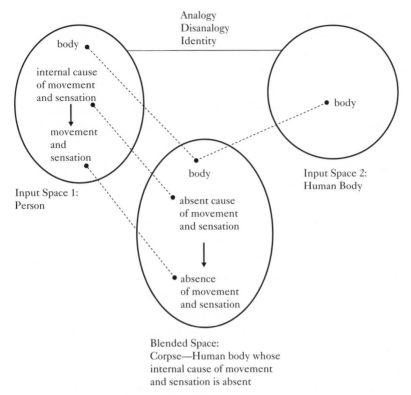

FIGURE 9 **Blend—Corpse**

on the concept of the absent soul to produce the blend in which the soul is not merely absent but now *departed*. The new stuff in this blend can include the notion that when the soul is absent from the body, it is because it is present somewhere else; that the soul is in a single space-time location; that death is the departure of the soul from the body as it journeys to another place. In the case of the Talbots, it journeys through the sky, presumably to heaven. This notion of the departure of the animating element fits nicely with other ideas in the elaborate mental web. For example, we can get out of the clothes and costume and go to another location, leaving the clothes or costume behind, and when we do, the clothes or costume are without humanesque movement. We depart from inside the clothes or costume, and we go to another place.

There are kindred blends that lend additional support to the concept of the *departed soul*. We know that when we dream, we have perceptions that do not fit our surroundings. Often, in our dreams, we are someplace other than the place in which our body is located. The sleeper's body seems to be in one place but the mind seems to "be" in "another place." We can project this idea of our mind's ability to "go somewhere else" to our idea of the soul. Since the body is left behind, the soul is something immaterial, not part of the body. Being immaterial, it can be lighter than material objects and so float up; it can go in and out of the same body, indeed in and out of different bodies (as in reincarnation and possession); it can be free from physical objects altogether, and so penetrate walls and ceilings; it can be impervious to material objects and so invulnerable to blows.

Figures

Classical rhetoricians noticed many different blending patterns involved in forbidden-fruit blends and gave them names like metonymy, synecdoche, and metaphor.[7] These mental patterns, and their expression in language, arise from the compressions that blending creates.[8] Consider the phrase "a loud man." In the mental web, there are quite a number of causal relations. A man performs actions. The actions make noise. The noise is heard by other people. The other people make judgments about the volume of the noise and rate it as "loud" on a mental linear scale. This is a small story all on its own. All of these causal relations across the mental web are compressed in the blend to an abiding feature for the man. Now, in the blend, the man has a feature: He is characteristically "loud." And we can project this "feature" to any story the man inhabits, even one in which he makes no noise. We are used to the idea that people and objects have features: the wooden chair, the tall man, the round wheel. We use this idea of features for objects to help us think of the man. Classical rhetoricians had a word, "hypallage," for this kind of compression: "Loud" applies not to the man but to the sounds he makes, but we move it instead to apply to the man. Some kinds of hypallage are called "transferred epithets." An example would be "a restless night." In the mental web, there is a small story in which a person who is trying to sleep just can't manage it, and these events take place in a time interval that we compress to a *night*. Now we compress these vital relations between the person and the time interval he inhabits into a feature for the night itself: In the blend, the night has a feature—*restless*. Again, we are not deluded, but we do not need to activate and carry the entire mental web. We can make use of the tightly compressed blend, in which the night has a feature: restless.

Once we become aware of these sorts of compressions, we see them everywhere, as part of everyday thought and language. We need "a warm coat" against "a cold wind." Of course, in the mental web, unless we have actually warmed the coat, it is not warm. In fact, it can feel cold when we first put it on. Rather, the coat is an insulation device that causes *us* to feel warmer because we retain more of our body heat. We are the ones warming the coat with our bodies, not the other way around. But the coat is an insulator and so preserves the warmth. The coat is a cause and the warmth is an effect, but we compress this cause-effect vital relation to a property of the coat: a warm coat. And the reason the wind is cold is that it removes the air around us that we have heated with our body and so it takes away an invisible insulation that would have kept us warmer in the absence of the movement of the air. Again, the cause-effect vital relation between the wind and the cold is compressed to a feature for the wind: a cold wind. In this way, we have happy mornings, bitter afternoons, early graves, guilty pleasures, grateful memories . . .

Suppose a president vetoes a foreign aid bill that would have provided funding for food for children. The chain of relations in the mental web for this understanding is vast. It includes many sequences of actions across time, space, causation, and agency. The number of children fed and the kinds of food provided are many, and the times and places quite numerous. The chain of causes and effects is also vast. The newspaper can claim that the president is "snatching the food out of the mouths of starving children." An editorial cartoon can show the president, in suit and tie, snatching a single rice bowl out of the hands of a single child.[9] The mental space in which one adult takes food away from one child is already tightly compressed. It is mentally tractable. We blend it with the great mental web involving the legislation and the veto. The result is that the blend borrows the compression from the mental space with the two people and the single act of snatching. Such compressions sometimes seem "metaphoric" to people, especially when the ideas connected in the mental web come from very different domains of thought (for example, American legislation versus taking away a bowl) and when the vocabulary for the compression is not routine in our language ("intellectual progress" strikes most people as less metaphoric than "mental journey").[10] The case of the president's snatching the rice bowl may at first seem "metaphoric," but in fact *depriving children of food* in one of the input mental spaces connects to *depriving children of food* in the other, and this relation does not meet any of the usual definitions of metaphor. The relations connecting the president in all the mental spaces of legislation and the president in the mental space of snatching the rice bowl are *identity* relations, not metaphoric. The relations across all the children are *analogy* or *category relations*. In this case, all those children and all those relations are compressed into a single child, just as we saw for the dinosaur that turned into a bird. The compression of indefinitely many children to one child is just another example of compressing all the analogical relations in the mental web to *uniqueness* in the blend. That does not strike us as metaphoric, either. The part that strikes us as metaphoric is the blending of legislative acts with snatching a rice bowl.

In blending theory, metaphor, metonymy, synecdoche, and many other rhetorical figures of thought are analyzed as resulting from the compressions brought about by blending. The classical rhetorical labels for all these things are useful as shorthand for picking out different reactions, but yet, that long list of labels can obscure the common underlying mental process. A given blend usually does not fit under the definition of just one of these terms. The blends of the cyclic day, the Buddhist Monk, the *lionman,* and so on do not seem to involve any compressions that strike us as metaphoric, and the blend of the president's snatching the rice bowl has many compressions that do not strike us as metaphoric, although it has one that does.

Elsewhere, I have argued that *category* connections (e.g., between two stars) and *analogy* connections (e.g., between a carpenter's toolbox and a photojournalist's jacket with lots of pockets designed to hold lots of equipment) differ not so much in the processes by which we invent the category connections and the analogy connections as in how we weigh and evaluate the products,[11] and that analogy very often (but not always) involves blending. In particular, the analogies that analogy theorists prefer to analyze typically rely for their most important inferences on blending.[12] A perhaps compatible view of analogy can be found in Douglas Hofstadter's *Fluid Concepts and Creative Analogies.*[13] Part of the blending project is to look at the scores of names and labels that rhetoricians, literary critics, and linguists have invented for different products and to investigate the underlying mental processes. Many of the blends that we have seen in this chapter might be given one or another of these various labels, but the underlying processes for all these examples may be much more unified than the long list of labels would suggest.

The History of Forbidden Fruit Is the History of Modern Human Beings

Genesis 1 has no human beings for the first 25 verses. When people who have bodies like us show up in Genesis, there is not much happening. They start out as forms, utterly boring and unlike us. These anatomically modern human bodies perform some operations as the story continues through Genesis 2. But there are no fully cognitively modern human minds like ours, even though they can talk! But then, the serpent shows up, in the first line of Genesis 3, and everything happens in 200 words. There we stand: "And the eyes of them both were opened, and they knew that they were naked."

It is brilliant of Genesis to have placed the plucking of forbidden fruit as the origin of ideas and the birth of the modern human mind. People pluck forbidden mental fruit, they embrace forbidden ideas, and the results are often extremely useful. People blend together what should not go together, they grasp the blend, pluck it, make it their own, and it gives them knowledge. They get ideas, new ideas, ideas that they can manage even though those ideas are embedded in mental webs that themselves arch over time, space, causation, and agency.

Science faces severe challenges in studying this plucking of forbidden mental fruit, for the simple and obvious reason that there are no robust animal models. Science depends upon animals in comparative research. Patients are often willing to take prescription drugs because those drugs have been tested on animals. We reason like this: For the relevant biological systems, those animals work the way we do, so a test on them is a pretty good indicator of how the drugs would work on us.

When we encounter a nonhuman animal that works the way we do for some aspect of our existence—like vision or drugs, for example—we say it is a robust "animal model." The problem is that there is no animal model for advanced blending, for plucking forbidden mental fruit. Animals are great, they can do many things we cannot, and we are on a gradient with mammals, including for operations like blending, but we find elsewhere in life no equivalent ability for advanced blending.

We have at last in science come to a moment where we might begin to peek into the principles of advanced blending, the mechanisms that make it possible, the pattern of its unfolding in the human infant, and the path of its descent in our species. This is a challenging research program, one that will require the combined efforts of cognitive scientists, neuroscientists, developmental psychologists, evolutionary biologists, and scholars of story. Any human child can pluck forbidden fruit, but we are only now beginning to figure out what happened in the Garden of Eden.

6

Artful Ideas

[T]he greatest riddle of archaeology—how we became human and in the process began to make art—continues to tantalize.

DAVID LEWIS-WILLIAMS, *The Mind in the Cave*

In the discussion of *Harold and the Purple Crayon*, we considered the blending of two mental spaces connected by a vital relation of *representation*. We are going to look at that pattern of blending here, especially in art and in our ideas of art.

Mentally, we can relate one idea to another idea. For example, we think of the child as related to the adult it became. Vital mental relations connect the child and the adult: *time, change, identity, analogy,* and *cause-effect.* Mentally, Ohio and California are connected by a vital relation of *space.* Ohio and the United States are connected by a vital relation of *part-whole.* Mary and a picture of Mary are connected through conceptual relations of *representation* and *analogy.*

Picture World

It is common in art to work with many blends, and to make blends of blends, called "hyper-blends." A hyper-blend is a blend that has as at least one of its input mental spaces something that is already a blend. Hyper-blends occur routinely.

We saw already, in chapter 3, how blending works to let us attribute mind to a seal, and how even more blending can create the idea of a selkie. There is a story—"Aunt Charlotte and the NGA Portraits"[1]—in which the idea of a selkie is elaborately developed, in ways that seem to be easy for children to follow. NGA is the acronym for "National Gallery of Art," the one in Washington, DC. It sits on the National Mall, between the Capitol Building to the east and the Washington Monument to the west.

"Aunt Charlotte and the NGA Portraits" has a character named Olga Weathers. Halfway into the story, the reader discovers that Olga is a selkie lacking her coat. The word "selkie" never occurs in the story, and no prior knowledge of selkies is required to understand the story. Indeed, when I first read the story, I had never heard of a selkie and assumed that the shape-shifting Olga was entirely the author's invention.

Olga has the mental character of a woman but, understandably, no native taste for the human world. She would prefer a life of swimming in the water. Wearing her coat, she would have something like the body of a seal, naturally. But not quite, since her coat can be removed, and when it is, she becomes a woman. But not quite, since, when she is a woman, she retains her knowledge of the sea and retains, too, the remarkable instinctive capabilities of a marine mammal.

Olga Weathers has features possessed by no seal. Neither seal nor woman can lose its skin or assume the skin of another species. Neither seal nor woman can be transformed into a member of another species. And Olga is not the only person in the world of this story who is impossible in ours. A real man in our world cannot obtain a wife by stealing the skin of a seal, but in the world of this story, a man can try to get a wife by stealing the coat of a female selkie and demanding that she marry him if she ever wants to have her coat back.

These things are possible in Olga's world. She switches from species to species according to whether she is wearing her coat. She is never either woman or seal, but always something different, and this difference counts in the story as her "magic." A mean man, it turns out, did steal her coat. He hoped she would marry him in order to regain her coat, but she refused to marry him, because she knew he would have kept her coat forever, and she would never have been free. "He thought I was helpless and had no choice, but I am not powerless, and I have a few friends," she says. Her friends helped her make a home on Ocracoke, a seaside town off the coast of North Carolina, where she earns her living by helping the fishermen. Olga can tell where the fish are, and she can foretell the weather, and she has a sense for the conditions of the sea. The fishermen therefore pay her for advice. In Olga's world, it seems, boats have an intentional nature, too, or at least, they can hear a selkie, and they are happy to comply with her requests. She can call the boats home when they are lost.

As luck would have it, the man who stole her coat was injured while hunting narwhals. The wound turned septic and he died without telling Olga where he had hidden her coat. So there is Olga, beached on Ocracoke.

In the blending web that produces this selkie, the shape and movement that are projected from the "human being" input and from the "seal" input to Olga do not make her lithe and frisky. That is sometimes how selkie blends end up. But in this case, Olga's body is massive, like a seal's, and she has relative difficulty moving on land, as a seal might. She is hefty. Her long hair combs out in perfect waves. She is herself a kind of undulation whenever she passes over the sand.

Olga's world, inhabited by selkies, includes the magic of shape-shifting, the magic of moving from one category to another, the magic of blending incompatible elements such as *woman* and *seal* to make not just an imaginary mental blend but actual elements in the world of the story. For us, a selkie is a fictional blend. In Olga's world, she is a selkie. (One wonders whether there is an imaginary world in which the lionman can meet Olga.)

There is another magic pattern of blending in Olga's world, and this additional magic is also based on a familiar pattern of blending, one that concerns our everyday, entirely pedestrian concept of *representation*. This familiar pattern of blending is a general blending template used widely in art and in everyday life. I will call it "Picture World." It works as follows. We routinely put something and its representation into a mental relation. The representational element is understood as "representing" a world or a scene or an element in a scene (figure 10).

It is extremely common for us to blend these two related mental spaces. One typical way to do so is to fuse, in the blend, the represented element with the representing element. This turns them into a unique thing in the blend (figure 11).

For example, a person and a photograph are two quite different things, but we can blend the photographic element and the person. We point at the picture and say, "This is Mary." Of course, we are not deluded in the least: We know

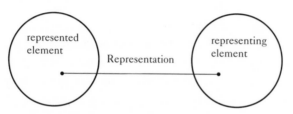

FIGURE 10 **Representation Relation**

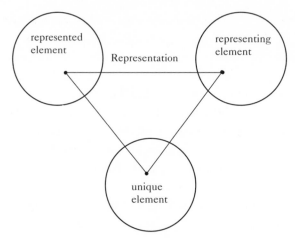

FIGURE 11 Compressing a Representation Relation to a
Unique Element in the Blend

that, in the input mental space with the person, Mary is three-dimensional
and moves. We know that the photograph is two-dimensional and does not
move. But the mental blend in which the representation of Mary is fused with
Mary is extremely useful. We can talk "to the picture" because, in the blend,
we are calling up some of the emotions of talking to Mary. People apologize,
confess, or propose to pictures, upbraid and accuse pictures, insult pictures.
They feel ashamed or proud when a "picture" looks at them. They throw darts
at pictures. They are not crazy. They are just using the blend.

Most blends of this sort, but not all, have connections not only of representation but also of analogy between the representation and the element
represented. That is, the visual image that is the representation of Mary is visually and topologically analogous to Mary herself: There are two images of eyes
in the representation and two eyes in Mary's head; the two images of eyes in
the representation are above the image of the nose in the representation just
as Mary's actual two eyes are above Mary's actual nose; and so on (figure 12).

In addition to the one idea of the representation and the other idea of
what is represented, there is yet a third idea that can be brought into this common "compression of representation" blending web. This third idea is the idea
of a portal through which one can see. The blending works in the following
fashion. A window, or a gap in the curtains or in a fence, or a portal of any
sort gives us a view. When we catch only a punctual view through a portal, we
get a framed glimpse. Many mental webs contain a relation between a framed
representation and a framed glimpse. For example, a photograph of a person
and a framed glimpse of the same person are strongly analogous not only in

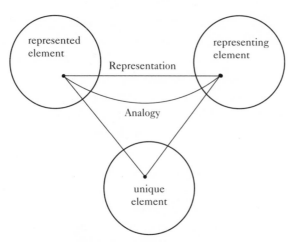

FIGURE 12 **Compressing a Representation Relation and an Analogy Relation to a Unique Element in the Blend**

the content of what is viewed but also in the fact that there is a viewer of that content. It seems to be common to blend the photograph of a person with a framed glimpse of the person, so that, in the blend, the entire photograph becomes a framed glimpse of the part of the visual field the photograph represents, including the person. We often say not only that the photograph gives us a "glimpse" but also that a true visual glimpse is a "snapshot." This blend of *representation* and *framed glimpse* is especially irresistible in the case of cameras that allow us to look through the lens just before we snap the picture. The connections between the photograph of John and the glimpse of John are then thorough.

So, we can take the blend of the representation and what it represents (like "Mary" in the blend), and we can call on what we know about a framed glimpse, and project some of that knowledge to the blend. What do we know about a framed glimpse? Principally, we know that what we see in a framed glimpse is only part of a world—the world around the framed glimpse is bigger in both space and time. The ability to conceive of a framed glimpse as part of a larger world in space and time may be common across all mammals that have vision, and this tendency to take a limited percept as implying a larger context may extend across all sensory modalities. For example, if we feel something small for a brief moment in the dark, we take it immediately to be part of a larger spatial and temporal world. Human beings, and perhaps dogs and dolphins for that matter, are very adept at conceiving of rich dynamic scenes with full spatial and temporal continuity on the basis of very partial perceptions.

When we blend a framed representation like a photograph with our concept of a framed glimpse, the photograph thereby becomes, in the blend, a
spatially and temporally limited part of a rich dynamic world with temporal and spatial continuities and changes that are not directly represented. Of
course, the photograph itself does not extend in space beyond its borders, and
it is static rather than dynamic, so although the photograph itself lasts in time,
what it represents does not extend in time: It represents just one moment.

When we blend the idea of the photograph with the idea of a framed
glimpse, the blend can have new stuff. In blends, the most minimal, but often
important new stuff is a conjunction of elements that in fact do exist in the
input spaces but are not conjoined except in the blend. An example of a conjunction in a blend is the conjunction of an ascending monk and a descending
monk. Each of the monks is available from an input space, but their conjunction is not.

But in this book, we typically emphasize new stuff that goes beyond
cut-and-paste conjunction. The conjunction of a bird and a pig, or even wings
and a pig, is just a conjunction. But when we have a flying pig—an utterly new
species—or two identical monks *meeting themselves*, that goes far beyond
conjunction. We can conjoin a talking person and an animal, as we do when
we have the idea of a person talking to an animal, but a talking animal, a flying
pig, or a person meeting himself is radical new stuff, not mere conjunction.
Of course, once we embrace and remember these new ideas, these products of
blending, they become old ideas and, as we have seen repeatedly, can in turn
serve as inputs to yet newer blends and newer ideas.

In the blend of the photograph with the framed glimpse, something truly
new emerges. We have a persistent view of a dynamic and changing world
that nonetheless does not change no matter how long we stare at it, no matter how much we inspect it; and this view is directly connected to existing
spatial and temporal extents we cannot see. Outside the blend, the idea of the
photograph does not offer such a view, because the view available in that case
is emphatically not a sustained view of a dynamic and changing world and is
not directly connected in our embodied and interactive perception to spatial
and temporal extents. Outside the blend, the idea of the framed glimpse does
not offer such a view, because the view in that input in fact changes if we stare
at it. The blend we are considering does not merely conjoin these two views. If
we had a mental space with a photograph of a portal, sitting on a windowsill,
and an actual view of the portal of which it is a photograph visible outside
the window, that would be a conjunction. Other conjunctions might be a
memory of the photograph as we look at the portal. But in the blend of the

photograph and the framed glimpse, we have not two conjoined views but a single view, a single experience, a single viewer, and the nature of the view is utterly unavailable from either input.

If we see a photograph of the middle of a bridge, we routinely and naturally activate the blend of the photograph and the framed glimpse, to conceive of the bridge as extending beyond the frame. We conceive of a person on the bridge as obscuring elements behind her, even though those elements of course have no representation in the photograph. If we were actually looking at the bridge instead of a photograph, and we were not making a blend of a photograph and a framed glimpse, we could move our viewpoint so as to see what is behind the person or is in other parts of the world near the bridge; but in that case, as we stared at the bridge, the whole visual field might change. In the blend of the photograph and the framed glimpse, the real dynamic world, with all its connections, does not change no matter how long we look at it. That is an utterly new kind of view.

Of course, we usually construct a similar blend when we see a painting or a sketch. We can project to the blend elements that correspond to our understanding of the reality of a framed glimpse even though there is no visible counterpart of them in the painting or sketch itself, and we can do this even when we know that the representation is fictitious. In the blend, the painted woman on the painted bridge is obscuring something from our view even if the painter invented both her and the bridge. We can also prolong our view, if we like, and yet the woman and the bridge will never move.

So, would we want to call these blends of paintings, what they represent, and framed glimpses of what they represent "imaginary"? Sure, for us. But inside Olga's world, they can be real. The paintings that exist in Olga's world have the same names as some actual paintings in our world, and most of the people in Olga's world who see those paintings see exactly what people in our world see when they look at the counterpart paintings. But in Olga's world, in contrast to our world, paintings, or at least some paintings, are in fact—not just in imagination—framed glimpses of other worlds. What worlds? Picture Worlds, of course! In Olga's world, those paintings actually are rich dynamic worlds of their own, and the few elite viewers in the world who in fact see properly, that is, with intelligence and open-minded insight, can indeed stare attentively through the portal of the picture frame to see those dynamic painted worlds. When these expert viewers look at paintings, they see—with effort and practice—the people move, the sea roll, the wind blow, and vehicles enter and depart from the scene.

This is great new stuff in the blend—rich, dynamic worlds inside the paintings. It comes in part from projection from what we know about a glimpse through a window or portal. We know that if we prolong the glimpse to a stare, we might, looking through the portal, see change, dynamism, movement. Just so, in Olga's world, if you are talented and trained and you stare at the painting, you might see change, dynamism, movement. Why do you see it? In Olga's world, the answer is straightforward: because it is *there*, although not everybody can see what is there. In fact, very few people can.

Olga, of course, is one of those who see properly. When she looks at a painting, or at least the right kind of painting, she can see the people in it move, breathe, and act, because in the blend they in fact do, and in Olga's world, the blend is real. In the blending web that blends the painting, what it represents, and a prolonged framed view of what it represents, the representation of a person has received very full projections from our notion of staring through a window at a world: The blended painted person can move, converse, think, plan, become hungry, eat, and so on. Yet the projections from the mental space of the real-world person are not complete: In this blend, these painted people do not age. With a few exceptions, they are unaware of anything outside the world of the particular painting they inhabit.

We are all familiar with a basic "Picture World" blending template. We use it routinely. Suppose that in our real world we have a bridge over a canal. Well, an object can literally be part of that scene, part of the real world. A person can walk onto the bridge and leave a picnic basket there, for example. If the physics works out right, such a thing can literally be put into the scene or removed from the scene. Similarly, we can row a real gondola into the real scene. Over in the representation, that is, the picture, there can be little images that are created there; they can also be erased or otherwise made invisible. So, for example, the painter can do something with paint and a paintbrush that results in the existence of a representation of a gondola "in" the represented scene. There is a mental relation between the two acts, that is, between putting something into a real scene and taking some action, like painting, that results in a new element in a representation. This relation connects two caused changes in the two scenes and it connects their visible results. This relation can be compressed in our routine "Picture World" blending template to yield, in the blend, a blended causality. The blend fuses these two caused changes, so that the performing of actions that result in a representational element in the representation is fused with "putting" what it represents "into" the "scene." We say, "The painter put a gondola into the painting." Of course, we are not at all deluded: Whereas a gondola must exist before it can be rowed into the

Grand Canal, the exact flat composition of paint that represents the boat in the representation does not in fact exist as such to be "put" into the picture until the artist is quite finished taking the artistic action. We use such expressions all the time, as when we say that the artist "put some flowers into the sketch" but then "took them out," or "Hey! You forgot to put Grandma into your sketch." The blend that fuses the representation with what it represents gives us a natural way to think and speak about representations at human scale. It lets us recruit—for the purpose of talking about representations and their creation—the deeply understood logic of manipulating objects. So our notion of the creation of a representation already has some structure that can be projected to the blend to support the idea of "putting" an element "into" the representation. This blend has some remarkable new stuff: We can, for example, "put" a "mountain" into the picture. Indeed, we can "put" "the moon" or "the sun" into the picture, even though in the real world we cannot perform the corresponding action.

There are other forms of art in which the notion of "putting" "something" "into" the representation is more direct. For example, children can make pictures by putting prefabricated stickers or plastic laminations onto a surface. There are additionally genres of adult art in which the artwork may have a real dried flower or some other real element right in the picture, placed there by literally taking it and sticking it into the artwork.

There is yet other stuff we know about looking through a portal onto a scene that we can use in the blend. For example, one of the things we know about a window or portal on a real scene is that we can throw things through the window or portal or go through it ourselves, and then be part of what we previously only saw. We can project to the blend this action of "entrance," to give, in the blend, the possibility of moving something from our world into the Picture World.

In fact, we have all had the experience of extending this standard "Picture World" blending template by imagining that we are entering the representation, or interacting with what is in it. Perhaps we imagine taking our place at the luncheon on the grass, or dining on the food in the painting, or walking down the street in the Dutch village, or even saying something to one of the characters, who then responds to us. The cosmopolitan glut of well-produced photographs of smashingly good-looking people posed receptively and (in the blend) "looking at us" (or even "beckoning us with their eyes") owes its existence to our mental ability to enter the scene and interact. When you think of it, our ability to be transfixed and absorbed by a very small, two-dimensional, static photograph of a beautiful human being is a deep enigma, explained,

I propose, by the uniquely human ability for advanced blending, and in particular for the construction of a blend in which the representation is the thing represented and we can interact with this representation. We are not deluded, but the effect is undeniable.

This enigma is no less enigmatic in the case of real-time video, with which, of course, we cannot actually interact. Although any mammal, looking at a video, might respond to cues that suggest that a train is rushing toward it, and might attend to cues that suggest that it is looking at a member of its species, could a dog or a chimp, when presented with the appropriate video image, mentally insert itself into an imaginary blend and mentally interact with the elements of the blend, knowing that the interaction is imaginary? Could it visibly act out that interaction, as in imaginative play?

In Olga's world, the "Picture World" blend is real. It provides the possibility of moving an object from our world into the Picture World. The man who stole Olga's coat as a means of compelling her to marry him hid it not under a rock or up a tree or in any other normal locale in our world, but instead inside a painting of Venice by Canaletto. Within the logic of Olga's world, he literally "hid" it "in" Canaletto's painting. The coat is there, in the painting, in the exact sense that it was here, outside the picture, where any actual coat ought to be, but he moved it from here to there, and now it is there and not here. He did not paint it into the picture. Instead, the picture is a portal into a Picture World, and he moved it from this world into that Picture World. Olga's coat, in accordance with the physics of our world, can be in only one location. But when we blend Selkie World with Picture World and so get Olga's world, the location of the selkie coat can literally be inside a painting, and there is a means of moving things from locations outside the painting to locations inside the painting.

Projection to the blend is always selective, so not all Picture World blends are the same. Consider, as a contrast to Olga's Picture World, the Picture World in *John's Picture*, by Elizabeth MacDonald, a book for younger children. John receives a new set of colored pencils and draws a house on a piece of paper. He draws a little man standing in front of the house. Then he puts down his pencils and goes to have his supper. It turns out that he has left behind him a Picture World, but one quite different from the Picture World in Olga's world. In John's little picture, the little man can perceive the pencil that is left lying on the paper, and he can bring it into his world, and he does. Because he feels lonely, he draws a little woman to be his wife. She is evidently aware that she is being drawn and is quite happy about it, and even as she is being drawn she is just as real as he is. This little wife, with some help from her little husband, draws a little boy and a little girl. The husband draws some extra rooms for them at the back of the house. Then the whole family draws a backyard. The boy draws a dog. The girl draws a cat. The cat, as it is being drawn, draws a mouse to chase. Life goes on. Why not?

Later on, after many domestic adventures, the little man is standing in front of the house, thinking of how empty it looks, when John returns and picks up his pencil. The little man's wide-eyed expression, pursed mouth, and hands-on-hips posture as he looks in the direction of John's fingers suggests that the little man can perceive at least something of the outside world. If we take that interpretive line, then we are projecting to the residents of Picture World at least constrained abilities to perceive at least parts of the external world, to interact in at least limited ways with the external world, and even to understand some of the causality of representation and its role in their existence. Indeed, they can themselves take advantage of those causal patterns and change their world by drawing it from the inside. By contrast, the residents of the Picture World of Venice in Olga's world do not seem to have these abilities. In *John's Picture*, it is unclear whether John can himself see that his drawing is a Picture World. At the moment when John returns to look at his picture, there are no changes to be seen: the little man is in front of the house, standing in exactly the spot where he stood when John left. The little man's new family is inside the house, hidden by happenstance from view. All the new drawing done by the little man and his family lies behind the house. So, conveniently and intriguingly, there is nothing new for John to see. Would the cosmos allow John to draw a new little wife for the little man? What would happen to the other wife if he did? I have heard children explore these possibilities. But not to worry: John draws only a garden and then, like all good children, goes contentedly to bed. The little man then draws a note for the milkman and fastens it to the door and goes to bed, too. How many days could they all go on living this way?

Olga's suitor, having hidden her coat in the Canaletto painting, went on to hide the painting itself. When she at last locates the painting, she faces a far greater challenge. As the suitor-thief had anticipated, it is not so easy for the land-bound selkie to take the coat out of the painting. To get to it, you must first physically enter the painting. But Olga cannot do that; she is too stout to squeeze through the frame. More daunting still, there is nothing but water across the bottom of the picture. Olga, massive and cumbersome, would fall into the water, and, unable to swim in her present unfortunate form, would drown. It is extremely witty to manipulate a selkie through fear of drowning. What better way to remind her of her vulnerable state? But why can't she simply remove the frame, add more canvas, paint more picture, including a walkway to the quay, and walk in? Apparently, the portal to a Picture World is set by the original creator and cannot be changed. Presumably, if you create a new picture with a new portal, even if it incorporates the old one, and enter it, then you are in a different Picture World, not the one created by Canaletto, and not the one where the coat is hidden. Or perhaps this is a question we never think to explore.

It is common in the world's cultures to create a blend that contains a representation into which objects can be placed and out of which they can be taken. Examples include myths in which people die and "become" constellations, and cartoons in which "cartoon characters" throw something at what are represented to be members of their audience, only to have these represented members of the audience leap into the frame of the television to interact with the "characters," to chase them, even sometimes to drag them out. Such artful tricks are widely deployed and remarked.

Olga's world is a blend of two blending webs. One is the blend in which there are selkies, Selkie World. The other is a Picture World blending web in which representation is compressed to uniqueness. In this Picture World web, the relation between two separate input mental spaces is compressed to uniqueness in the blend, so that the representation and what it represents are fused there into a single element. In this Picture World blend, the painting of the water really is water, for example, even as it is part of the painting. The Picture World blending web in Olga's world has, as mentioned, yet another input mental space on which the blend draws: the concept of a portal, such as a window, on a real scene. Projecting *portal* to the Picture World blend results in a Picture World that is much fuller than our view of it, a Picture World into which we can insert elements from the external world, such as a coat.

In Olga's world, which is a blend of the general Selkie World blend and the general Picture World blend, there is a selkie, and her coat can be hidden inside a painting (figure 13).

In Olga's world, there are many paintings, in fact all the paintings that are in our world. And in Olga's world, each of them is a Picture World. These individual paintings, these individual Picture Worlds, are indeed very rich, but they do not possess anything like the completeness of our world. Someone who enters one of these Picture Worlds from the outside will find that the world inside the Picture World fades out at its edges. If you are in the Canaletto Picture World, and you walk through the marketplace to where the side streets lead deeper into the city, you are then confronted with "impenetrable grey mist." Open the door to a wineshop, and you encounter "the

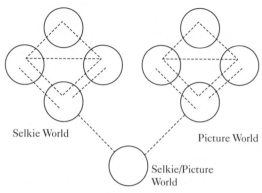

Selkie World

Picture World

Selkie/Picture World

FIGURE 13 Blending Two Blending Webs, Each with Its Own Blend

same thick grey fog." There isn't anything there, you see. As a character in the story says, "It's a painting. It only goes so far." This is remarkable new stuff: In neither of the input spaces—the representation or the world it represents—can you walk to where the world fades out. There are other ways in which a Picture World in Olga's world is unlike our world, some of them influenced by projections from the painting (that is, the representation input). For example, one can enter the Canaletto Picture World, and take a cooked chicken away from the marketplace and dine on it. But when you return, the chicken is still there. "It's a painting," a character in the story explains. "When you go back, everything will be just exactly as it was before you came."

Not exactly. Olga recruits a young girl to help her. This girl, Charlotte, is a talented but solitary child, adept at solving puzzles. She is visiting Ocracoke in November with her adequate but bored mother and adequate but distracted father. Through Olga's tacit coaching, Charlotte learns to see the people moving in the Canaletto painting. It is not clear to the reader that even a talented and motivated human child could perceive the Picture World of Canaletto's painting of Venice without Olga's training and influence: Charlotte encounters the painting in Olga's home, which is perhaps a magical place itself. Olga sings, puts her arm around Charlotte, and unpins her own long hair so its smooth waves brush across Charlotte's bare arm. Charlotte sees, and a few minutes later goes through, the frame of the painting to retrieve the coat. Charlotte is much smaller than Olga, and she can swim very well.

In general, "Picture World" is a general blending template. We use it all the time. It is always at our disposal whenever we see any representation: We can imagine that the representation (painting, photo, sketch ...) actually has a world inside it. This general blending template does not dictate the details of any particular Picture World. For example, some Picture Worlds can be entered by outsiders, others cannot. In some Picture Worlds, a visitor from outside the picture can be perceived by those who inhabit the picture, but in other cases, the visitor is invisible to the natives.

In Olga's world, the Picture Worlds can be entered, at least by those who have the knack to see that they are Picture Worlds. Insight brings new possibilities, a central theme of this story. In Olga's world, the usual blend of understanding and seeing that we all know and deploy ("I *see* what you are saying") undergoes remarkable conceptual development. Charlotte must work on her literal ability to see. She must strive to attain superior vision. As she looks at the painting, its elements and their movement become clearer and clearer. Seeing better, she understands more deeply. She already had, as Olga knew, talent in that direction: Solitary and friendless, Charlotte spends her time on jigsaw puzzles, looking at each piece, seeing its significance, recognizing its place. After their first meeting, Olga and Charlotte work together on jigsaw puzzles, and Charlotte improves. The idea that Olga might possess superior perceptual abilities is naturally projected to her from our knowledge of a seal: We are familiar with the idea that many animals have perceptual abilities we lack— the ability to hear sounds we cannot hear, to see patterns we cannot see. Olga explains to Charlotte why she watches people: "I like to piece together their actions in order to understand their thoughts." Charlotte has honed the same knack through inspecting her mother and father. She turns it on Olga, too, and figures her out. She sees. She looks at the Canaletto painting, and she sees.

Charlotte hooks her foot on the frame, which turns out to be as solid as a stone banister (because, in the blend, it is a stone banister, and in Olga's world, the picture blends are real), and throws herself over the banister through the frame into the Grand Canal. When she splashes down, she can indeed swim to the side of the canal. Good thing!

Needless to say, there are problems. She is nearly run over by a gondola, because in this world, the residents of this Picture World cannot perceive the visiting girl. She is in their Picture World but not fully part of it. She has some abilities they do not, which come from her powers when she is not in the painting. But she also has some abilities they do have, such as the ability to move about in their three-dimensional space. The fact that they can neither see nor hear Charlotte is evidence of the selective nature of the projection to the blend and the fact that from identical input mental spaces we can develop quite different blends. There are many examples of Picture World blends in which the natives can interact with the tourists. And indeed, Charlotte can interact with them bodily: She must clear out of the way of the pedestrians as she is walking down the street or they will bump into her, and she must avoid being run over by the gondolas or poled down by the gondoliers.

In Charlotte's Venice—that is, the Venice she enters by splashing down into the Grand Canal—all the elements are truly there, in the sense that, as bodies, they take up space and conform to familiar physical patterns of mass and force. Nobody moves by flying, for example, and the characters imported from outside the painting cannot walk through walls. If you fall into the water, you must swim. The one exception to this logic is that someone in the picture who has been imported from the world outside the picture can leave this Picture World through the picture frame, the portal, but to do so must reach the frame and propel herself through it. Visitors to Charlotte's Venice from outside that particular Picture World can perceive everything in it, but the Venetians themselves cannot perceive what has entered their world from the outside. If this seems to make sense to you—and of course it does—it is because you have a cognitively modern human mind, and so can do advanced blending.

Charlotte, having landed in the Grand Canal, does manage to avoid being run over by the gondolas and poled down by the gondoliers. But then she arrives at the edge of the canal, and the water level is 2 feet below the street level. How can she get up?

At this point, the story needs yet another crucial blending web in order to proceed. This new blending arises in the following way. Paintings form a category. For each of those pictures, there is a specific Picture World blending web. Those Picture World blending webs *also* form a category, with analogy connections *across* all the webs. Mentally, we are free to take any number of Picture World blended spaces and blend them together. When we have finished, elements from the different Picture World blends will now inhabit the same Picture World. Each of them was an element in an individual Picture World, for an individual painting, but now they can be elements in yet a further blend, in which elements from different Picture World blends are blended together into a kind of overall Picture World. The new Picture World is a kind of global village of pictures. Of course, projections from an individual Picture World to the blend of several Picture Worlds will be selective.

For example, I have often seen a particular advertisement in airports that represents such a blend of several blending webs. The advertisement shows images taken from many famous paintings, of people playing musical instruments. In the advertisement, they are all newly arranged as a little orchestra whose members look quite different from one another, because they keep the artistic style of their original paintings even as they are projected into this many-input blend. The slogan of the advertisement asks whether you, the traveling business manager, have all of your resources playing together in harmony. I forgo analyzing the staggering creativity of the blend in which the resources of the traveling business manager are all people playing musical instruments, and in which differences between the business resources are differences of artistic style of representation. Then, of course, there is the blend in which I, the viewer of the advertisement, am the traveling business manager.

One inference we can make from this advertisement is that resources that are perfectly good in themselves can be quite uncoordinated when assembled, so it is not sufficient in business merely to gather good people and resources; you must also put them together just right. Therefore, you need to hire a consultant. Indeed, you need to hire a consultant from the company that placed the ad. In the world of art that is assumed by this blend, there is stylistic consistency within each painting, and the artistic style used for representing the musician in each painting is consistent with the artistic style of representation used generally throughout that whole painting, but assembling the different musicians can create stylistic inconsistency, a clash, through no fault of the individual elements. In the blend, where each resource is blended with a painted figure, the resources, which are internally consistent, each within itself, fit badly with each other. Similarly, in the world of music, the musicians who play in tune in the scenes from which they are drawn can be jointly and relatively out of tune when assembled. And the visual style of each painting might in itself be fine, but mixing them together might create a visual horror. Again, we can infer from the blend that the resources work fine by themselves but nonetheless fail to work well together. So you need a consultant to ensure harmony.

Here is how Olga's world involves just such a blend of many Picture World blends: Charlotte, having swum to the edge of the canal, and struggling to scale the 2 feet of smooth, wet stone between the water line and the street level, is assisted by Antonio, Rannuccio, Celeste, and Catherine, all children about her age. Why can they see her? Because they have been sent by Olga from *other paintings,* that is, from portraits of themselves, into Canaletto's Venice, expressly to help the adventure. More accurately, they have been projected from their own Picture World blends into the Venice Picture World, so that it becomes further blended, including elements from other individual Picture Worlds. The Canaletto Picture World blend supplies the principal setting, but it is blended with elements from other Picture Worlds.

Antonio, Rannuccio, Celeste, and Catherine are visitors, like Charlotte, and as such cannot be perceived by the Venetian residents of the Canaletto Picture World. But they can perceive other visitors, and so can see both each other and Charlotte. They retain features of their own Picture Worlds: They are ignorant of historical events after the period of their paintings; they wear the costumes of their portraits, although they can change clothes; and they have the manners of their epochs. Rannuccio is from Florence and Antonio from Milan, and they accordingly participate in the city-state rivalries of their period. When Charlotte, realizing that they are not native denizens of Canaletto's Picture World, asks, "You are…paintings?" Rannuccio responds, with a certain amount of disdain, "Of course. We are not Venetians." The story explains, "Neither of them thought much of any city besides their own, although for the sake of politeness, Rannuccio said nothing of Milan and Antonio said only that he preferred Florence, of course, to Venice." These five children, united in the goal of restoring Olga's coat to her, become fast friends. This multiply blended Picture World develops all-important new stuff: Charlotte now has friends, for the first time in her life, and understands what it means to have friends. This is one of the two great realizations she achieves during her adventure in this Picture World, realizations that guide her for the rest of her life.

But however real these friends are to Charlotte, they still come from Picture Worlds, and so can enter only those realms of a Picture World that belong to a Picture World. This is why they have never found Olga's coat, we learn. As the children scour the city, Charlotte, with her ability to see, stops outside an arched doorway without knowing consciously why. At the back of the archway, in the shadows, it turns out, is a glass door. As she walks closer, she sees a tiny electric doorbell, and then above the door an address: 5478-B. Puzzle-solver that she is, she understands immediately that Canaletto's Venice certainly never contained an address like that, much less a tiny electric doorbell. She of course seeks to enter:

> I turned the knob and pushed open the door. Celeste, Antonio, Caroline, and Rannuccio came behind me, but when they reached the doorway, they found they could go no further.
> "This is not the painting," said Antonio.

At the heart of the story, once Charlotte, in a dusty room full of hunting trophies, has assured herself that a bundle on a table is in fact Olga's coat, and has started with it for the door, we are confronted with the most challenging blend in this story. A previously unnoticed harlequin, obscured by the dust as he sits mostly hidden in a chair in the corner, asks her, "What would you want with that old thing?"

Physically, it is clear that the harlequin presents no threat to Charlotte. At one moment, he is propping his elbows on his knees, at another, flopping wispily back in his chair. He is disarming yet spooky. He and Charlotte hold a conversation, an odd one, in which Charlotte actually speaks aloud only the first of her many lines. After that, he responds directly, it seems, to whatever she thinks. He knows, too, all the facts about Olga, Ocracoke, and Charlotte's life. Why not stay? he asks Charlotte. After all, Olga hasn't changed anything: Charlotte still has no friends back home and she is doomed back there to accompany her mother to endless boring tea parties. But, ah, if she stays, she will have friends, and no one will miss her at all. So goes the harlequin's logic: Olga doesn't really care about Charlotte; she only wants the coat. Olga cannot fit through the frame. She can't actually force Charlotte to leave then, can she? Stay, he says—you'll never grow old.

That last line is his mistake. It might have been a good argument for an adult, but Charlotte realizes when he says it that she wants to grow up, she wants to tell her mother she won't go to her stupid tea parties anymore, she wants to go to college—an amazing thought for a girl in her era—and she wants to find real puzzles to solve. She bolts out the door hollering, "No, thanks."

Is the harlequin real? If so, he is a fabulous blend of many things: an actual Venetian Mardi Gras harlequin wearing a mask, a mind reader, a being whom the hunter has captured and transformed into a trophy, maybe a puppet or some similar toy or automaton, perhaps even the hunter himself. The harlequin has many of the hunter's goals, strategies, preferences, and tricks, but none of his predatory behavior. He has the spooky aura of a harlequin but the rootedness of one of the hunter's stuffed animal trophies.

But there is another way to think of the harlequin. He could be a figment of Charlotte's mind or a symbol that "speaks" her mind. Remember, he seems to know what she is thinking. How can that be? A blending web compresses elements and relations to a blend, but we can also decompress, unpack, expand an element so that it corresponds to multiple related elements in the web. We can think of ourselves as unitary, or alternatively disintegrate ourselves into two different input mental spaces: self now versus self 10 years ago; practical self versus passionate self; self in New York versus self in San Francisco. And just as we saw in the case of the woman talking to her younger self in the mirror, we can reblend those separate elements with the mental input space of a conversation. That could be what is happening with Charlotte: Parts of her mind are separated in the blending web, and she ends up having a debate with herself. Just as part of the woman talking to her younger self in the mirror is blended with the image in the mirror, so part of Charlotte could be blended with the harlequin. Such blending and disintegrating and reblending is common. For example, imagine a train conversation in which some imaginary traveler is a truth-teller, able to see and express to us one of our most closely held desires, maybe even one we somehow knew but were not willing to admit to ourselves. The harlequin in Canaletto's Venice can be interpreted as, in part, just such a figure: He can express Charlotte's doubts. Is this because he is a literal mind reader, or is it because he is a product of Charlotte's mind? The story does not specify.

Coat under arm, Charlotte parades with her friends back to the Grand Canal, where they all hop on a gondola headed toward the picture frame, which is of course still suspended over the canal, invisible to the Venetians. Her friends, with goodbyes all around, push her up and through it.

The story of the Ocracoke selkie is an aggressive and explicit blend of two general blending templates. The first is the general Picture World template, which has a representation, what it represents, and a glimpsed view through a portal of what it represents; and the second is the Selkie World template, which blends an animal, in this case a seal, and a human being. These two blending webs are blended with each other. Not only is the hyper-blend creative and entertaining, but it also speaks directly to the heart of the psychological matter.

In "Aunt Charlotte and the NGA Portraits," Charlotte, in advanced age, tells the story of Olga and the coat to her great-niece Marguerite, a child. The events—meeting Olga, going into the painting, retrieving the coat—took place during a visit in Charlotte's childhood with her mother and father to Ocracoke one November.

But the narrator of the overall story, that is, the person who speaks to the reader, is Marguerite, when she has grown to adulthood. In Marguerite's telling of the story, Aunt Charlotte took her, when she visited as a child, by taxi to the National Gallery of Art, the NGA, on the National Mall, in Washington, DC. During the taxi ride, Aunt Charlotte recounted the story of her childhood visit to Ocracoke, where she met Olga, entered the painting, and retrieved the coat.

So we have Marguerite in adulthood narrating the story of Aunt Charlotte's narration of the story of Ocracoke. Aunt Charlotte, now no longer the child of jigsaw puzzles but instead Marguerite's revered and slightly distant ancestor, begins by saying to the child Marguerite: "I was just about your age the year that we went to Ocracoke for Thanksgiving. My only brother was away at college, so it was just my father, my mother, and myself." And, a little later, speaking of her home life, she reveals, "I had a governess to teach me, so I didn't go to school and I didn't have any friends. I had never had friends, and I didn't know that I was missing them. In fact, I'd have to say I was something of a lump." Marguerite the child is being invited to make a blend that literary critics call "identification" but that I would call a compression of the analogy between Marguerite the child in one input mental space and Charlotte the child in another input mental space.

In the blend, by identifying with the child Charlotte as Charlotte makes friends with Antonio, Rannuccio, Celeste, and Catherine, Marguerite can understand imaginatively what it is like to have friends. She can have a sense of who she is, and develop ambitions about growing up, and in fact grow up a little, or at least be set on a path in that direction. When Marguerite and Aunt Charlotte reach the National Gallery of Art, they enter, where they see the portraits of Antonio, Rannuccio, Celeste, and Catherine, which do in fact exist, not only in the nested worlds of the story, but in reality. I have now seen some of them, in the National Gallery of Art.

The implied reader of the story is, of course, just about the age of the child Charlotte and the child Marguerite. A potential basis of the psychological power of the story for the implied reader lies in the three-way blend of Charlotte as a child, Marguerite as a child, and the actual child reader. The child reader, projecting herself into a fabulous and impossible blend, can imaginatively take on the experiences, dispositions, and perspectives of both Marguerite and Charlotte, and make great realizations while inside this fantasy, and, further, project those realizations back to her own "real life." Blends need not be false to be true or powerful. But neither complete truth-value with respect to our world nor even mere possibility as judged by the principles of our world is crucial for the power of the blend as a human tool of reason, judgment, and decision. Through advanced blending, fiction can deliver truth, with influence on our lives. It gives us new ideas, and those new ideas can change who we become.

How to Ski

So far, we have seen a number of blending webs that compress *representation* relations, as in *Harold and the Purple Crayon, John's Picture,* and "Aunt

Charlotte and the NGA Portraits." But there can be different levels of representation in a work of art or fiction or just everyday communication, and blending can also work across those levels. In one way, we just saw this: child Charlotte on Ocracoke is at one level, child Marguerite in the back seat of the taxi is at another level, and the child reader of "Aunt Charlotte and the NGA Portraits" is at another level, and none of these children is actually at the same level of nesting as any of the others in the telling of the story. The child reader of the story is not in the world of child Marguerite, who is not in the world of child Charlotte. But all three of them can be blended by the child reader, to give the child reader some guidance, or at least stimulation, in life.

Complicated blending across levels of representation is everyday stuff for people. I analyzed in *The Literary Mind* some of the extremely sophisticated cross-level blending that takes place in the *1001 Nights*.[2] But young children watching cartoons blend across levels of representation no less readily than adults transfixed by thoroughly adult literature like the *1001 Nights*. (If you think *1001 Nights* is a book for children, check out the original!) Disney short cartoons routinely rely on the humor and creative pleasure that comes of these compressions across levels of representation. In "The Art of Skiing," a 1941 short running 7:57 minutes, a pompous, earnest, stentorian narrator in voice-over explains the elements of alpine skiing. The explanation is general, without reference to Goofy, the character we see. This cartoon sets up several levels of meaning and representation: the fictional activities of Goofy in the alpine environment, the animated audiovisual representation of those activities, the general conceptual frame of alpine skiing, and the narrator's verbal description of that frame, connected implicitly to the fictional activities of Goofy. Our general understanding of voice-over description by an omniscient narrator includes the knowledge that it has *no place* inside the fictional activities themselves; it is on a different level of representation; it cannot be heard inside the world of the fictional activities. (To be sure, there are many other kinds of arrangements: The voice-over can be framed as expressing the silent character's simultaneous thoughts, or the character's retrospective thoughts about this moment in time, and so on.)

But in "The Art of Skiing," the mental space of the narrator and the mental space of Goofy's activities are partially blended. We infer that the narrator can perceive the cartoon representation from his evident increasing frustration at Goofy's radical failure to do what the narrator says the alpine skier always does. At one point, the narrator is discussing how the alpine skier leaps from his bed at sunup in joyous anticipation of the thrills that lie in store for him. But Goofy is dragging. Goofy puts on his skis, but then goes back to bed. The narrator says, "And now...and now..." but Goofy is snoring. So the narrator yells, "NOW!" and Goofy hears. It also seems that Goofy can understand at least part of what the narrator says. When the narrator, having described the sequence of dressing, says, "Now, we are completely dressed...," Goofy seems to have been misled into thinking that he is completely dressed, and heads out, so the narrator must add, in a slightly corrective voice, "with the exception of the trousers," and Goofy, embarrassed at wearing no pants, slinks back to try to put his trousers on over his skis. Routinely in this cartoon, separate mental spaces connected by a *representation* relation are compressed to a blend in which the separation is not entirely maintained.

The Book, the Bear, and the Blustery Day

The Disney enterprise has legendarily produced one tour de force after another of blending across levels. "Winnie the Pooh and the Blustery Day," a Walt Disney classic that won an Academy Award in 1968 for Best Cartoon Short Subject, requires the child to blend multiple levels repeatedly. Inside any of these levels, there is already elaborate blending. We can mention a few of them before continuing with the analysis of blending across representational levels.

Owl tells Pooh and Piglet that his aunt visited her cousin, who, being a screech owl, sang soprano in the London opera. The cousin's constant practicing so unnerved Owl's aunt "that she laid a seagull egg by mistake." This blend works inside the level of the fictional world of Winnie the Pooh, without involving the kinds of compressions of *representation* relations that we have been considering and to which we will soon return. To create the reality of that fiction, owls are blended with human beings to produce talking owls. The voices of talking animals typically arise by projection not only from people but also from the noises made by the kind of animal in question (remember Goofy and Scooby-Doo), so it is fitting that a talking "screech" owl in the blend would be prone to bad operatic performances. Now for the mistaken egg part. We have a notion that a mother bird gives birth to eggs belonging to her species. We have a notion that distressing conditions, including sounds, can conduce to mistakes, whether in thought or action. We also have the notion that environmental causes afflicting the mother can lead to misbegotten offspring. If we blend these notions with Owl's talking aunt, we can make a blend in which distress and shock lead a mother to a misbirth. The mother's "mistake" is produced by blending intentionality with procreation. Instead of a mistake in intentional thought and action, she commits a mistake of procreation: She lays a seagull egg. This is wildly new stuff, a new idea, not found in any of the input mental spaces, and certainly not found in reality.

One more: The wind blows Piglet so hard that eventually he becomes airborne. Winnie grabs Piglet's scarf to rescue him. It unravels to become a string, with Piglet at the end of it, like a kite. Given the aerodynamics of Piglet's form and the blusteriness of the wind, this would be impossible under everyday physics, but Disney cartoons specialize in such "plausible impossibilities," in which a real-world constraint is not projected to the blend, so the blend achieves the plausible physical impossibility. We have all seen Daffy Duck's head, when slapped, spin on its axis several times before rotating back, presumably driven in reverse by the potential energy stored up in highly elastic neck muscles. Roo says to Kanga, "Look, Mom, look! A kite!" The Piglet-kite is a blend we can easily recognize to be a blend. But at just the moment of Roo's call to his mother, there is an equally complicated but unnoticed bit of blending: The viewpoint shifts so that now we are "looking through Roo's eyes" and focusing on the Piglet-kite. Visual and literary representations always carry an implicit point of view and focus for the audience. As we watch, hear, or read, we respond to usually unnoticed prompts to move our viewpoint and our focus. In the case of "looking through Roo's eyes," we understand the visual representation by blending our viewpoint and focus with Roo's, for just a few seconds, before we move to a different viewpoint blend.

The famous dream sequence in "Winnie the Pooh and the Blustery Day" involving the song "Heffalumps and Woozles," complete with such classic blending web props as mirrors and spirits, offers an amazing sequence of "in-the-fictional-reality" blends that could support a series of book studies in themselves.

Here are some of the levels in "Winnie the Pooh and the Blustery Day," many of them already blends:

- The perhaps fictional activities of a boy with his toys, including stuffed animals. In the opening credits of "The Many Adventures of Winnie the Pooh" (which includes "Winnie the Pooh and the Blustery Day" as a "chapter"), we see in the background a nonanimated boy's bedroom, which contains stuffed toys that correspond obviously to the animal characters we will see in the animated cartoon that follows. For something to count as a "stuffed animal," it must already be a material anchor for a blend in which inanimate stuff is blended with an organism or a generic concept of an organism. Achieving this blend does not mean that we are deluded: Stuffed animals don't really talk, but children channel their voices. The blend is psychologically powerful and useful.

- The fictional activities of Christopher Robin, Winnie the Pooh, Eeyore, Piglet, Owl, Kanga and Roo, Rabbit, and others. The blending needed to produce this fictional world is elaborate. To achieve it, the already-blended stuffed animals are blended with concepts of both animal and human behavior. The landscape and environment also show sophisticated blending.
- The mental and psychological states of all these characters.
- A. A. Milne's stories representing these fictional activities.
- The writing that expresses those stories and also presents a frame story about the "real" boy who is the "basis" of the stories. It is presumably this boy's bedroom we are seeing in the opening credits to "The Many Adventures of Winnie the Pooh."
- A person who reads these stories aloud.
- A child to whom these stories are read.
- The printed and bound book that includes the writing. Interestingly, the boy's bedroom represented in the opening credits includes a copy of this book.
- The static illustrations in the bound book of the fictional activities of the characters.
- Our imaginary perception of these activities in the mind's eye, prompted by the verbal and printed representations.
- The perception of such a book as we turn its pages.
- The film, representing many of these levels, from the boy's bedroom to the fictional activities of the characters.
- The voice-over narrator, whose voice is represented in the film.
- Music, which, through blending, we can interpret as "programmatic" and as carrying "mood" and "tone."
- And very many others. For example, in the DVD version, there is a "menu" that allows one to select scenes. Merely dealing with this menu involves elaborate blending and compacting of different levels of representation.

Here are some instances of the blending across various levels of representation:

- The static illustrations in the book are connected by *representation* relations to the dynamic fictional events they represent. In "Blustery Day," we see a copy of the book, and as the pages are turned, we see illustrations. Periodically, one of the illustrations becomes animated. This blend compacts dynamic features of the represented scene with the static illustration, to give an animated illustration in a printed book. This very cleverly provides the transition in "Blustery Day" from the book to the animated cartoon. We zoom in on the now-animated illustration until we lose the frame of the printed book and are immersed in the animated representation of the fictional reality.
- The talk in the fictional reality is blended with the now-animated, previously static illustrations so that the characters in the illustrations not only move but also speak.
- The voice of the person reading the words on the pages (we can see the pages turning in the cartoon) is blended with the voice-over of the narrator of the cartoon. At various points, we can see that although the voice-over is speaking some of the words on the printed page, he is in fact abbreviating considerably.
- The level containing the voice of the reader/narrator is on occasion blended with the level of the fictional reality and the book: When the voice starts talking about "the next chapter," Pooh says, "But I haven't finished yet!" and the narrator replies, "But Pooh, you are in the next chapter." Further, this is also blended with the level of the book: The page containing the now-animated illustration is occluded because the page has been turned to the next chapter; Pooh's voice comes from that animated illustration in the book, and so the page is partially turned back so we can see Pooh speaking. This compresses the fictional reality, the inside of the book, and the world outside, since Pooh is in fact leaning to see past the half-turned page that would occlude his view of the person reading the book.
- The fictional reality is blended with the mental space in which the book is being read: When the wind blows in the blustery day, and we are seeing the book within the cartoon, the wind turns the page of the book! This blending is helped by the prior blend of the fictional reality with the static illustration, so that the now-animated illustration has projected to

it movement and sound from the fictional reality, and if there is "wind" and the sound of wind already "in" the page we are looking at as the pages are being turned, our notion that wind can move in a continuous physical environment makes intelligible the movement of the wind off the page and into the space in which the book is being read, to turn the page. This blending is subtle here, but is used to noticeable effect in the prior Winnie the Pooh cartoon: When Winnie is catapulted "in" the now-animated illustrations, Gopher says, "Sufferin' succotash, he's sailing clean out of the book! Quick! Turn the page!" The turning of the page makes it possible for Pooh to land in a suitable place "back" in the book, which is simultaneously the fictional reality.

- The elements of the fictional reality, blended with the now-animated illustrations, can also be blended with the elements of the rest of the printed book. When the wind blows, it blows the leaves gradually off the tree, and then the letters printed on the page are blown just as the leaves are blown. In the animated illustration in the book, the huge rain cloud releases the rain into the lake, which is above the text. This influx drives the water right down the page, which swamps and displaces the letters to the bottom of the page, but not, this time, out of the book.

When Tigger leaves Pooh's house, he is singing his signature song:

> The wonderful thing about Tiggers
> Is Tiggers are wonderful things
> Their tops are made out of rubber
> Their bottoms are made out of springs
> They're bouncy, trouncy, flouncy, pouncy
> Fun, fun, fun, fun, fun
> But the most wonderful thing about Tiggers is
> I'm the only one
> I'm the only one.

At "trouncy," Tigger bounces from the animated reality into the now-animated illustration in the book, suggesting that the animated reality and the book are alternative views on the same world. As Tigger goes over the horizon, the printed lyrics lie above the illustration into which he has bounced—except that the last line of the lyrics ("I'm the only one") is not yet on the page. As Tigger sings this last line, the words in "I'm the only one" appear one after another from beyond the horizon. The movement of the *printed words* is compressed with the travel of his *voice* back above the horizon and toward Pooh's viewpoint. The printed words travel up to take their appropriate place in the book! So the activity of the fictional reality is blended with the text itself, and causality in the fictional reality is blended with causality for the book and its print.

The Wild Squatter

When we perceive a leaf twisting in the wind, we see it as one integrated leaf, one movement, one "wind." When we look away and back, we think we see the "same" leaf before and after. This is a miraculous compression of perceptual diversity into unity. In all such cases, whether we are at rest or in action, we face a chaos of perceptual data. Bombarded by this diversity, we perform the highly impressive mental trick of compressing great ranges of it into manageable units. We parse an ocean of diversity quickly and reliably into a few elements coherently arrayed.

Typically, we are unaware that we face this perceptual diversity. When we look at the serene marble statue, it appears to us to be a single unit, without fragmentation, instability, or diversity, despite the fact that the perceptual data we are compressing to achieve this comforting and useful recognition of an abiding, unvarying statue are themselves shifty and uncoordinated.

At moments when we actually do manage to recognize that we confront shiftiness, we nonetheless feel—provided we are not in that instant afflicted with a cerebral hemorrhage, a drug-induced breakdown, or a chronic neural pathology—that the unities of the world shine through, fundaments of perception, essentially impervious to accidents. We ascribe the tiny fraction of shiftiness that we do detect consciously to changes of viewpoint on our part or to motion or transformation on the part of the unity we perceive—events that, in our conception, leave the perceptual coherence of the world intact. The cloud moves in the wind, perhaps our view of it is blocked entirely while we walk past the tree, and probably we are looking at the road for the most part anyway, but no matter, the cloud's unity is clear to us. This mental creation of stability is profound and evident in everything we human beings do, despite our obliviousness to it. It is only under sedulous discipline during an ingenious experiment, for example, that we can begin to detect hints of the literal blind spots in our vision, caused by gaps where axons dive through the retina.

The challenge of mastering spectacular perceptual diversity and churning out of it a regular, constant, stable reality is faced by very many species. Human beings compound the difficulty of this challenge in art. First, there are compressions of viewpoint. In Pablo Picasso's 1907 *Les Demoiselles d'Avignon*, one of the five women represented in the painting—Leo Steinberg calls her "the wild Squatter"[1]—has a face presented in full frontal view, with two eyes, but a nose in profile, a back view of a torso, and various other anatomical components seen from disparate viewpoints. We see just the same blending of viewpoints in Picasso's 1937 *Marie-Thérèse Walter*.

Compression of viewpoint over time rather than space is exemplified in Marcel Duchamp's 1912 *Nu descendant un escalier*. In this case, the compressed blend has elements that come from different temporal moments of watching the nude as it descends the staircase. In the blend, but in none of the inputs, we have an extremely familiar conceptual unit, the *descent*, which remains connected to the different temporal moments. This unity-out-of-diversity can be expressed visually in Duchamp's fashion or linguistically by means of a definite noun phrase: "the descent." Duchamp's blend has emergent properties not possessed by any of the inputs. For example, in the blend, but in none of the inputs, we have a static form for the line of descent of the head.

Such compressions have occurred throughout human art since the Upper Paleolithic. A painting from the Hall of the Bulls in the Lascaux Cave shows the bull's head in exact profile, with one eye and one nostril, but also shows the horns from something like a three-quarters view. Similarly, we see the bull from the side but the bull's cloven hooves from nearer the front. This painting points not to an abstraction but to a compression over many quite diverse views.

In the cases of *Les Demoiselles d'Avignon*, *Marie-Thérèse Walter*, and *Nu descendant un escalier*, we recognize immediately that something is cockeyed, jumbled, or lumped. But in the case of the Lascaux bull, most people do not seem to be consciously aware that there is any compression of viewpoint at all until it is pointed out. This lack of recognition cannot be ascribed to ignorance of actual horns and hooves. If anyone ever saw a similar animal with horns and hooves disposed the way they are in the Lascaux bull, they would be astonished.

The routine utility of blending in art over times, spaces, viewpoints, and agents can be seen in many traditions, such as the tradition of paintings of the Annunciation. In an Annunciation painting, we typically "see" the Virgin holding, anachronistically, a lectionary, often opened to the narrative of the Annunciation. In Rogier van der Weyden's Annunciation, the medallion on the bed represents the Resurrection. The painting in this way gives us a compression of eternity, or, at least, a compression of the time span from not yet being born to being raised from the dead, all in one momentary scene. We have no trouble interpreting this representation as evoking a blend of a young girl and the Mother of God, which is already a blend. The Virgin's bedroom may additionally have features of a church—the lectionary stand and veil that are part of the furniture of an altar, trinitarian tracery windows as in Broederlam's version, a full Gothic church interior as in one of Jan van Eyck's versions. Annunciations may have a representation of God in the upper left, although we do not interpret this to mean that God was just up and to the left of the bedroom. In the Mérode Altarpiece, a homunculus already tolerating his own miniature cross is flying on a sunbeam from God toward the womb of Mary. All representations of the Annunciation evoke a blend of girl with Mother of God, and some of them evoke other blends, such as the blend of bedroom with church.

These Annunciations take concepts incredibly diffuse, foreign, and difficult to understand—eternity, divinity, theology, the Church, and the relationship of the immortal to the mortal—and compact them to an extremely familiar scene: a room, a woman reading in the room, and someone addressing her, in this case, the angel of the Annunciation, who informs Mary, the girl, that she is the mother of God. Such art is superb at compressing over time, space, causation, and agency, and delivering the compressed, tractable product for understanding at human scale. How else could we understand life, the universe, and everything? What otherwise would lie beyond human understanding is compressed via blending to human scale. In these cases, plucking the forbidden fruit through art is meant to give us an understanding of the greatest possible ranges of time, space, causation, and agency, and of ourselves. The blend compacts into one room, with two agents, the whole of the cosmos, the whole of the human relationship to divinity, and all of time.

7

Vast Ideas

Biologically, we resemble other animals, but mentally, we leave them in the dust. The sweep of human thought is vast, arching over time, space, causation, and agency. Why are we so different?

Animals—including us—live, think, and feel in the here and now. Living, thinking, and feeling are biological events, existing only in the present. When we think about the past or the future, or anything distant or outside our present situation, the thinking and feeling are not distant—they are right here, right now, present, confined to our local, human-scale situation, conducted through here-and-now biological systems.

In this regard, we are like dogs, dolphins, corvids, chimpanzees. A human being may have been alive 10 years ago and may be alive 10 years hence, but our brain activity of 10 years ago or 10 years hence does not exist. The only systems for living, thinking, and feeling that human beings possess are run by their bodies here and now.

This picture, as we saw, was sketched by Sir Charles Sherrington, who described the brain as an "enchanted loom" in which "millions of flashing shuttles weave a dissolving pattern, always a meaningful pattern, though never an abiding one."[1]

Dissolving, never abiding. Yet our thought ranges over time and space, over long-range causal chains and possibilities, over present and potential absences, and over mental stories that include, in our imaginations, thousands, maybe billions, of human agents whose minds we also imagine to be like ours—full of beliefs, desires, plans, decisions, and judgments, all with the same easy power for vast scope that we ourselves command. The contents of our thoughts do not seem to us to be dissolvingly evanescent. It is true that other species seem to have single-point memories of previous events—and in that way they have some grip on previous experiences—but people are utterly different in this regard. We can conceive of great entire expanses connecting up any single points of memory, and we can conceive of the future, too. We often ask young people headed into a career, "Where do you want to be 5 years from now?" Try asking that of your favorite animal. It's not just that they won't understand your language; they seem to have no conception of the future in this sense.

Scientists have pondered the scope of human thought and tried to explain its origins. Antonio Damasio, in *The Feeling of What Happens,* speculates on how neurobiological development could have made "extended consciousness" possible:

> Extended consciousness still hinges on the same core "you," but that "you" is now connected to the lived past and anticipated future that are part of your autobiographical record.[2]

Endel Tulving[3] was absorbed with our ability for mental time travel, our capacity for episodic memory and autonoetic ("self-knowing") consciousness. In autonoetic consciousness, we can recover the episode in which something occurred. "Autonoetic consciousness…allows an individual to become aware of his or her own identity and existence in subjective time that extends from the past through the present to the future."[4]

Ulric Neisser notes just such remarkable capacities in his classic article, "Five Kinds of Self-Knowledge."[5] Hundreds of other scientists have participated in the inquiry. Here is one of the most recent:

> A self can feel like such a singular fixture, hugging one's here-and-now like a twenty-four-hour undergarment, but actually it's a string, looping back and forward in time to knit together our past and future moments.…A self is a Tardis, a time-machine: it can swallow you up and spit you out somewhere else.
>
> Charles Fernyhough,
> *The Baby in the Mirror: A Child's World from Birth to Three.*[6]

Naturally, there are some objections that immediately confront the idea that there is anything extraordinary about the human capacity for vast thought. After all, it does not feel extraordinary to us that we can think this way. It seems utterly humdrum. Let's go through a few of the main automatic objections:

> Objection 1: What's the big deal? How can it be so astonishing and difficult if everyone, even children, can do it?

Cognitive science has shown repeatedly that seemingly simple human behaviors are far more complicated than we might have imagined and that our folk theories purporting to account for them are in many ways wrong from the start. The cartoons we have in consciousness that we use for dealing with the world are very useful and impressive, but they do not count as an elementary version of science. Cognitive science has turned out not to be a mere improvement on our cartoons. Mostly, it has tossed them out entirely. We of course feel that common sense is basically right, and that cognitive science will give it nuance and depth. But it turns out that what seems simple to us is anything but. What seems given to us is anything but. How we feel about our mental performance does not provide a good guide to what we are in fact doing mentally. In short, our feelings and intuitions are completely unreliable as science. What we think we are doing mentally we mostly are not doing. The vast scope of human thought is a recognized major problem in the science of the mind. It lies far beyond the abilities of other species and we have no consensus on what makes it possible.

> Objection 2: Doesn't evolution build us so that our actions here-and-now have long-range consequences? Doesn't instinct provide the connection between here-and-now and the rest of our lives?

It does. Instinct can cause a squirrel to bury nuts without any need for the squirrel to cogitate upon hunger; instinct can lead a person to lust after a member of the opposite sex without any need for that person to cogitate upon cute great-grandchildren. But whether evolution can build us to work this way is not the issue. Of course it can. The question is, how can people *think* about mental webs of such vast connections, including past and future states of their own minds and the minds of other people?

> Objection 3: What about memory? Doesn't memory solve the problem of continuity over time, at least? Doesn't memory bring the past into the present?

No. Memory is of course only in the present, and a particular memory is only in the present, even though it seems as if the detailed memory comes winging in from long ago, carried to our present minds on winds from yesteryear. Both our memory as a system and any particular memory we experience are present biological events. The universe does not bend back upon itself when we remember, to make two different times intersect in one time. That is an illusion. This sense of the intersection of past and present—one of the basic mainstays of life and art, from Homer to Proust, from the witches in *Macbeth* to Dr. Who, and a key part of our mental apparatus for dealing with reality—is an adaptive delusion. Moreover, our memories are not static: We rebuild them every time, often differently from the way we rebuilt them last time. To say so seems like a radical insult to our mental ability, but there is no scientific doubt that it is so, and everyone, on reflection, already suspected that it was so. There are also benefits that come from this reinvention of memory. Our memories themselves are often new ideas, or include new ideas.

> Objection 4: Are we really so special? Don't other animals show signs of thinking beyond the here-and-now?

This objection is very serious and important. The studies on this topic are fascinating. As listed in chapter 1, there are hints that dogs have some human-like social skills; that rats have some recollection-like memory retrieval; that scrub jays have some episodic-like memory; that chimpanzees have some understanding of conspecifics as possessed of goals, intentions, perceptions, and knowledge; that Santino, the Swedish zoo chimpanzee, stores rocks as part of a plan to throw them at human visitors later; and so on. There is considerable evidence for the weak form of this objection, and we learn more about animals all the time. But the strong form of this objection does not have a leg to stand on. Other species show severe limits in vast thinking that human beings blow past at full and accelerating speed without even noticing that there were any limits. Other animals seem to have some single-point memories, but that is minor compared with the human faculty for complicated, detailed stories, with many agents and events, and with sophisticated webs of causation, that we take to be "memories" of the "past." How did those two people meet and get married? The human being answers instantly with a complicated representation that stretches across a large span of time.

What makes the vast scope of human thought possible? Nonhuman animals often seem to possess impressive rudimentary abilities for blending, but human beings have the advanced form, advanced blending.[7] Advanced blending gives us the ability to conceive fully of other minds, and our own minds, and to grasp extended mental webs that would otherwise lie beyond our cognition.

What Are We Built For?

A person in the local, present moment has, like any mammal, a brain in a certain state of activation, with integrated systems for affect, perception, inference, and construal. Human brains are built to conceive of scenes that are at *human scale*. At human scale:

- We operate within limited ranges of space and time.
- We partition our sensory fields into objects and events.
- We interact with objects locally.
- We recognize some of those objects as agents.
- We interact with a few agents in patterned activity: eating, moving, fighting, mating.

That is pretty much what we are built for. In one sense, it is what we are.

For other animals, this scale, or a similar scale, seems to be pretty much the entire story of existence. No nonhuman animal, for example, seems to be able to understand that other animals hold systems of belief, or what those systems of belief might be. The pet ferret recognizes its owner's scent, but that recognition has none of the rich connection across time, space, causation, and agency that the human recognition of a face clearly always has. No nonhuman animal seems to be able to wonder what its life might be like if it had done something different 10 years ago. No nonhuman animal seems to be able to wonder what will become of its as yet nonexistent offspring.

People, by contrast, have:

- an idea of self as possessed of a *characteristic* personal identity running through *time* and *space*, including time and space that has not yet been experienced.
- ideas of other agents as similarly possessed of *characteristic* personal identities running through *time* and *space*, including time and space that has not yet been experienced.
- ideas of other agents as possessed over time with the standard system of elements in folk psychology, that is, emotions, goals, and beliefs that drive actions and reactions.
- an idea of oneself that includes relationships with the psychology of other people, and ideas of those other people as themselves possessed of ideas of self that contain relationships with the psychology of oneself.
- an idea of self and one's personal identity as richly inhabiting both the past and the future.

It is a scientific puzzle that human beings are the sole species that seems to be able to *think* and feel beyond the limits of the scale for their species.

Human scale is fundamental for human thinking and feeling, but we go beyond our scale in ways that no other species can, ways that place us in a different galaxy of thinking and feeling. We are like Dr. Who, the Time Lord of science fiction, who can use his Tardis to move across ranges of both time and space that go beyond human scale. People have a mental Tardis, an internal Tardis. Our mental Tardis is what we are trying to come to grips with.

Human Scale and Web Scale

The blending hypothesis takes the view that it is our ability for advanced blending that gives us the capacity to create vast mental webs with extended vital relations that are served by, organized by, and held together by blended scenes that are themselves at human scale. The scale of the mental web can be vast because it is served by a blend that is itself at human scale. The *human-scale* blend that serves the mental web provides us with a platform—a scaffold, a cognitively congenial basis from which to reach out, manage, manipulate, transform, develop, and handle the mental web.

It is of the utmost importance that once we have achieved a human-scale blend, it can be used as an input mental space to a new blending web. So blending can work like a cascade. Achieving a blend at human scale extends our human-scale knowledge. It's as if we manufacture a stepping-stone, place it ahead of us, and then step from where we are to that new stepping-stone. And we can repeat the procedure, stepping from blend to blend. So what counts as human scale can be repeatedly extended, on and on. This can give us a cascade or sequence of blends, each depending upon previous blends. We saw just such a step-by-step cascade of blends in the case of Death the French Warrior, with all those levels, where one blend is the input to the next. Blending is recursive, in the technical sense that an output of the process can be an input to the process. Compact, human-scale blends can be used as grist for other blending webs. What was once beyond human scale is now transformed to human scale. What counts as human scale is repeatedly extended over the course of a lifetime. What once was impossible is now possible. This is a major benefit of the human spark.

Packing the Universe and Time

Consider an example: Toward the end of the film version of his slideshow presentation on global warming, Al Gore shows us a picture of Earth, the pale blue dot photographed in 1990 by Voyager I from 4 billion miles out in space. He explains,

> Everything that has ever happened in all of human history has happened on that pixel. All the triumphs and all the tragedies. All the wars, all the famines, all the major advances. It's our only home. And that is what is at stake: our ability to live on planet Earth, to have a future as a civilization.

Concluding, Gore states,

> Future generations may well have occasion to ask themselves, "What were our parents thinking? Why didn't they wake up when they had a chance?" We have to hear that question from them, now.

In Gore's example, for both time and space, we have diffuse, extended, vast webs of mental spaces, all of them wildly, unimaginably far from human scale: a distance of *4 billion miles*, and *all of history* plus *all of the future*. Try getting that across to a dog, lemur, chimp, raven, beaver, bat, rat, anything. But people, through advanced blending, can get it easily, because we compress these otherwise unimaginable arrays to human scale.

First, let us take the spatial compression. Think of our embodied viewpoint on space: We have a bodily notion of vision, at human scale, which we take from our local visual experience. In this notion of vision, the farther we back away from an object, the smaller the angle it subtends in our field of vision. This is a human-scale, experienced idea. We experience it very often. We all have it, just from seeing the world and moving closer to an object or farther away from it. We also have the idea of the universe, with the Earth somewhere in it. The incompatibility of these mental spaces—human vision for what we see around us, and the scale of the universe—is obvious. For starters, human beings cannot walk backward 4 billion miles from Earth to have a look, the way Gore suggests that we do. Even if we could, it might be that vision from 4 billion miles away does not work quite the same way as vision in our front yard. Imaginatively, it might be that sight across the universe works differently from sight across the street. Many aspects of physical reality at great spans of distance and time in fact do not fit human intuitions, and there are science fiction books in which perception does indeed work differently across such distances. But we can use our human-scale notion of vision to make sense of it all: We can make a blend. In this blend, we compress local vision with the universe. In local vision, we can see a bird in a tree. In the blend, we can see the Earth from 4 billion miles away, just the way we might see a bird in a tree from 40 meters away.

The blend holds amazing new stuff, inconceivable to any other species. In the blend, the Earth is one small, fragile thing. In this blend, everything human is contained on a dot that is hard to see. In this compressed blend, we have an understandable scene in which the entire Earth subtends a small angle in our field of vision. Our world is just a pale blue dot, in the blend. Of course, for no human being is the Earth a pale blue dot in experience. But it can be in this blend. What a new idea! In the compact blend, the idea of viewing the Earth from 4 billion miles away has inherited the human-scale structure of human motion and human vision from our everyday experience, so what never happened seems normal, and at human scale.

One of the input mental spaces to this blend of "normal vision of the Earth from 4 billion miles away" is the everyday idea of looking at something that is near to us. We have some power over what is near to us, and maybe we feel some responsibility. In the everyday scene of vision, we have some local relationship to the person, the tree, the lake. What lies in our everyday field of vision is to an extent local to us. We can act upon it; it can act upon us. But what lies very far away is very different in that regard. It might seem too large for us to make a dent in, too vast to be subject to our actions. But when we blend it with everyday seeing in order to create a little Earth that we can see—to make a little undifferentiated pale blue dot—then we can think of the Earth as under our thumb, subject to our actions. It's right there: We can see all of it. Better do something! This conception of the Earth as local and subject to our actions can stimulate a feeling of human-scale power, responsibility, and duty.

To be sure, there is diversity on Earth, as Gore describes, but in the blend, all this diversity is unified as our common place, our home, the home of our children. The emphasis is on commonality rather than diversity. There is diversity at home, but home is a rock-solid human-scale idea. We are responsible for our home.

Outside the blend, the Earth can seem to be too big for us individually to change. How could any one of us individually have any effect on the Earth, as opposed to, say, our yard, or at most our street? But in the compact human-scale blend, the whole Earth is right in front of our nose. We are plenty powerful enough to affect it. It is small and vulnerable, just as our home is small and vulnerable. In the blend, NIMBY is NOPE: "Not In My Back Yard" is "Not On Planet Earth."

Gore intends to lead us to perform a mental compression of space, and of all the agents and causes on Earth, so that we will carry around a new tight idea of the Earth. His hope is that we will carry that new tight idea with us from situation to situation, and unpack it to hook up to new situations, so that we will think and act differently in those situations. He wants to change what we do by changing what we think, by giving us a new idea of the Earth. Our actions and decisions in this or that local spot, at the hardware store or the gas station, will be connected to this small idea of the Earth, making the local global and the global local.

Gore's "pale blue dot" also urges us to compress time to human scale. Just as the blend compresses spatial expanses of Earth to human scale, contained in our field of vision, so it compresses vast expanses of human action over *time* to one chunked unit, expressed in phrases like "history" and "Everything that has ever happened." The Earth over all human history can seem much too complex and diffuse to comprehend. But in the blend, it is unitary, simple, and visually homogeneous.

Compressions of time are in fact utterly routine, part of our everyday understanding of ourselves. They are all around us, everywhere, even in the room in which we are sitting. They are with us when we look out the window, or when we turn on the television, or go to work, or go to church, or pay our taxes. We live by these compressions, which we never notice. But in Gore's entertaining and artsy blend, there is one compression of time that we actually can notice: a strange blend in which unborn descendants actually talk to us—how bizarre!—and we hear them—even more bizarre! Talking with someone who asks us questions is utterly at human scale. We understand this scene immediately.

Even more, when we are talking in an everyday conversation about something we can all see, like a pale blue dot, we are in a scene of "classic joint attention." Joint attention refers to an activity at which human beings excel: Different people are attending to something in their environment, and they all know they are all attending and that they all know this, and that they are interacting with each other by joining together in attending to it. In classic joint attention, there are only two people, or maybe a few more, and they are communicating about what they are attending to. Gore blends all of future humanity and all of present humanity by blending them with two, or a few, people in a conversation. The blend itself stretches across generations, compressing billions of agents and centuries of causation, stretching across the entire planet, to a human-scale scene of a little conversation. The blend is fantastic: In the mental web that the blend serves, there are many reasons that we cannot actually hear all those future agents. The first rock-solid reason we cannot hear them is that they do not yet exist. Second, there are far too many of them—and not just a few too many, as when you are in a chatty meeting, but instead *billions and billions* too many. Third, they are not in one human-scale auditory field, but rather distributed around the entire Earth. Who knows, they might even be in a colony on the moon. Fourth, they are not in a human-scale interval of time but instead stretch across many generations, so their yack no longer takes place even during an individual human lifetime. If we listened to them all our lives, we would never hear everything they had to say on the subject, because the conversation goes on for generations. Fifth, they do not all speak in languages we understand. Sixth, they might not be speaking at all, but instead only writing, or even thinking. And so on and on.

But all that future—diffuse, complex, hypothetical, unknowable, so very far from human scale—can be blended with the basic scene of human questioning. Now, in the compact blend, all the individuals of future generations are packed into one human voice, the voice of our child. The emergent structure in the compact blend is amazing: Now, in the blend, each of us can hear the voice of our descendants, even if in fact some of us, in reality, have no children at all. And we hear their question now.

Packing the World

Consider an editorial cartoon, "World Food Crisis," which appeared in *The International Herald-Tribune*.[8] It shows a bland, fat, middle-aged American pumping fuel—"Bio-ethanol"—from a green and tan gas pump into the tank of his green car. The car's bumper sticker says, "Go Green." The gas pump has a sign presenting an image of a half-shucked ear of ripe corn. This fat American is looking over his shoulder at two emaciated people, one vaguely Asian—with minimally Asian eyes, a stereotypical woven bamboo peasant farmer horn hat, and a shift—the other wearing only low-hanging shorts, his body deformed by the stereotypical edema potbelly and thin hair of children suffering from protein-deficient diets. The vaguely Asian character is lifting a rice bowl with both hands in a classic gesture of supplication. The edemic character, lethargic, dangles his hands at his sides and watches wide-eyed. The American says, casually, one hand in his pocket, "Sorry, I'm busy saving the planet."

We think that expressions—speech, signs, gestures, cartoons, paintings—have meaning. They do not. They are sounds or visual marks or whatever that prompt *us* to construct meaning. That is a causal relationship, and we compress it, so that, in the blend, we have the new idea that the expressions "have" meaning. The expressions are causes; the meaning is an effect. We compress the cause-effect relation so that now the expressions "have" meaning. In fact, obviously, these prompts invite us to work on knowledge we have with processes we already possess. Inevitably, because different people have different knowledge, and even the same person activates different knowledge at different times, different people in different moments may activate somewhat different knowledge to build a meaning from the prompts.

My purpose in talking about this cartoon is not at all to provide an "interpretation" of it. All its readers are already very good at doing that. Instead, what we want to see is how the mind works to build a meaning when it is prompted to do so by such a cartoon. Interpretation itself varies, and our models must allow for that variation. Different people might construct different interpretations of this prompt.

So let us take one interpretation of the cartoon and look at some of the mental work needed to produce that meaning. The cartoon is easily taken as suggesting two stories. One of these stories involves the typical behavior of Americans who disregard the needs of the world's starving populations while assuaging their guilt, or, anyway, manufacturing a nice self-image by participating in activities that count popularly as helping the environment, even when those activities are in fact self-serving, useless, or deleterious. The other story involves the needs of impoverished and deprived people worldwide that go unheeded by the developed nations.

In the mental web containing these two stories, we have a vast range of individual American behaviors, the many different ways these behaviors affect the environment, the consequences of American governmental policy, the psychology of self-delusion, and the scientific and technical details of inventions such as ethanol, as well as their actual effect on the environment. We also have the foreign needy, deprived of not only food but also shelter, health care, education, and security. From all these ideas, we project selectively to the blend, and create a compact scene at human scale. In the blend, the world situation becomes an exchange between one American filling his car with ethanol and two deprived foreigners requesting food.

There are clear prompts in the cartoon for the blending and compression of these two distinct stories. The landscape over the shoulder of the American who is fueling his car is barren except for a line that looks like the curved horizon of planet Earth. The feet of the foreigners lie below that horizon, but their bodies rise above it, as if they are standing on the other side of the planet but visible right here at the gas station. In the story of the world's food crises, it is impossible for any of the destitute, emaciated, hungry foreigners to make a direct personal appeal to an unexpecting individual American at a gas station. In the story of the American consumers, it is impossible for any of them to speak directly from the gas pump to individual hungry foreigners in other countries, and the hungry foreigners stereotypically do not understand English in any event.

The blend in which America says "Sorry" at the gas pump draws on our idea of a simple conversation in which somebody asks for something but is denied. In this scene, the people can see each other and communicate with each other directly through speech, vision, and gesture. So, now we have three inputs to the blend: the story of self-deluded Americans who convince themselves they are helping the environment, the story of America's disregarding the needs of the world, and the small story of request and denial. It is this last story that does most of the heavy lifting in providing a compressed human scale for the blend. In the blend, there is a simple gesture of request, a simple denial and its rationalization, and only three people. It takes only a few seconds.

We are not deluded: We know this blend is completely fantastic. It is strictly impossible that an American in America fueling his car could see in his actual visual field (without distance technologies) two foreigners who are in fact not in America, who are continents away, who are appealing to him directly to provide them with food (many kinds of basic food around the world are compressed in the blend into rice, which alone, for example, would not solve the problem of protein deficiency). It is geographically impossible that two impoverished and hungry people who are on different continents can be standing next to each other in any event. It is strictly impossible that the American could utter (without distance technologies) a spoken expression in English that would be heard by them on separate continents, none of which is North America. The American moreover has no rice, certainly no cooked rice to put into the rice bowl.

There are many other items in the cartoon that are at least implausible. Yet no one encountering this cartoon expects it to represent a scene one could actually see on Earth. For example, the "Bio-Ethanol" pump carries the label, "Pure Corn." The cartoonist is exploiting a linguistic accident here: Corn can be thought of as a sustainable agricultural product, as opposed to petroleum resources, and corn happens to be used in the production of ethanol. And so the American, eager for any token of environmental sensitivity, can take the view that the fuel is somehow eco-friendly, despite the arguments that net consumption of petroleum is increased by the manufacture and use of ethanol instead of gasoline. The word "pure" can be taken as the kind of thing the willfully self-deluded American wannabe environmentalist likes to associate with his activities, the way American suburban adolescents who know nothing about combat wear military fatigues or martial arts paraphernalia as indications of their personal identity. But of course, the phrase "pure corn" in American vernacular English means "nonsense." No vendor of a commercial product is going to label his product in such a way as to indicate that the rationale of its provision is fraud, nonsense, pure corn (except ironically, for consumers who will pay for irony, and then the product is the irony itself). We recognize immediately that the use of "pure corn" involves a projection from a *fourth* mental input space, the one in which an editorializing voice is communicating directly with us, the reader of the cartoon, to tell us his opinion. The cartoonist is exploiting the accident of the existence of *corn* in one of the narratives to do some editorializing. The entire scene is, if taken as a representation of an actual event, crazy.

But no one reacts to this cartoon as if it is surreal or mentally taxing, a jumble of impossible conflicts, because no one takes it as a representation of an actual event. Its impossibility is no problem. In many ways, its impossibility is a virtue in trying to communicate truth about actual reality. The cartoon is embraced instantly, and with no feeling of mental effort, as a coherent snapshot, a vignette as recognizable as a lightning bolt, summing up the gist of the matter, connecting the newspaper reader, the American populace, the world's needy, and the cartoonist's opinion.

This blend compresses domino-trains of causality. Those causal chains, across very many agents, are compressed so that in the small blended narrative, the causality is direct, between few agents, and the cartoonist's implicit editorializing on that human-scale scene can be expanded to indicate his editorializing on the world food crisis.

Packing a Species

Feeding is a human-scale scene. Although there is debate about the origins of the domesticated dog, *Canis lupus familiaris,* there is consensus that people and dogs have been domesticating each other and themselves for at least 10,000 or 15,000 years, possibly longer. It is a human-scale idea to feed a pet, or a work animal, or other companion animals like birds in the yard, rabbits, even squirrels. Mostly, we think this kind of *feeding* is good: We are doing the animals good, much as we do good when we feed children and guests.

This human-scale idea of feeding animals created big headaches for the population of Lake Tahoe, because it led people to feed the bears. Much of this feeding was deliberate, and friendly, but the bears also ate food that was not deliberately left for them—picnic food, garbage, birdseed... There are many problems that result from conditioning bears deliberately or inadvertently to prowl human environments for food, but the most dramatic among them is that the bears become bolder, perhaps even bring in other bears, such as bear cubs, and then the frightened tourists call the California Department of Fish and Game to come kill them. In particular, it was reported that a summer tourist complained that his property had been damaged by bears, with the result that a federal trapper trapped and killed a mother bear and her cub. Another cub climbed a tree to avoid capture (or at least, that's how a person projects mind to a bear cub).

The human-scale idea of feeding the animal runs up against big complexities, elaborate causes and effects, and the result is dead bears in Tahoe. The Bear League of Lake Tahoe created an information campaign intended to produce a new blend, a new idea about what happens when you feed the bears. This new blend was intended to give an opposing human-scale idea, one that could be carried around as part of our mental traveling kit when we go to Tahoe, and expanded to produce quite different behavior. The campaign was in its small way a parallel to Gore's attempt to lead us to think of the Earth as a pale blue dot. The Bear League tried to give us a new human-scale idea to displace the one we were using.

The Bear League produced an advertisement in which someone is feeding a small bear by hand, or rather, offering the bear a snack.[9] The bear is much smaller than the person doing the feeding. The little bear is standing on its hind legs and reaching up for the treat. But the person doing the feeding is The Grim Reaper, its hand made of bones, its face hidden behind its black cowl, its other hand holding the scythe. The little bear is smiling. There is lettering running down the black cassock sleeve of The Grim Reaper, reading *Garbage, Birdseed, Pet Food, Food in Cars, Picnic Baskets, Fruit Trees, Etc....*

Lower down, overprinted on the figure of The Grim Reaper, runs the warning:

Feeding Our Bears and Cubs Any Time, Anywhere, with Any Food Will Get Them Killed.

Ann Bryant, the Bear League's executive director, explains on its website:

We gave up on trying to talk to people or on expecting them to read our warnings, and instead decided to go with a powerful image getting the message through.

The text accompanying this image announces:

A Fed Bear Is A Dead Bear

The blend is false, or rather, it would be if we did not understand that it is a blend meant to serve us in understanding a complex mental web of causes and effects. First, there is of course not only no such thing as a Grim Reaper, but also no special-duty Grim Reaper who goes around feeding little bears, so what is the point? Second, I come from California and know Lake Tahoe and can say that it is hard to imagine that anyone, even a 2-year-old, upon seeing a bear, would be crazy enough to try to feed the bear, even a cub, by hand. Anywhere close up, bears are amazingly frightening. Third, it is not true that a fed bear is a dead bear. Plenty of bears who eat human food get away with it just fine. Fourth, the bears that die might not be the bears that were fed; perhaps a mother who has been fed brings a cub; the cub never feeds, but is trapped and killed. Fifth, the Grim Reaper is intentionally feeding the bear, but the human beings have perhaps simply failed to dispose of their garbage in a way that prevents the bears from eating it. Sixth, we recognize instantly the lethal intentions of the Grim Reaper, and its intention to trick the bear, whereas presumably none of this applies to the human beings. Indeed, that's the point—the tourists do not realize that they are being the Grim Reaper. Some of them think they are being nice to the bears. Seventh, the image presents only one bear, a cub, whereas in fact the problem is distributed over the entire community of bears in the area. And so on.

But the image of the Grim Reaper feeding the bear prompts us to conceive of a compressed, human-scale, immediately intelligible, memorable blend. One input mental space to this blend is the compact, human-scale scene of well-intentioned hand-feeding of an animal such as a dog or a horse. Another possible input mental space is setting out poisoned food for a nuisance animal, like a rat—something that presumably does not happen at all in the mental web in which tourists end up providing food for bears. The idea of the Grim Reaper is an input to the blend: The person doing the feeding is blended with the Grim Reaper. Elaborate and extended chains of cause and effect in the mental web are compressed in the blend to direct bodily action: One person feeds one bear by hand.

We talked before about cascades of blending, like placing a stepping-stone onto which one steps to place another stepping-stone, and so on. We saw a cascade of blends for Death the French Warrior. The Grim Bear Feeder relies on such a cascade of preexisting blends. One of the preexisting blends is the blend just for The Grim Reaper.[10] This blend is a sophisticated achievement, but once it has been constructed, it can be used as an input to new blends. For example, there are several magazines and news publications that name a "Person of the Year." One year, when an exceptionally high number of celebrities seemed to have died early in the year, one of these publications announced that

> As of this date, the Person of the Year for 2005 is…the Grim Reaper.[11]

We have another pre-existing blend used as an input for The Grim Feeder. We saw it used before for the dinosaur evolving into a bird, and for the North American pronghorn. This blend, or rather, this general blending template, gives us one organism, one particular individual animal (the dinosaur, the pronghorn, the bear) into which are blended lots of such animals. This generic blending template is a superb tool for compressing over time, space, causation, and agency.

There is an additional, phonological compression evident in The Grim Feeder. At least in English, compressing a conceptual connection into a rhyme (or other phonological similarity) can prompt us to tighten the conceptual relation. "Traduttore Traditore" is a chestnut example in Italian, "a translator is a traitor." "A *Fed* Bear is a *Dead* Bear" uses sound to create a similarity link between the words that the Bear League want us to take as cause and effect: feeding and killing. Note that "A *Fed* Bear is a *Killed* Bear" would have been just as accurate, perhaps even more alarming, but would not have had the additional phonological compression of the rhyme. To prompt us to compress the cause-effect relation, the Bear League rhymes them.

All this packing, compression, blending! You would think we would become mentally exhausted. But, on the contrary, blending does not appear to be costly at all. It is not something we fire up for special purposes. It is running all the time. It is the big bass rhythm of our lives. The human mind is built for it. We can have vast thoughts—going far beyond anything available to any other species—because we can create tight, compressed blends that are congenial to our minds, and carry those packed little blends with us from situation to situation, to be expanded when we need them, to hook up with whatever we want to think about.

8

Tight Ideas

All animals have bodies, and their brains are built to run those bodies. Human beings have tight, efficient, functional bodies, and the way we think is built to match how our bodies work. Biological evolution is really adept at setting that up. Thinking for the purpose of running the body is already automatically at human scale.

Getting a new idea that goes beyond our bodily scale is often a matter of creating a blend that uses some pattern we know from our own bodies. Let us look at one of the most basic of these patterns—symmetry.

Hermann Weyl, a mathematician, explained that a body in the world innately incorporates its environment.[1] An unmoving little organism that floats in the ocean at a depth where gravity and water pressure balance out is pretty much spherical, because for such an organism, all directions are the same. Its experience has spherical symmetry and so does its body. A plant fixed to the ground—like a tree—is asymmetric top-to-bottom because gravity creates an environment where all directions are not the same, an environment characterized by differences. The gravity vector points down, not up; water has to be pumped up, but it flows down; a tree's structure needs to be much stronger at the bottom than at the top. At the same time, trees have mostly equivalent environments in any direction perpendicular to the vertical gravity vector. (I say "*mostly* equivalent" because I am leaving out of account the path of the sun, the flow of water, and so on.) So trees pretty much have bodies that are the same in all directions perpendicular to that axis. An animal on the ground that moves has different experience in the direction it is headed than it has from the direction whence it came, and so has a body that is different front to back. We run into things we are moving toward, not things we are moving away from. We experience gravity and we move. So our bodies are, on the outside, anatomically, pretty much different up-down and front-back, but not so much left-right. What can happen from the left can happen from the right. What we can do to the right we can pretty much do to the left. Except for our bodies, we can reverse what is on the left versus right just by doing an about-face. We are set up for this: It would be extremely inefficient if we had to learn everything twice, once to the left and once to the right. Instead, our brains are built to be able to map left to right and right to left and pick out the midline, the axis, about which the pattern is symmetric. This kind of symmetry is called "bilateral symmetry," or "heraldic symmetry."

We have several immediate, human-scale ideas that come from our bodily knowledge of bilateral symmetry. Most important, we know that when we are symmetrically positioned about the plane that separates the left side of our body from the right side of our body (called the "sagittal" plane), whether we are sitting or standing or even moving, then we are stable, balanced, able to deal with the world, ready with power to engage what is in front of us. We know that the same is true of other people, because of course we can make an easy mental blend of our body and their bodies to have an idea of how their bodies work. We also know that we most easily attend to something by facing it, standing full-frontal to it, with it in our sagittal plane directly ahead. And of course we know, by blending, that other people have this experience and behavior. Just by putting our two hands against each other and pressing with equal force, we understand the equilibrium and stability that comes from equal opposing forces. And we understand that there is a linear order from one side to the other that advances to our sagittal plane and then reverses to reach the other side. Stretch out your arms, like Leonardo's Vitruvian Man, and mark off from left to right—fingernails, dactyls, palm, wrist, forearm, elbow, upper arm, shoulder, pectoral, neck and head, pectoral, shoulder, upper arm, elbow, forearm, wrist, palm, dactyls, fingernails. It is like a bodily palindrome. A palindrome is a piece of writing that reads the same backward and forward, like "able was I ere I saw Elba," or "Madam, I'm Adam." Whether you start on the left or the right of the human body, one side is the mirror image of the other.

This bodily knowledge of symmetry is used to make new, tight ideas that go far beyond human scale.[2] An institutional power, like a king, is frequently represented by bilateral symmetry, as we see in the Lion Gate at Mycenae, where two beasts (scholars debate whether these beasts are actually lions) in heraldic symmetry lean rampant against a central pillar. We understand immediately a "stability" and "power" that goes a vast distance beyond our human-scale idea of symmetry, because we have blended a vast mental web of political and institutional power with that human-scale, bodily idea of symmetry.

Vast conceptions are often given an artistic or poetic or symbolic presentation that starts at the periphery, works toward the center, and then works back out toward the periphery. When Odysseus meets his mother Anticlea on a visit to the underworld[3], he asks her six questions, which she answers in reverse order, something like this:

A.   What killed you? (171)
  B. A long sickness? (172)
    C. Or Artemis with her arrows? (172–173)
      D. How is my father? (174)
        E. How is my son? (174)
          F. Are my possessions safe? (175–176)
            G. Has my wife been faithful? (177–79)
            G'. Your wife has been faithful. (181–83)
          F'. Your possessions are safe. (184)
        E'. Your son is thriving. (184–87)
      D'. Your father is alive but in poor condition. (187–96)
    C'. Artemis did not kill me with her arrows. (198–99)
  B'. Nor did a sickness kill me. (200–201)
A'. But my longing for you killed me. (202–3)

What falls at the center of this orderly symmetry is the great theme of the *Odyssey*. Odysseus will fight his way back to Ithaka, discover that Penelope has been faithful, and, against the greatest odds, regain his position with her, his son, and his people.

This may seem at first to be the stuff of old epic, but a few minutes' reflection will bring to mind many examples from current political rhetoric, advertising, and popular entertainment that use such heraldic bodily balance.

Much of the virtue of this blending is that, instead of having to think about many things simultaneously, we can think of one thing—the blend—and use that one thing to help us key into this or that part of the mental web that is so vast. This gives us a tight idea instead of a diffuse bunch of ideas.

Here is a demonstration of the power of thinking about one tight thing instead of two.[4] Consider the sequence 1, 3, 5, 7, 9 … What is the next number? It's easy: 11, followed by 13, 15, 17 … Now consider a second sequence: 2, 4, 6, 8, 10 … What is the next number? It's easy: 12, 14, 16 … Hold those two sequences in mind. Now alternate between them, starting with 1. That is, take the first element from the first sequence, then the first element from the second sequence, then the second element from the first sequence, then the second element from the second sequence, and so on, like this: 1, 2, 3, 4, 5, 6, 7 ... How does the sequence continue? It's easy: 8, 9, 10, 11.

But now, using the same two sequences, combine them again, in just exactly the same way, but instead start with the second sequence rather than the first: 2, 1, 4, 3 ... How does the sequence continue? Well, uh, 6, 5, ... uh, uh, um, 8, 7, ... I have run this demonstration many times, in lecture halls full of very clever people. They end up laughing at how quickly they stumble over the sequence.

Why? Both tasks have the same input mental spaces, that is, the two different integer sequences. Both tasks have the same rule for constructing the third sequence—or rather, the same rule except for where you start. To that extent, the tasks place identical demands on the mind. The obvious difference is that for the first task, there is a unified blend of the two sequences, a blend in which the sequence proceeds by taking one number, and adding one, and doing that again for the next number, and so on. That blend of the two sequences can be held in the mind all at once, and we can think about this one thing instead of having to alternate back and forth between two. But in the second task, it is much harder to get a single, unified blend that can be used to juggle and access the input mental spaces.

If we want to put some stuff into a room and it does not fit, there are in general two different ways to succeed: First, get a bigger room; second, change the stuff so that it will fit. These are very different, if complementary, strategies. Changing the stuff can include folding it, packing it, stacking it, filtering the stuff so as to throw away what we do not need to keep, and so on. Most interesting, changing the stuff can include adding things to it, like, say, stackable storage bins. If we want to stack a lot of fine wine in a small space, it might be best to build good racks for it. This may seem backwards, because adding racks increases the amount of stuff we must fit into the room. But that is often the right strategy. The specific details of the packing can vary. Here is an analogy: In Robert Crichton's *The Secret of Santa Vittoria,* the Italian villagers have hidden very many bottles of local wine underground from the German army at the end of the Second World War. They stacked it tightly. To mislead the Germans, they also stacked a lot of wine above ground, in plain view, but stacked it using a method that requires a great deal of space per bottle. So you can store a lot more or a lot less, depending on how you arrange it. The same is true of numeric sequences. One way to arrange the combination of the two input sequences 1, 3, 5 ... and 2, 4, 6 ... is to create the blend 1, 2, 3, 4, 5 ... This is a tight blend that can be held as a unified blend in the mind: Instead of working in the mental web of inputs, you can work in the blend. The other way to arrange the combination of these two sequences is to create the blend 2, 1, 4, 3..., but that attempt to blend is poor. It produces something that does not fit so well in the mind.

Of course, we have heard and memorized the sequence 1, 2, 3, 4...many times, and never heard or memorized the sequence 2, 1, 4, 3...Accordingly, somebody might legitimately object: Does the difference in our ability to manage the two sequences stem from the fact that in the first we are reciting from long-term memory, but in the second we lack such assistance? Does this exercise merely demonstrate the obvious: that we know what we have memorized but do not know what we have not?

Good question! We can run a different demonstration to answer the question. We can show the same effect without calling on long-term memory, by working with sequences that we have never heard or memorized. Consider a sequence defined by this rule: Take every other even number, beginning at 256. So, 256, 260, 264...What is the next number? It is easy to generate it, because there is a unitary rule: Just add four to the last number. This rule makes the sequence seem like one thing. Now hold that sequence in mind. At the same time, consider a very similar sequence with the identical rule: Take every other even number beginning at 254. So, 254, 258, 262...What is the next number in this sequence? It is easy to generate it, because there is a unitary rule, and it is the same unitary rule: Just add four to the last number. This rule makes this second sequence seem like one thing. Now hold that second sequence in mind along with the first. What is the sequence that consists of numbers taken sequentially in alternation from the two sequences, beginning with 256? So, 256, 254, 260, 258, 264, 262...What is the next number? Keep going. Everyone finds it difficult not to stumble almost immediately. A computer would have not the slightest difficulty.

Why is that? We have no difficulty holding *each* of the sequences in mind because for each we can make a simple blend: The blend has only two numbers, and the second is four more than the first. Wherever you want to be in the sequence, project it to the first number in the blend, and project the next number in the infinite sequence to the second number in the blend, which is four more. So just add 4, and you are done. That little blend gives you the entire sequence, or rather, you can expand from the human-scale blend to any part of the infinite sequence you like. The mental web has an infinity of numbers, but the blend has only two elements, and it repeats. So there is no difficulty in keeping either one of these sequences in mind, because we can use the little blend. If we could hold *both* of the input sequences in mind and go back and forth between them, choosing at each turn the next number for the new sequence, we could answer the question and continue indefinitely, switching back and forth in working memory. But we stumble almost immediately.

But now, here is a similar question that is much easier to answer. This time, start the new sequence at 254 and switch back and forth. Then the resulting sequence is 254, 256, 258, 260…What is the next number? Of course, the answer is 262, and then 264, and then 266, and so on forever. Everyone finds it very easy to continue this sequence indefinitely, even though we haven't forgotten that the inputs are two separate sequences, the first one being 256, 260, 264…and the second one being 254, 258, 262…Why is it so difficult to run the sequence 256, 254, 260, 258, 264, 262…but so easy to run the sequence 254, 256, 258, 260…? The answer is not that we have already heard one but not the other! It is not that in one case we are reciting from long-term memory but in the other case we are not! The answer is not that they are put together from different inputs. Again, a computer would not have the slightest difficulty running either of these sequences, and indeed, a mathematical ranking of the two sequences would assign them equal computational complexity. How does our mind work so that running the two sequences feels so different?

Everyone knows the answer immediately. In both cases, we have the same two input sequences, and in both cases, we have the same sequence rule: Take numbers sequentially in alternation between the two input sequences. Or at least, we have the same sequence rule except for where we start. The computer would easily generate the needed parts of the two sequences and just alternate between them. But that is not how we do it.

For a person, there is a big difference between the two tasks. Starting with one of the two inputs makes it very difficult to keep going, and starting with the other makes it very easy, because in the second case, there is a single, tight blend, namely a single, unitary sequence defined by a rule: Start at 254 and keeping adding 2 to the last number. We can use the tight blend to do our thinking, and expand it to the input sequences when we want to. (Of course, there is a rule for the sequence that starts with the other input, but the rule is more complicated and not everyone finds it, and even when they do, they can have difficulty running it.) When we start with 254, there is a congenial, unitary blend, and running the blend makes immediate sense. The blend serves the web of two different sequences, and lets us keep connected to not only the blend but also the two input sequences we started with. In that case, we run in working memory three things rather than two, but running three things is easier than running two because the third thing is a compact blend that connects to and organizes the web involving the other two. Running the blend lets us run the input sequences by inference. More is easier, if the more is packed in a congenial way. More is easier if the more is a packed blend that lets us grasp and manipulate whatever we were trying to hold in mind. More is easier if the blend lets us generate most of the web on the fly instead of having to hold it explicitly in mind. For working memory, more is better if the more comes about by good blending. Blending changes the task; it leverages working memory. On the fly, blending and working memory are a much stronger tool than working memory alone.

Which Way Do You Turn?

Here is a much simpler visual exercise to demonstrate how blending helps us manage a diffuse mental web by creating a compressed, congenial blend that serves the web and makes it possible for us to grasp it. The mental web we are about to look at is overarching, diffuse, difficult. But the blend is compact and congenial.

Imagine a line of identical interlocking gears lying flat on a table that stretches for miles, or, if you are anyplace but the United States of America, kilometers. If the first gear turns counterclockwise, which way does the 173rd gear turn? The 256th? It is not so easy to reach the right conclusion for these big numbers.

But think of it: Any two gears separated by only one gear must turn in the same direction. So project all the odd-numbered gears in the infinite sequence to the same gear in the blend, the first gear. And project all the even-numbered gears in the infinite sequence to the same gear in the blend, the second gear. Now, in the blend, instead of an infinite number of gears, there are only two interlocking gears, the first turning counterclockwise and the second turning clockwise (figure 14). In imagination, all the odd gears in the line are projected onto the first gear, and all the even gears are projected onto the second gear. The blend has only two gears, and two directions, but it can be expanded to help us deal with any part of the infinite sequence of gears. The blend organizes a mental web much too diffuse to be held in working memory. From the blend, we can manipulate the mental web of the infinite sequence, and even rebuild it. Now we know that the 173rd gear must turn just like the first gear, which is to say, counterclockwise. Using the blend, we know that the 456,251st gear turns counterclockwise, too. And we know that the 256th gear must turn just like the second gear, which is to say, clockwise. We know that the 12,345,678th gear turns clockwise, too. *Blending leverages working memory.* Blending makes working memory more powerful. It even saves us from having to carry the

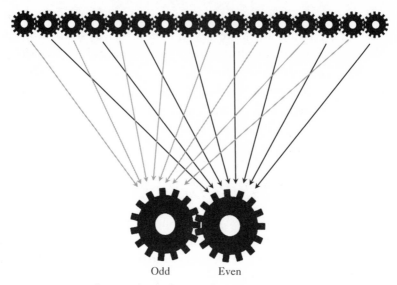

Odd   Even

FIGURE 14 A 2-Element Blend of an Indefinitely Large Mental Web

contents of working memory around with us all the time. Because of blending, we do not need to hold the entire mental web in working memory. We can reactivate parts of it on the fly as needed by working from the blend.

Out at Sea

Blending makes it possible for the human mind to go places it has never gone before. In a nutshell, this is what makes us human. We are living beings, in many ways very much like other living beings. Like plants, we are made of cells. Like mammals, we breathe air. Like primates, we have not only two arms and two legs, but also the common primate brain. In the big picture, what we share with other species is surely the largest part of the human story.

But there are other things that we do not share with other living beings. We do not share photosynthesis with plants. We do not share echolocation with bats. And they do not seem to share advanced blending with us. Advanced blending provides us with extraordinary flexibility and a unique power for innovation.

Blending lets us, for example, go to sea.

Start on land. Land is the kind of place we are built to be able to understand. Imagine that something in our field of vision comes straight at us. That is, we look in its direction, keep our gaze fixed, and this object we see stays in the same place in our field of vision, but it keeps getting bigger. We know that we need to get out of the way. That understanding is at human scale; it requires no big thinking. It takes only basic cognition.

Next, suppose that whatever we are looking at on land stays in the same spot in our field of vision but gets smaller, or stays the same size. Put another way, its image subtends an ever-decreasing, or an invariant, angle of our visual field. We do not need to move, because it is either moving away from us or staying at the same distance from us. This understanding is at human scale; it requires no big thinking. It takes only basic cognition.

Since motion is relative—we, in relation to the thing we are looking at—there are actually two or three ways to understand what is going on when we see these objects getting bigger or getting smaller. In one way, the object is moving while we remain stationary. In the other way, the object remains stationary while we are moving. There is also the possibility that both we and the object are moving. Any of these three scenes might fit what we see when the object seems to get closer. No matter which of these three scenes you are imagining, suppose that the object is staying in the *same spot* in your field of vision and *getting bigger*. In that case, you know you are going to collide with the object. In any of three scenes, we have the same little physical story: the story of a collision. We are going to collide with the object.

Throughout this book, I have been stressing the ways in which advanced blending makes it possible for us to go far beyond mere instinct. I do not mean to dismiss instinct's contributions: Our immediate response on land to something in our visual field that is getting bigger as we look at it may well be a case where instinct has given us a deeply human-scale understanding. Sure. But now let's look at how we go beyond that instinct. To do so, all we need to do is to go to sea.

Landlubbers might find it difficult to imagine how ambiguous and uncertain a boat's location can seem to be when one is on it out at sea. Let me tell you, it is wild. In our time, the problem of locating the boat relative to the Earth is solved by signals from Global Positioning Satellites. But only a few decades ago, GPS was not available, and even now, GPS can fail, requiring the sailor to use other methods. There are charts, but it can be a very hard job to establish the relationship of the boat's location to the images on the chart, especially out of sight of land, at night, under overcast skies.

Suppose we see another object out on the water—a boat, a buoy, a board, a green or red or white light. Is it moving? Will we collide with it? There can be a considerable lag between a pilot's action and a vessel's response. The larger the boat, the greater the lag, for the most part. And there is even more bad news: A great deal is going on while a boat sails along a bearing out at sea. Maybe it is not so easy for the sailor to change bearings. Maybe there are obstacles preventing the sailor from going some of those ways. Maybe the conditions are better over here than over there. It might not be so easy to make a course correction later. What should we do?

The sailor can try to compute in working memory all the relative positions of objects on the water and their futures, but that results in a diffuse, distended mental web, reaching over time, space, causation, and agency. Such a web is very hard to hold and manipulate in working memory. There is a lot at stake. A mistake could be fatal. I mean, you and those for whom you are responsible could die in the next 15 minutes because you didn't figure it out.

This at-sea mental web of possible actions and possible consequences stretches far beyond anything at normal human scale. The collision could be an hour away, or 2 hours away. We have to think about it. How can we get a handle on this problem?

First, there is the simplest case, in which something is close, straight ahead of us, and getting bigger fast. We have to get out of the way. Move that tiller, rotate that wheel.

But suppose the object is not straight ahead of us, or is getting bigger only slowly. We are not moving directly toward it. It is off the port or starboard side of the boat. Now we have to do some blending.

We can start to think about this process by remembering what we know about basic mammalian movement on land. We are very good at understanding movement along a path—a skill we share with other mammals. We are good at picking out in our visual field something that moves fairly quickly along a path: a bird, a fly, an ant. Often, the object leaves a trace along the path, as when a child rides a bicycle through the beach sand. Activate this idea of something moving along a path and leaving a trace of its movement. At the same time, activate the idea of a boat moving on the ocean. The movement of the boat will take a long time, and we do not see the trace made during all of that time. But if we blend these two ideas—the relatively quick movement along a path that leaves a trace, and the boat's movement—then, in the blend, the boat has motion along a path, and we can see that path all at once. In the blend, we now have a boat, its entire movement along a bearing from past through present to future, and its trace.

Notice what is happening here: In one of the input mental spaces, we see the entire movement and its trace in a very little bit of time—as when the bicycle goes through the sand—but in the other, the amount of time is immense. When we blend these together, we can see in the blend something happen fast that we know takes a long time. This is a compression of time. We perform such compressions routinely. When we look at the calendar, for example, the whole month is right there; the movement from day to day takes no more time than is required for our finger to go from one spot on the calendar to another. In the blend, the movement of the boat that might take hours takes only a few seconds. That is a time compression. And even though we see no lasting trace on the water, since the wake disappears, in the blend, we have the boat's trace mentally available as something to be used.

We are not deluded: When we expand the blend, we realize that it contains a compressed mental representation of time. In the blend, the extended activity of the boat has been blended with our simple notion of quick movement along a path that leaves a trace. The blend uses something with a basic, at-home structure to let us conceive of a far-from-home mental web of ideas.

Now that we have this blend for our boat's movement along its bearing, we can find a way of dealing with the question of whether we will collide with something else we see out there on the surface of the water. First, make not just one, but two of these boat-on-a-path-with-a-trace blends. In each, there is something moving along a course, both under severe time compression. One blend has our boat. The other has whatever object we are looking at, out there on the surface of the water. In fact, it could be that the "course" of the other object, or even our own course, is to stay motionless in one spot on the water. Either we or the other thing could be anchored, for example, or becalmed. But when we are out at sea, we cannot tell just by looking whether one of us is not moving. So, imagine that what we see is a boat out on the water. Then in each of two boat-on-a-path-with-a-trace blends, there is a boat and a course for the boat along a bearing, and in each blend, there is a static line, a trace.

Now, blend again. Blend those two boat-on-a-path-with-a-trace blends into a hyper-blend, so that in the new blend, we have two bearing lines. Do those bearing lines intersect? If so, do the two lines, or, more accurately, the two boats, arrive at the intersection at the same time? If so, then there is a collision coming. Move that tiller, rotate that wheel. But how can we think about whether the two boats arrive at the intersection at the same time? That point of intersection could be a long distance from where we are, and we do not know that distance. It could be a long time from now, and we do not know how long.

Here, what we know about the human-scale scene of colliding with something or someone comes to our aid. In our human-scale scene, we know that if we keep our angle of vision just the same as we look at the other object, then the other object must move "forward" in our field of vision if it is going to get to the intersection before we do. That is, it must look as if it is "gaining" on us, shortening the distance to the intersection faster than we are. Alternatively (assuming, again, that we keep our angle of vision just the same as we look at the other object), the other object must move "backward" in our field of vision if we are going to reach the intersection first. That is, the other object must look as if it is "losing" because we are shortening our distance to the intersection faster than the other object. If the other ship is moving "forward" in our field of vision, it is beating us to the intersection. If it is moving "backward" in our field of vision, we are beating it to the intersection. In either case, there is no problem, because the two objects will not arrive at the intersection simultaneously.

But if the other object stays in just the same spot in our field of vision and gets bigger, then we are going to reach the intersection at the same time. Boom! Collision!

Baseball fielders use this "gaze heuristic" to catch a fly ball: They run toward where they think the ball might be headed, but keep looking at the ball flying through the air with the same angle of vision, and speed up or slow down so as to keep the ball in the same spot in the field of vision, neither advancing nor falling back. That way, they will intersect with the ball, and perhaps catch it.

Blending what we know from our human-scale experience of movement and collision with the vast at-sea web of objects in the distance, we can understand, in the blend, something that we cannot actually see. In the blend, there are intersecting lines and everything else we need to decide whether to deviate from our course or not. In the case of the gaze heuristic, it may be that instinct has built the right tool into lots of mammals. That is very impressive! But what we are interested in here is the way in which advanced blending can make this kind of idea available for scenes far beyond the local area and moment.

For those who are interested—this is going to be technical—it can be shown that the same blending provides the basis of the mathematical understanding of the situation as it is usually taught in navigation classes for sailors. The geometry goes like this: We can mentally draw an imaginary triangle in the blend. One vertex is the position of boat A, the other vertex is the position of boat B, and the third vertex C is where the two bearing lines intersect. If both boats arrive simultaneously at C, then each boat, sailing at a constant speed along an unchanging bearing, traverses its leg of the triangle in the same amount of time. In that case, boat A traverses x% of its course to C in the same amount of time that boat B traverses the same x% of its course to C, and therefore we have at each moment a triangle, ABC, and all these triangles are similar: They all have the same, unchanging interior angles, and the three sides always stand in the same proportions. So, for all these triangles, the angle—that is, the bearing—from boat B to boat A stays the same. In other words, all these different static triangles can be packed to a blend in which there is *one triangle* that is *shrinking over time*. This blend is, in visual imagination, something direct and human-scale. Of course, it is not something one can see in the visual field. The triangle in the blend changes in a manageable amount of time. It can be unpacked to the entire diffuse web of locations in time for both boats.

Will we collide with the other boat? Now we can see the math that can be applied to the blend: As we stand on our boat, we gaze at the distant object and ensure that our gaze is constant relative to our boat, by, for example, picking a point on our gunwale and looking out over it at the object, and not moving our head or our eyes. If the distant object remains in the same spot in our gaze and grows larger, we are going to hit it, so we should change course.

The "shrinking triangle" blend for determining whether we will collide uses an extremely common pattern of blending: In a big web, find the analogies and disanalogies across lots of mental spaces; pack the analogies and disanalogies into the blend, with the result that the blend has one thing that changes. There can be very many conceptual inputs in such a web, with analogies and disanalogies connecting them. The analogies are compressed to a single entity—in this case, the *triangle*. And the disanalogies are compressed to *change* for that one thing. In this case, the change for the one thing is that the triangle is *shrinking*. The triangle keeps its proportions as it shrinks, and shrinks down to a single point: the point of collision. So if there is a collision (in the blend), then the bearing from boat B to boat A *stays the same* and boat A gets closer to boat B because the leg of the triangle that connects them is shrinking. This implies that boat A subtends a larger angle in the visual field of the sailor on boat B. This situation is called by sailors *Constant Bearing, Decreasing Range*. The mnemonic is Charter Boaters Detest Returning. To the sailor, it means: If there is a constant bearing to the other object, and the range to the other object is decreasing, alter course or the two of you are going to collide.

Of course, if what you want to do is collide with or meet the other object, then the shrinking triangle blend is exactly what you want.

By using this blending web, the sailor creates a manageable mental scene—the shrinking triangle of doom. It can be easily grasped. The shrinking triangle blend enables the sailor to make a human-scale decision. That decision can be expanded to manage a diffuse mental web that otherwise could not be mastered within working memory. This is new stuff, on a grand scale, and lets us boldly go where we were not adapted to go. Dogs, wonderfully talented as they are, so flexible that they can learn to work on a boat in blue water, seem to be equipped with the gaze heuristic: Some breeds are good at catching fly balls and Frisbees. But never expect a dog looking at a dot on the sea a long way off to start barking to alert you that you and the dot are going to collide.

The shrinking triangle blend lets us think far beyond human scale. It lets us think at web scale, about a future that is only slightly specified. But in all versions of that future, with different triangles, there is a collision if we have constant bearing, decreasing range, and no change of course. The blend organizes and serves the diffuse mental web. We conceive of the blend, and it allows us to grasp the mental web, to reason in the mental web, and to draw inferences for our present action.

The blend delivers new stuff that is amazing, once we think about it. To begin with, there is of course no triangle except in the blend. Imagining a single triangle on the water is already an impressive compression.

Moreover, this conception of the triangle on the water is not actually an idea of a specific triangle. Instead, the imagined triangle is a potential, generalized triangle, with some constraints. Why is it not a specific triangle? Because the sailor does not know the lengths of any of its legs! Therefore, what she knows is not a triangle, but rather a set of constraints on the relevant (but unknown) triangle. There is an uncountable infinity of triangles fitting those constraints, and an uncountable infinity certainly cannot fit inside working memory, but that uncountable infinity of triangles is all compressed into *one* triangle in the blend.

The next compression we achieve, a compression that is quite different from the compression of all the possible static triangles into one static triangle, is the *shrinking*. Over time, there will be an uncountable infinity of such similar triangles. But each of them is static. There is no shrinking in reality. The shrinking is new stuff in the blend. It arises as new mental structure in the blend, much the way the monk's meeting himself arises as new mental structure in the Buddhist Monk riddle. The new stuff in the blend is not itself shared by the ideas that we call into use to make the blend. In none of our ideas of reality is there a shrinking triangle. But we make one in the blend, and it helps us understand reality. The blend originates a new idea that helps us manage the vast mental web.

It is not even given that there is a triangle that results in a collision. The entire blending web for the collision triangle is held as potentially counterfactual with respect to another blending web in which the two lines that are the courses of the boats either do not intersect or have an intersection that is not a simultaneous location for the boats. It is no problem if the courses intersect—this happens all the time. The only problem is if their intersection is a *simultaneous* location for both boats. The monk has to meet himself in the riddle, but out at sea, we are trying to arrange for two boat courses *without* the boats' meeting.

Managing the mental web of events on the water depends upon having a blend at human scale, one we can mentally grasp. From the blend of the shrinking triangle, we can manage the out-at-sea web it serves.

Do You Remember?

The evolution of an advanced blending capacity and the evolution of memory capacity could have bootstrapped each other in the evolution of human beings, in two different but related ways:

1. An expansion in working memory—where by "working memory" we mean the capacity to hold information in mind for processing—would have made more mental stuff available to the process of advanced blending. So, other things being equal, an expansion in working memory would have been more useful, fitter, if that blending capacity was already strong enough to handle the new load and deal with the range of new material.

2. Long-term memory might have evolved to provide some mental input spaces to the advanced blending mill that are *not compatible* with the present situation. That is, contents of long-term memory might be incompatible with the present situation, so long-term memory could be a great resource for blending if blending can work with incompatible input spaces. The present situation we inhabit has stuff that is pretty much compatible—after all, it is all right here right now together. So where would a capacity for advanced blending that is superb at blending incompatible ideas get the incompatible ideas? One answer is an evolved long-term memory that is freed from submission to the present situation. In cognitive science, a memory incompatible with the present situation is called "decoupled." The more capacious the power of long-term memory, the greater the range of the conceptual material it can supply to blending.

In the cases of both working memory and long-term memory, we have an evolutionary bootstrap: An expansion of blending capacity makes it fitter for working memory to expand and for long-term memory to expand; and an expansion of working memory or long-term memory makes it fitter for the blending capacity to expand.

What Key Are You In?

One great difference between our species and all other species is our capacity to manage complex, diffuse mental webs that range far beyond the here and now. Our ability to manage these mental webs depends upon our ability to compress them into congenial, human-scale blends.

Here is a snippet of a sequence of integers:

2 2 1 2 2 2 1 2 2 1 2 2 2 1 2 2 1 2 2 2 1 2 2 1 2 2 2 1...

It can be quite difficult to grasp this sequence, but a first step is to recognize that it is a repetition of

2 2 1 2 2 2 1

like this (figure 15):

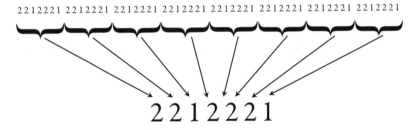

FIGURE 15   Blending an Indefinite Mental Web to a 7-Element Cyclic Blend

If one memorizes "2 2 1 2 2 2 1" in an auditory loop, it might be possible to write out a lot of this sequence by repeating it and writing as one repeats.

Musicians may recognize that this sequence defines the major diatonic scale: Its numbers give the number of steps (semitones) between notes in the major diatonic scale, beginning on any note. For example, the major scale beginning on C is

C D E F G A B C D E F G A B...

The number of semitones between C and D is 2; between D and E is 2; between E and F is 1; and so on. This is a spectacular mental compression not just of the major diatonic scale beginning on C, but of *all* major diatonic scales, regardless of the beginning note. For example, the major scale beginning on G is

G A B C D E F# G A B C D E F#...

Of course, this major diatonic scale has the same repeating pattern as any other: Beginning at G, take 2 steps to A, 2 steps to B, 1 step to C, 2 steps to D, 2 steps to E, 2 steps to F#, and 1 step to G, and then repeat indefinitely.

Children studying music chant, "Whole Whole Half Whole Whole Whole Half," which is another way of saying "2 2 1 2 2 2 1." This chant triggers a compressed blend that can be expanded to help us understand the major diatonic scale, *any* major diatonic scale.

You can get a grip on this sequence by looking at a piano keyboard (figure 16). On the piano keyboard, the sharp and flat notes are the black keys. The key of C major has no sharps or flats—so just white keys. If you start at C, you have to make 2 steps (first to the black key, then to the white key) to reach D. Then 2 steps to E, then only 1 step to F, then 2 steps to G, then 2 steps to A, then 2 steps to B, then only 1 step to C. 2 2 1 2 2 2 1, or "Whole Whole Half Whole Whole Whole Half." If you find the keyboard representation confusing, look at the neck of a guitar. Play a C, then move up 2 frets, and play a D, and so on up the scale.

But the 2 2 1 2 2 2 1 recurring sequence is good for *any* major scale. If we blend it with a specific beginning note (like C), then the new blend is a more specific compressed blend—compressed not least because it has only 7 elements in a repeating sequence, whereas the actual scale itself goes on indefinitely in either direction. This new specific compressed blend can be expanded to give the entire major diatonic scale beginning on that note.

It gets better. Inspection shows that the sequence that consists of repetitions of the period 2 2 1 2 2 2 1 is the same as the sequence that consists of repetitions of the period 2 1 2 2 1 2 2. And if one starts at the beginning of the

C D E F G A B C

FIGURE 16 C Major Scale on a Keyboard

period 2 1 2 2 1 2 2, one has the natural minor scale. Accordingly, every major scale has a relative minor scale that has the identical notes, but that begins on the sixth note of the major scale. The C major scale is

C D E F G A B C D E F G A B ...

and its sixth note is A, so the A minor scale has the identical notes

A B C D E F G A B C D E F G ...

The difference is only where one starts. Everyone hears and feels that musical difference immediately. Both scales have 2 steps between their first 2 notes, but where the major scale has 2 steps between its second and third notes, the natural minor scale has only one step between its second and third notes.

There is a further packing scheme that creates a blend of great importance: All the structure of all the major diatonic scales and their relations to all the natural minor diatonic scales can be conceived of as an expansion from a compressed blend known as the "Circle of Fifths" (figure 17). A circle is very much at human scale, and the idea that you go from one spot on the circle to the next spot in the circle by repeating the identical operation is also at human scale. Of course, in music, the keys are not actually arranged in any physical circle, and one does not actually move from one physical location in the circle to another when one "changes keys," but the blend can recruit both the idea of the circle with steps and the idea of moving from one spot of the circle to another.[5]

Teachers of music create further blends to help students reconstruct this blend. "Fat Cats Go Down Alleyways Eating Bread" gives, in the first letters of its words, enough of the structure of the circle to get the student rolling in generating the rest: F C G D A E B. (It's like the mental blend of the DC Metro map.) If one remembers the mnemonic phrase, and remembers that the relative minor scale starts on the sixth note of the major scale, one can generate all the relative minors. There are even more powerful mnemonic blends: "BEAD Girls Can't Fight BEAD Girls" provides the sequence of all the major scales all the way around: B E A D G C F B^b E^b A^b D^b G^b.

A professional musician with a solid formation no longer needs to do all this expansion from the Circle of Fifths on the fly, because so much has been entrenched in the musician's long-term memory and muscle memory that the musician can call up any scale on its own. But even the professional musician was once unable to call to mind, much less hold in mind, the entire structure of tonality so as to work within it and manipulate it, and needed these

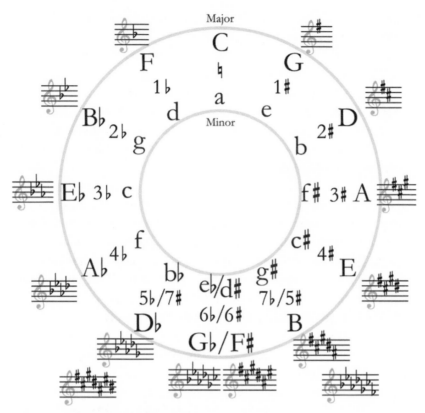

FIGURE 17 The Circle of Fifths

compressed blends to get through the music. Blending and memory complement each other in human thought.

It might seem at first blush as if creating the compressed blend and adding it to the mental web for the scale would only increase the mental load and so make it even more difficult to work with the diffuse mental web. On the contrary, the compressed blend can serve the mental web, allowing us to work in it and manipulate it much more powerfully and efficiently. The compressed blend can also serve as a tool of long-term memory, to be used for on-the-fly regeneration of the diffuse mental web.

Blending is the lever of memory.

Inchworm, Inchworm

A familiar, comfortable blend almost never looks like a blend. Artifacts like the lionman are the rare exception rather than the rule. Usually, blends become second nature, direct and familiar, obvious. New ideas quickly look as if they have been there all along.

Think of the *number line*. What could seem more natural than that the integers lie on a line? Start at 0, then take a step to 1, then a step to 2, then 3... Or go in the other direction. Start at 0, take a step backward to −1, then another backward to −2... Teachers show schoolchildren "sliders" that move "back and forth" on the "number line" to help them get the blend. It is so natural to think of the number line that some researchers propose that there is a mental number line that is part of the genetic human endowment.[6] But it is not so clear why having two beans in your hand can be thought of as a linear distance. What has 2 spaces along a path got to do with beans? It took culture a long time to invent the number 0. It is not so clear why we would now think of 0 as a point on a line, a specific point, namely the beginning point for applying the metric that tells us that the integers are evenly spaced on the line. There seem to be many concepts floating around the idea of *number*: a container with objects in it (a container like your hand, holding a few beans); tallying (I, II, III, IV...), and distances along a line.

To be sure, we now connect these ideas immediately: We know the connection between 2 beans in the hand, the second point in a tally, a line segment of a certain distance, and 2 paces from our starting point. These different ideas correspond to one another. But again, we do much more than simply connect these ideas. We *blend* them. In the blend, 2 is indeed that specific spot on the number line.

There is an emerging view in cognitive science that some capacities for numerosity are part of the human endowment and have been here for a long time, evolutionarily. The main example is subitizing—our ability to make rapid, accurate, and confident judgments of the quantity of items in an array up to three or four.[7]

Is the mental number line something like subitizing, or is it a relatively new idea in our descent that originated by blending? Rafael Núñez argues that the neurobiological and psychological evidence for an abstract, hard-wired, innate mental number line is weak, that the hypothesis of an innate mental number line is implausible, and that Old Babylonian mathematics had no number line.[8] Núñez writes,

> Explicit characterizations of the number line seem to have emerged in Europe as late as the 17th century, and only in the minds of a few pioneering mathematicians. It was apparently John Wallis in 1685 who,

for the first time, introduced the concept of number line in his *Treatise of Algebra*. Earlier precursors may have paved the way, such as John Napier with his 1616 diagrams used to define the concept of logarithm. The number line mapping, however, was not a common idea among mathematicians....

It is important to point out that Wallis's and Napier's texts, intended for readers with advanced knowledge in mathematics, proceed with detailed and careful—almost redundant—explanations of how to generate and use a number line mapping. These explanations are not "formalizations" of the idea of a number line, but rather, they are elaborated presentations of a new meaningful and fruitful idea. The hand-holding narrative, however, is similar to what we see in many elementary school classrooms today, showing just how unfamiliar the idea of a number line was to 17th century mathematicians, let alone to the rest of the majority of illiterate citizens in Europe at that time. Taken together, these facts from the history of mathematics—from Old Babylonia to 17th Century Europe—are simply at odds with the idea of a hard-wired MNL [mental number line] that would spontaneously manifest in *all* humans.[9]

Can this be? Can it be that a concept that seems so natural as the number line is actually a relatively recent achievement of cultural innovation, through blending? Núñez argues that there are human beings alive today in remote indigenous groups who do not have a mental number line: "Uneducated Mundurukú adults dramatically failed to map even the simplest numerosity patterns—one, two, and three—with a line segment, and a high proportion of them only used the segment's endpoints, failing to use the full extent of the response continuum."[10]

How we grasp the number line is evidently an open question in cognitive science. I review it here to emphasize that our intuitions about the origins of a very clear idea—such as the idea of the number line—might be very far off base. Although the mental number line seems to us to be inevitable and inescapable, perhaps it originates in cultural time through blending.

Let us take one step further in looking at the ways in which we blend number and motion along a line. In particular, let us look at something that everybody knows arose only very recently, inventively, and among a select few thinkers: the concept of *number* as a *limit*. Brilliant high school students, for example, are often stumped, and argue, touchingly, about whether the infinite decimal .9999 ... is a number, and if so, which number.

We can think of .9999…as a number by putting together a particular mental blending web. Imagine a conceptual web consisting, potentially, of an infinity of numbers, each with one more decimal place: .999, .9999, .99999, .999999… These are different finite decimal numbers, and there is an infinity of them. How shall we make sense of this web of numbers? It is obviously much too big for working memory to handle by listing all the elements and remembering individually their order. We must do something to compress all this stuff into a tight idea. There are analogies across all the numbers, and disanalogies across all of them, too. If we compress the analogies to a unique element—a point—and compress all the disanalogies to *change* for that element—so the unique point *moves*—then we have in the blend a point that keeps hopping toward 1 but never goes past it. This compressed blend has one entity, a number-point on a line, and that entity is changing—it is moving along the number line toward 1. Good job! Now working memory is adequate to grasp what is going on. Working memory has now been provided with something that is compressed, manageable, familiar, at human scale, and congenial to the human mind. Working memory can now use that blend as a platform from which to grasp, manipulate, and work on the full web, a little at a time. The job becomes tractable. It is like stacking all the wine bottles in a nice rack.

In the blend, we can now ask about *the point* that is *moving toward a fixed point*. Does it grow ever closer to that point and never go beyond it? If so, then we can think of it in the compressed blend as *approaching a limit*.

Advanced mathematics provides much more sophisticated tools for measuring whether something approaches a limit, but in this case, we do not need those tools. In this case, we have the very simple compact blend in which each additional decimal place *advances the moving point closer to the fixed number-point 1*, and does so for an infinite number of steps.

Because, in the blend, the infinite decimal *approaches a limit* that we already take to be a number, we can blend again to create an even greater compression—the infinite decimal can be fused with the limit it approaches. Then, in the blend, we can stipulate that .9999…is indeed a number, and we know exactly which number it is: .9999… = 1. In the blend, the infinite decimal is fused with the limit it approaches.

High school students confronted with such analyses sometimes feel that the analysis is just an arbitrary trick, a rabbit out of a hat. The effective but incomplete answer to the high school student is, "Well, if you think .9999…is less than 1, how much less than 1 do you think it is?" But the more fundamental explanation we should offer to the resisting high school student is that in the discipline of mathematics we have chosen to call .9999…a number and to fuse it in the blend with the limit "it" "approaches" because such fusions produce a mathematical system that is truly useful both in theory and in practice. Blending is the origin of the idea that $.999\ldots = 1$.

We take one last step in the mathematical blending that blends motion and number. This one last step is on the same path, but is known only to those who have studied calculus. Riemann sums and Riemann integrals provide examples of the ways in which blending to a compressed mental space helps us invent mathematical structures, operations, and knowledge. The blending that produces Riemann sums and integrals is clearly a matter of innovation, not of the genetic human endowment. Indeed, very few human beings alive today have the idea of a Riemann integral. James Alexander argues that mathematics as a formal system routinely deploys blending, in an iterative manner, to develop the rich structures of "higher" mathematics, and that mathematics has developed strong controls on the use of blending so as to maintain the rigor of the innovations.[11] His central point is that blending and other such mechanisms are incorporated into the formal structure of the discipline of mathematics.

So let us take a simple look at Riemann sums and integrals as an example of the origin of new mathematical ideas by blending. Riemann sums are sums of the areas of rectangles—that's all. Take a curve in the Cartesian plane, like the one below. What is the area under the curve between two given points on the x-axis? We can approximate that area under the curve by fitting adjacent rectangles to the curve, where one side of each rectangle lies on the x-axis and each rectangle has the same width. The width is the "domain" of the rectangle. The height of the rectangle can be taken in any of several usual ways: The height can be the height on the leftmost point in the domain, the height on the rightmost point in the domain, the average of those two heights, the maximum height over the domain, or the minimum height over the domain. For our purposes, it doesn't matter. In figure 18, I have chosen the height of the rectangle to be the height on the leftmost point in the domain.

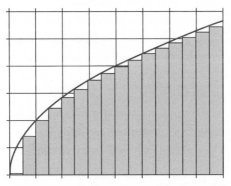

FIGURE 18 A Riemann Sum = The Sum of the Areas of Rectangles Under the Curve

When we divide the domain of the function into n equal subintervals like this, we have specific values for the endpoints of the subintervals, and a specific, invariant value for the width. All n rectangles under the curve have the same width. The formula for the summed area of the rectangles (figure 19) is then:

$$S = \sum_{a}^{b} f(x_i)(x_i - x_{i-1})$$

FIGURE 19   Formula for a Riemann Sum

This just means the sum of all the rectangles, computed as follows. We divide the horizontal distance on the x-axis under the curve into n equal widths. This gives us $n + 1$ equally-spaced points along the x-axis: $x_0, x_1 \dots x_n$. For the first rectangle, the one on the left, take its height, which is just the value of the function at x_0. We write that $f(x_0)$. Now take its width, which is just $x_1 - x_0$. Because the area of a rectangle is the height multiplied by the width, the area of the rectangle is the product $f(x_0)(x_1 - x_0)$. Now move to the rectangle that sits between x_1 and x_2, and take its area, and all the way down to the rectangle that sits between x_{n-1} and x_n. Now add up all the areas. That's all there is to it. More technically, the invariant width of the rectangles is $(x_{i+1} - x_i)$. So the area of the rectangle sitting on the subinterval that starts at x_i and ends at x_{i+1} is just the width times the height of the rectangle, namely, the product of $(x_{i+1} - x_i)$ and $f(x_i)$. The sum of all these rectangles is the Riemann sum, and it is our approximation of the area under the curve.

To obtain a more accurate approximation, we increase the number of subintervals, that is, we make n larger, thereby shortening the width of the rectangles. When we do so, we have a second Riemann sum. But then we can repeat that process again and again. We can increase the number of the rectangles an infinite number of times, just by making n larger each time, each time narrowing the width of the rectangles. As we increase the number of rectangles so that it goes beyond just a few, we get a mental web of lots of rectangles much too big to manage in our thinking.

But now, we use standard mathematical blending. In fact, we use once again the very common general blending template we have already seen many times: Blend the analogies together into an identity and the disanalogies together into a change for that identity. In this case, take all those

Riemann sums and compress them to *one* Riemann sum in the blend. In that way the analogies across all these input Riemann sums are compressed to *uniqueness*: We have one Riemann sum in the blend. And the disanalogies across all those input Riemann sums are compressed to *change* for that one unique entity in the blend: The Riemann sum changes; it *approaches a limit*. Note that we say "the Riemann sum": language here marks that we have created a compressed blend, and we can refer directly to the compressed blend. When we say, "the Riemann sum," no one responds, "What do you mean, '*the*' Riemann sum? Every time you increase *n* by 1, you have a new and different Riemann sum, with a different number of rectangles, and probably a different value. Which one do you mean?" Instead, we know that "*the* Riemann sum" refers to the compressed entity in the blend, the one that "changes," the one that "approaches a limit" by "moving" along "the number line." Analogy and disanalogy across the web are compressed to the blend, where we now have a unique element that changes. This general blending template is a strong tool of cognition, used widely, no matter what we are thinking about. That is why it is available to higher mathematics in the first place.

The blend has new stuff, that is, something that cannot be projected to it from any of the input mental spaces in the web. A blend is almost never just a cut-and-paste reassembly of elements from the inputs. We run and develop the blend mentally, creating new stuff in the blend. In this case, the crucial new stuff in the blend is the *limit*. This limit becomes a new mathematical structure: a Riemann *integral*. Blending provides us with the origin of this idea. If *a* and *b* are the endpoints of the domain for which we want to measure the area under the curve defined by the function *f*, we write the Riemann integral (figure 20) like this:

$$\int_a^b f(x)dx$$

FIGURE 20 Riemann Integral

We say that "in the limit," we get the exact area under the curve. This blending approach generalizes over any number of dimensions. We are already getting well beyond the general mathematical knowledge of even educated people, so we will stop with the Riemann integral. But mathematicians will be instantly able to rattle off hundreds of examples of such new stuff from blending, in algebra, geometry, analysis, set theory, and logic.

Common General Patterns of Blending

Blending is flexible, systematic, and principled. But it can produce many different blending webs. They do not separate into just a few kinds. There is no taxonomy or partition of the products of blending. Still, certain general patterns of blending arise so often that they have been given names. They are reference points in the theory of blending that stand out from the crowd. We have seen many of these. If we want to emphasize that one of the input mental spaces to a blend is already a blend, which is often the case, we call the resulting blend a *hyper-blend*. If we want to emphasize that what is being blended are a common mental frame and a mental space that has exactly the kind of stuff to which the frame is built to apply, we call it a *simplex* web. Consider the statement "Paul is the father of Sally." Obviously, the kinship frame is built to apply to people. In the blend, Paul is blended with father and Sally with daughter. If we want to emphasize that the input mental spaces to the blend all share a mental frame, or more generally, share the same organizing structure, we call it a *mirror* web. The name comes from the loose idea that the input spaces all *mirror* each other in their main organization. For example, the Buddhist Monk blending web is a mirror web: Both input mental spaces have a monk traveling along a particular mountain path from dawn to dusk, from one end to the other. When we want to emphasize that the analogy and disanalogy relations across the input mental spaces are blended to *change* for a *unique* element in the blend, we call it a *change* web.

Some names for blending webs are more specific. If we want to emphasize that agents who do not interact in the input mental spaces are blended to interact in the blend, we call it a *fictive interaction* web.[12] So, actually, the Buddhist Monk blend is also a fictive interaction web, because the two separate monks interact in the blend by meeting. This is not much of an interaction. An example of a fuller fictive interaction web would be the web in which the woman has a conversation with her younger self. A blending web that creates something in the blend that *repeats* is called a *cycle* web. When two input mental spaces have strong conflicts in their organizing structure but one of them controls the organization of the blend, we have used the name *single-scope* web. This comes from the loose notion that in such a web, one is "looking" mentally mainly through one of the input mental spaces. That input mental space is a lens on the organizing structure of the blend. But *single-scope* webs very quickly and easily become what I have been calling *advanced* blending webs, in which both of the organizing structures of the input mental spaces contribute to the organization of the blend, and the blend has new stuff of its own. *Advanced* blending webs have also been called *double-scope* or *vortex* webs.

Below all this, there are particular general blending patterns that have achieved strong status in one culture or another. For example, Cristóbal Pagán Cánovas has shown, in "The Genesis of the Arrows of Love: Diachronic Conceptual Integration in Greek Mythology," an article notable for its sensitivity to the role of historical context, how general blending templates underlie a new idea in Greek mythology.[13] He writes, "No symbol from ancient Greek culture seems to have been more successful than the arrows of love." There is a very common general blending pattern, the *Event-Action* blending pattern, in which we blend an event with an action—the action being one that would have led to the event. The result is that something from the input mental space for the event becomes, in the blend, an actor performing an action that leads to the event. We say, "Time is the best doctor." *Time* is causally related to the event of healing. In the blend, Time becomes an actor, a person, a doctor, who performs an action that is causally related to the event of healing. This *Event-Action* blending pattern is at work in Death the Grim Reaper. Death, the general cause of a category of events, becomes an actor, a person, a reaper. Pagán Cánovas explains that the Eros the Archer blend, in which Eros shoots someone with an arrow to cause love, is another example of this Grim Reaper pattern. He calls this general blending pattern *Abstract Cause Personification*. He finds another general blending pattern in classical antiquity—the *Erotic Emission* blending pattern. He locates another, specific blending web: Apollo the Archer, or, as he quips, "Death the Grim Archer." His analysis shows how the general blending templates *Abstract Cause Personification* and *Erotic Emission,* the Greek archaic idea of love as a punishment, and the idea of Apollo the Archer all blend to create the arrows of love. He writes: "A process of conceptual integration, taking place probably through several centuries of Greek culture, shaped and refined the religious symbol.... This magnificent blend...achieves human scale by compressing the multiple causes, effects, and participants of the erotic experience into a clear story of divine emission."[14]

Many such patterns have been located and analyzed, but it is important to remember that they overlap and can be used simultaneously and that blends constantly arise that do not fit into any of these particular boxes. Blending is an operation with principles and constraints, and it creates a great variety of blending webs. In the next chapter, we will look closely at *cycle* webs, which show an astonishing variety even as they derive from common principles of blending.

A Muse of Fire

Since antiquity, it has been recognized that the human body and brain are small, local, and limited. So is working memory, for no matter how capacious our working memory, human thought outstrips it very quickly, requiring us to find some way to transform what we want to think about into something that can be managed within the limits of working memory.

It has also long been recognized that one of the great open scientific questions—perhaps the greatest—is how people are able to transcend the limits of the body and the brain to achieve immense conceptual sweep, to attain to a scope of thought so expansive that many observers have taken it as evidence of our connection to divinity. Philo of Alexandria (c. 20 BCE–40 CE) wrote,

> How, then, is it natural that the human intellect, being as scanty as it is, and enclosed in no very ample space, in some membrane, or in the heart (truly very narrow bounds), should be able to embrace the vastness of the heaven and of the world, great as it is, if there were not in it some portion of a divine and happy soul, which cannot be separated from it? For nothing which belongs to the divinity can be cut off from it so as to be separated from it, but it is only extended. On which account the being which has had imparted to it a share of the perfection which is in the universe, when it arrives at a proper comprehension of the world, is extended in width simultaneously with the boundaries of the universe, and is incapable of being broken or divided; for its power is ductile and capable of extension.[15]

Like many others, Philo of Alexandria recognized the daunting scientific problem: A local human brain—which is what he means by "membrane"— in a local human body in a local human place manages to think with vast scope. Human thought runs over times, places, causes, agents, and every other sort of distributed meaning. Philo, again like many others, offers an explanation: Human beings are partly divine, having been touched by divinity. They retain something of this divinity. Since divinity spans everything, we accordingly have a scope of thought that would otherwise lie beyond us. Plato proposed something a little different: The human soul lived and thought under supernatural conditions before birth. What we are doing when we think and learn with such vast scope is just remembering what we knew before birth. We remember, by gists and piths, some of the sweeping knowledge we had before being born.

Another range of proposals has it that this sweeping knowledge is given to us by awesome messengers—muses, oracles, ravens who circle the world, aliens, ancient astronauts—all of which, of course, are products of blending.

In our scientific age, we have moved away from supernatural and divine explanations of the sort Philo offers. We are the originators of our vast and new ideas, and blending is the tool we mostly use.

9

Recurring Ideas

To see a World in a Grain of Sand,
And a Heaven in a Wild Flower,
Hold Infinity in the palm of your hand,
And Eternity in an hour.

WILLIAM BLAKE, "Auguries of Innocence"

What is a number, that a man may know it, and a man,
that he may know a number?

WARREN MCCULLOCH, *General Semantics
Bulletin* Nos. 26 and 27 (1961)

As we have already seen, one fine way to manage a recalcitrant mental web is to turn it into a *cycle* in the blend. The web has many different input mental spaces, but with our capacity for blending, we can reduce them all to one simple thing: a small, repeating cycle. We can then organize, understand, grasp, and work on the vast mental web by seeing it through the lens of the blend. We use this general technique constantly to create new ideas, including some of the ideas that strike us as most true of our world.

Cycles in Time

Blending a vast mental web to a tight, recurring cycle in the blend gives us our most common way of conceiving of *time*. Consider an expression like, "In a leap year, we add a day to February." It seems perfectly normal and uncreative.

How else could one think of it? Every 4 years, we must add 1 day to the year. Where is the new idea?

But we have that reaction because we are terrible at seeing into the workings of our own minds. What is a year? What is February? There is no *February* out there in the world and there is no single *year* out there in the world, either, even though it seems that way to us once we have learned the right cycle webs.

In the first chapter, I noted that, in our experience, there is actually just one day and then another day and then another day and then another day and then another day and then another day and then another day, in an endless sequence. And the days are all quite different. Again, once we have the cycle web, it might not seem as if there is just a sequence of days as opposed to a recurring structure of time and experience, but if we woke up today and it was exactly the same as yesterday because it was in fact the same day, we would wonder if we had lost our minds. And then, of course, it wouldn't be the same day, because we did not wonder yesterday if we had lost our minds. Day after day after day indefinitely, with all those differences between days, is too much to comprehend, too much to fit inside working memory, too much to carry around and manage. It is not portable.

Consider one day and another day and another day and another day and … How long can you go on and hold it all? The task overwhelms the mind. So we blend these different days into a conception of a cyclic day. We do this by using a general cycle template (figure 21).

There are analogies and disanalogies across different days in our experience. The analogies are compressed to one thing in the blend: *the day*. The disanalogies are compressed to change for that thing: The day *starts over* every dawn and *repeats*.

The number of parts in the cycle in the blend can be increased without creating too much problem for the mental web we are trying to understand, up to the point where the cycle in the blend itself becomes mentally unwieldy (figure 22).

Our flexibility for dealing with the vast mental web depends upon how much flexibility we can tolerate in the blend itself. At what point do we cough? How flexible are these cycles? What kind of structure can they have that remains congenial to the human mind? When does the complexity of the cycle itself become too much for us? What kind of structure for the cycle works well for human thought?

For thinking about time, we can build parts to the cycle: dawn, morning, noon, afternoon, dusk, night. We could even build more parts, but building more parts can create difficulties.

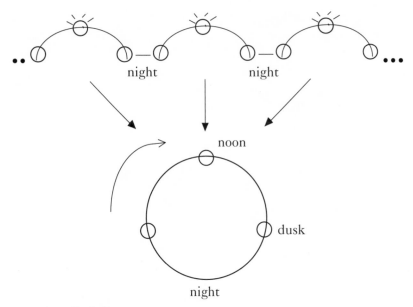

night   night

noon

dusk

night

FIGURE 21 Cyclic Day

Once we have this *cyclic day* web, we can speak directly about the blend, relying on people to make inferences about the web from what we say about the blend. We say, "Soon it will be morning *again*" and rely on people to understand that we do not mean that the specific morning that we just lived through is going to take place identically *again*. We do not think we will go backward in time to it, or that it will come forward in time for us to live through. We can say, "This park closes at *dusk*" and rely on people to know that each specific day contains a specific and distinct period that is analogous to but not exactly the same as other periods in other days, and that during that specific and distinct period, on each day, the park is closed to visitors.

Using the same general template to create a cycle in the blend, we can create a concept of the *cyclic year*, and exploit the same kind of flexibility to create a *cyclic year* that has a cycle with a linear order of parts that repeats. The parts in this case are not dawn, morning, noon, afternoon, dusk, and night, but instead fall, winter, spring, summer (figure 23).

Once we have this cyclic year web, we can speak directly about the blend, relying on people to make inferences about the web from what we say about the blend. We say, "Soon it will be spring *again*" and rely on people to understand that we do not mean that the specific spring that we just lived through is going to take place identically *again*. We do not think that we will go

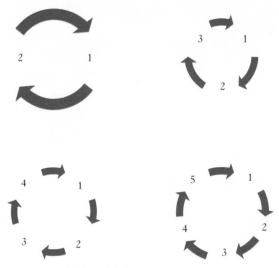

FIGURE 22 Cycles with Parts

backward in time to it, or that it will come forward in time for us to live through. We can say, "This park is closed during *winter*" and rely on people to know that each specific year contains a specific and distinct period that is roughly analogous to but not exactly the same as other periods in other years, and that during that specific and distinct period, in each year, the park is closed.

In fact, there exists a different cycle web for the year, one that has quite different uses. In this cycle web, the *repeating* subsequence in the blend is January, February, March, April, May, June, July, August, September, October,

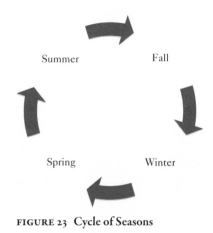

FIGURE 23 Cycle of Seasons

November, December. We work very hard to teach children this sequence, which places high demands on them. It has 12 parts. We practice and memorize structures to help us learn this sequence of 12 terms, so that long-term memory can help out.

It took a very, very, very long time historically to achieve this blending web and its internal structure of months. It did not happen by accident but instead required many ingenious people applying themselves over centuries. It is so difficult for children to learn this web that we establish schools to teach them devices for remembering how to structure this nifty blend. Such mnemonic devices include the rhyming poem "Thirty days hath September," which I at least can never remember, and the trick of placing our fists next to each other in front of our eyes, with the thumbs hidden away so we do not see their knuckles; then we see a line of knuckles and troughs, where the knuckle of the index finger on the left hand is next to the knuckle of the index finger on the right hand, with no trough between them. We then blend the order of knuckles (K) and troughs (T) with the order of months. We memorize that the knuckles correspond to the months with 31 days, and the troughs correspond to months with 30 days, except for February, which one must always remember as an outlier, with 28 days, except every fourth year, when it has 29 days. Here is a diagram of the sequence of months (figure 24).

This infinite sequence of months is compressed to the cyclic year, where now the single entity in the blend is a sequence of 12 parts, with a linear order, which *repeats*. This cyclic year corresponds to each of the infinitely many inputs (figure 25).

We can speak directly about this cyclic year blend, where the cyclic year has internal structure in the form of a sequence of 12 months, and we can rely on people to make inferences about the mental web, inferences deriving from what we said not about the mental web but instead about the blend that serves it. We say, "Soon it will be January *again*" and rely on people to understand

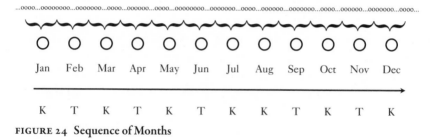

FIGURE 24 Sequence of Months

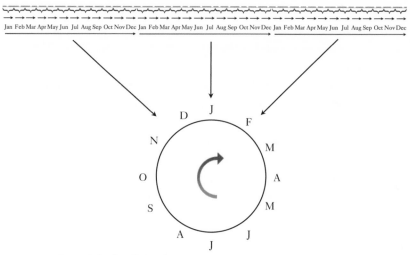

FIGURE 25 Annual Cycle of Months

that we do not mean that the specific January that we lived through some while ago is going to take place identically *again*. We do not think that we will go backward in time to it, or that it will come forward in time for us to live through. We can say, "This park opens in *May*" and rely on people to know that each specific year contains a specific and distinct period that is analogous to but not exactly the same as other periods in other years, and during that specific and distinct period, in each year, the park opens.

Routine

Actually, days, weeks, months, and years do not repeat, except in the blend. Life is not like the movie *Groundhog Day*, in which one particular day really does repeat—and even in that movie, the actions of the main character and the consequences of those actions do not repeat. The only thing that repeats is the identical state of the world every morning when his alarm clock goes off, at the same time. Also, everyone in the story except the main character has the same idea of what was happening 24 hours ago, and it does not match the main character's experience at all. It has never in our experience happened that on a January first, we awoke to see everything exactly as it was on the previous January first. For one thing, we are older. Every year is different. Every day is different. No day is the same day. No minute is even the same minute.

But often we project more to the cyclic day than just smaller temporal intervals such as mid-day and night. Often we project more to the cyclic year than just smaller temporal events like summer and winter. We have routines and habits, typical behavior, typical weather, typical holidays. Some of these typical events may have been attached to the cyclic year. Some of them may carry such an obligation of performance in a particular culture as to seem fixed—like Christmas or New Year's resolutions or the weekly Sabbath or the sound of the bells from the clock tower at noon.

Typical or habitual events can be installed with more or less connection to a cyclic time period. Someone can say that he did not have *his morning coffee*, or that he did not hear *the evening bells*. What we have in the input mental spaces to such a blend are just separate events—he drinks coffee this day, he drinks coffee the next day, he drinks coffee the day after that, maybe this day he doesn't drink coffee, and so on. The analogies connecting these events are packed into a single entity in the blend—*morning coffee*. So it is still there conceptually even if he does not have coffee on a particular day, but in that case, it is marked as an absence, a mismatch between the particular day and the habitual structures in a cyclic day. He says, "I missed my morning coffee." In this way, there is flexibility not only day-to-day, but also person-to-person. One person's cyclic day may include morning coffee, another's morning tea, another's morning juice.

Other animals may be conditioned to expectation at a certain time of the day, or may have instincts for such expectation. But we can do it at great scale: We can have an expectation for our fiftieth birthday; we can have an expectation for the gift we will give our first grandchild. The level of conceptual creativity and mental force required to manufacture some of the typical structure we find in cyclic blends is astounding. Consider that there is only one day on which a person is born, but that day is projected from the year in which one is born into the cyclic year, so that now in *every* year, one has a "birthday." No other mammal has the slightest idea of a recurring birthday, or could have such an idea. We live day after day after day, but every now and then, one of these days is marked as a special thing—our birthday. It is strange that on one day a person counts as "3," and the next day counts as "4"; that on one day one cannot legally consume alcohol because one is 20 (or 17 or whatever), but on the next day one can because one is, for example, 21. It is not even the case that everyone who turns a certain age has lived the same number of days. A child who is born

February 27 in a leap year turns 1 year old 366 days later, but a child born March 1 of that year turns 1 year old 365 days later. The same phenomenon occurs in the cyclic week. *Friday* seems so different from *Monday* not because of any natural meteorological or temporal conditions but because we have created the cyclic week mentally and freighted it with habitual and typical cultural and institutional events, and we have transformed our social world to follow those expectations.

These cycle webs make it possible for us to construct meanings in our lives and hold onto them by turning mere indefinite iteration into compressed and manageable blended elements that organize our existence.

Rough Cuts

Blending blends blends, too. That is to say, some of the input mental spaces to a blend may already be blends. As always, only some of the meaning from the input ideas is projected to the blend: compression is selective. And new stuff can arise in the blend that is not in any of the inputs. Here is an example.

One of our notions of a cyclic day has qualitative parts: dawn, morning, noon, afternoon, dusk, evening, night. These parts comprise the cycle. They are sequential, without gaps, but they do not have, or need to have, exact sizes. Between them, there are some gradual transitions. Are we in early afternoon or are we in mid-afternoon? Is it precisely noon right now or not? Two speakers do not need to agree on the answer in order to get along. For example, they might only agree that they are in the afternoon, that noon happened before, that evening is cycling toward them, that there is a transition through afternoon toward evening, and so on. That is quite enough.

We have another idea of the cyclic day in which there are parts with more exact and determined sizes: hours, or minutes, or other measured units of time. These measured parts comprise the entire cycle. They have much sharper transitions.

We can blend these two cyclic blends for the day to produce a hyper-blend that contains both kinds of parts: qualitative periods and measured units of time. In this blend of blends, the qualitative periods correspond roughly to the measured units of time, but we keep the gradient transitions between the qualitative periods. Afternoon is roughly the period from 12 p.m. to 5 p.m., but only roughly, and we do not feel that we need a sharper idea than that.

Similarly, we have an idea of the cyclic year with seasons—fall, winter, spring, summer—and an idea of the cyclic year with measured units of time—January, February, March, . . . We can blend these two blends, and the new blend has seasons that correspond roughly to periods of measured time. In this cyclic blend, we establish habitual or typical structure: "Winter" is "mostly" the period from December through February. Just as one can fail to have one's *morning coffee*, so now, in the blend, we can conceive of the situation in which "winter came early this year." This means that there is a habitual period for winter that corresponds to particular measured units of time in the cyclic year, but this year the transition to winter corresponded, atypically, to a period before its habitual onset. As winter approaches, we can say that nighttime *lengthens*. Here again, we see the familiar general blending pattern we use to pack analogies across many input mental spaces to a single thing in the blend—in this case, *night*—and to pack disanalogies across those many input mental spaces to change for the single thing in the blend: Night *lengthens*. Again, of course, in the individual inputs, there is no lengthening. It is only in the blend that the new idea of lengthening is available.

Things Fall Apart

A different and aggressive way to adjust the blend is to change the internal structure of the cycle itself. Then, although we still want to say that the blend is cyclic, we would not say that it is periodic, or more simply, we would not say that it has a fixed internal structure that repeats. The more you mess with a cycle, the harder it becomes to grasp it mentally and the less people are able to hold it all in mind. In those cases, we tend to invent external memory devices as props, and in some cases, we become completely dependent on those props.

Consider a leap year. In the blend for the cyclic year, but of course not in the input mental spaces in the mental web, we have this one thing—*the year*—consisting of monthly segments, and we have a *cycle of repetition*. It turns out that compressing time into cyclic years accurately requires some complexity and mental force. The problem is to make the cyclic year "start again" with more or less the same kinds of conditions every time. If we kept our years at exactly 365 days, then after about 360 years, fall would replace summer. That's blend-speak: Of course, there would be no "replacement" at all in the inputs. Instead, to cash this out into an explanation, we need to say that after about 360 years, during the part of the 12-month calendar that we associate with summer conditions, we would experience fall conditions. Winter would come very early indeed (in the blend), and earlier and earlier all the time.

To force all this detail into one compact cyclic year, we must assign to every fourth year in the sequence not 365 days but rather 366. In the blend, we have an easier way than this to think about it and keep track of it. In the blend, we have a single thing—the year. We compress the disanalogies between different years to a *change* for that single thing. We say we "add a day to February." This is quite congenial to human thinking. We have coffee in front of us, and we add milk. It is a little changed. Now, in the blend, the year is like coffee. Instead of adding milk, we add a day. No problem. Of course, it would actually be supernatural to add a day to the year. Some god would have to go to an alternative universe and steal a day and haul it back into our universe.

There is yet another amazing operation of blending required in thinking that "we add a day to February." Think of the range of agency and institutions around the world that it takes to bring about the remarkable social event of our calling a certain day not March 1, as we are conditioned to do, but instead February 29—a day that otherwise does not exist in the year. All these agents and institutions must be coordinated to establish that new mapping in the web and to hold it temporarily for the rest of the year. That agency is vast and distributed all around the globe, through people, institutions, objects, machines, and communications channels. But in the blend, all of that agency has been packed to a little congenial scene in which there is one multiplex agent—*we*. That single agent unitarily performs a single action: We add something to something else. The scope of human thought is vast, and we see here an example of how we do it. We can manage a very complicated mental web, stretching across time, space, causation, and agency, by carrying around only the compressed version, in which the agent does the adding. We carry this compressed version with us, and expand it to connect with the situation whenever we need to think about it. The result is a mental web that arches over time, space, causation, and agency.

Changes on the inside of the cycle in the blend present a challenge: If the cycle itself differs from here to there, how do we remember or infer the difference? How do we manage a mental web that has this kind of irregularity? When I was a child, we memorized arcane systems for remembering which years were leap years. We learned, for example, that it is not the case that every fourth year is a leap year. Exceptions are years that end in 00, except for those that are exact multiples of 400. But almost no one except someone born on February 29 ever remembered which year was a leap year or knew when the next leap year would "come," so we relied on communities of calculating experts to make calendars. We just looked at the calendar. These days, we just look at our electronic devices, trusting that some anonymous agents out there programmed the computers to do it right, where "right" includes not only astrophysical equations but also social and political negotiations. As I write, the experts are gathering in Geneva to debate the value of adding "leap seconds," a practice that is 40 years old. The rotation of the earth is slowed very slightly by gravitation, so every now and then, namely, 24 times in the last 40 years, a "leap second" has been added in Coordinated Universal Time to the time calculated on the basis of atomic clocks. When the authorities add a second, the world's computers must be adjusted manually, which costs time and money and conduces to error. Imagine the United States and France locked in debate with Britain, Canada, and China over the exact cycle.

Poetic Cycles

One of the most amazing feats of compression for us all occurs when an illiterate poet, bard, or singer—in Greek, Old English, or Serbo-Croatian—begins to recite a poem that goes on for thousands and thousands of lines, pretty much telling all of relevant history. In these cases, we typically see a use of a recurring idea that we do not usually see in everyday speech. At the larger level of discourse, there may be repetition: I speak, and then you take the floor, and you speak, and then I take the floor, and I speak, and then you take the floor... This can be compressed to a repeating cycle of 2 parts (I speak, you speak) or if you like 4 parts (I speak, you take the floor, you speak, I take the floor...). But how will the poet organize this massive performance and organize our attention to it?

One answer, which has been inherited by written poems, is to create a recurring structure at the very level of utterance. The *Iliad* and the *Odyssey*, for example, are written in dactylic hexameters. That means that each line has 6 feet, where each foot is a dactyl. "Dactyl" comes from the Greek word for your finger. If you hold out your finger, you see that the length from the first knuckle to the second is long, and the distance from the second to the third is short, and the distance from the third to your fingertip is short. So a dactyl has a long syllable followed by a short syllable followed by a short syllable: long-short-short. But now, for the most part, 2 short syllables can be replaced by 1 long one. So a dactyl's short-short can be replaced by a long, and the result is a foot that is long-long, called a spondee. In dactylic hexameter, the fifth foot is usually a dactyl, and the last foot is nearly always a spondee.

The result is that as the poet recites, he repeats every 6 feet! He doesn't repeat the words, but he repeats the meter. Just as with the cyclic day, or the cyclic year, there are some slight changes that may be made here and there. One line might have a dactyl for its third foot, and another might have a spondee. But that's about it. There are also some interesting internal structures in the cycle, governing where one places a break (a "caesura"), and also where one must not place a break (a "bridge"). The meter and its variations organize the poet's recital and our attention to it. Here are the first lines of the *Iliad*:

> μῆ-νι-ν ἄ-ει-δε θε-ὰ Πη-λη-ϊ-ά-δεω Α-χι-λῆ-ος
> οὐ-λο-μέ-νη-ν, ἥ μυ-ρί᾽ Α-χαι-οῖ-ς ἄλ-γε᾽ ἔ-θη-κε,
> πολ-λὰς δ᾽ ἰφ-θίμ-ους ψυ-χὰς Α-ϊ-δι π-ρο-ϊ-αψ-εν.

The first line has dactyl-dactyl-spondee-dactyl-dactyl-spondee (˘˘|˘˘|‾‾|˘˘|˘˘|‾‾). The second has dactyl-spondee-dactyl-spondee-dactyl-spondee (˘˘|‾‾|˘˘|‾‾|˘˘|‾‾). The third has spondee-spondee-spondee-dactyl-dactyl-spondee (‾‾|‾‾|‾‾|˘˘|˘˘|‾‾). So the bard has created a tight, repeating metrical structure with a little flexibility inside each repetition. The structure of the repeating dactylic hexameters was inherited in written texts such as Vergil's *Aeneid*:

> Arma vi | rumque ca | no, Troi | ae qui | primus ab | oris.
> Italiam, fato profugus, Laviniaque venit.
> litora, multum ille et terris iactatus et alto
> vi superum saevae memorem Iunonis ob iram;

The first line, for example, has dactyl-dactyl-spondee-spondee-dactyl-spondee.

A different kind of structure, but still a tight repeating structure for each line, is used in the Old English epic poem *Beowulf*, where each line consists of 2 parts held together by alliteration with a caesura in the middle. Here are the first lines, with an interlinear crib:

> Hwæt! Wé Gárdena   in géardagum
> Listen! We—of the Spear-Danes   in the days of yore,

þéodcyninga	þrym gefrúnon·
of those clan-kings—	heard of their glory.
hú ðá æþelingas	ellen fremedon.
how those nobles	performed courageous deeds.
Oft Scyld Scéfing	sceaþena þréatum
Often Scyld, Scef's son,	from enemy hosts
monegum maégþum	meodosetla oftéah
from many peoples	seized mead-benches;
egsode Eorle	syððan aérest wearð
and terrorised the fearsome Heruli	after first he was
féasceaft funden	hé þæs frófre gebád·
found helpless and destitute,	he then knew recompense for that:-
wéox under wolcnum·	weorðmyndum þáh
he waxed under the clouds,	throve in honours,
oð þæt him aéghwylc	þára ymbsittendra
until to him each	of the bordering tribes
ofer hronráde	hýran scolde
beyond the whale-road	had to submit,
gomban gyldan·	þæt wæs gód cyning.
and yield tribute:-	that was a good king!

In all these cases and many others, the poet has used a general blending template to create a cycle blend, but in a place we usually do not expect it, perhaps because we have been conditioned by our experience with writing. In a written text, we can glance back and forth, using the book to help us keep track of where we are and what is going on. That is not available in an oral poem that goes on for thousands of lines. The cycle web seems to have come to the mental rescue.

Cycle Blends in the Lab

Mathew D. McCubbins and I explored some of these cycle blends in the lab.[1] Which cycle sequences are easy for subjects to see? Which ones are they mentally disposed to see? We told subjects that they would be asked a set of questions about an infinite sequence, one with a rule that defined its elements. Each question about the sequence gives them a little information about the sequence, such as a subsequence. They can choose from five multiple-choice answers. For some questions, there is only one right answer. That is, subjects have enough information in the questions they have been asked about the sequence to eliminate four of the possible answers. For other questions, there is no right answer, but the answers follow different patterns, so asking these kinds of questions lets us investigate how the subject is mentally disposed to guess at the sequence. These questions are not memory tests: Subjects have all the time they want, see the information in front of them, and are provided with pencil and paper. Conducting a memory test with infinite sequences would be ridiculous, because it is impossible to hold such sequences explicitly in mind.

Consider a sequence that has period = 1, namely −2, −2, −2 . . . We tell subjects that "the following 5 questions all concern the same sequence. There is a rule that defines this sequence." One of the questions is "What is the second missing item in the following? −2, −2, −2, _, −2, _." A subsequent question is "What is the missing item in −2, −2, −2, −2, _, −2, −2, −2, −2 ?" Subjects have already seen that the fifth item is −2, so there is a right answer. But before we ask those questions, the first question we ask is actually "What is the missing item in the following? −2, −2, −2, _ ?" The multiple choice answers offered are −2, −1, 0, 1, 1. All the answers are possible. The *Online Encyclopedia of Integer Sequences* has not the slightest difficulty identifying a sequence containing any of the 5 strings produced by picking any of the 5 possible answers; for example, −2, −2, −2, 0 is a subsequence of the periodic sequence of order 4 whose period consists of the subsequence −2, −2, −2, 0. We ask a variety of such questions.

How do subjects do? For the sequence of −2 repeating, which is a sequence of period 1, 100% of subjects answer perfectly all the questions for which there is a right answer, and 100% of subjects choose −2 as the answer for all other questions, even though all the other answers are mathematically possible. The data are consistent with the hypotheses that people have a powerful grasp of infinite sequences of period 1 and that people are mentally disposed to grasp a sequence as a cycle of 1 with an unchanging interior cycle if this interpretation is not clearly wrong. People seem to find it easy to grasp an unchanging, repeating cycle of period 1. No one will be surprised to hear that every subject in our experiment correctly answered every one of the questions for which there is a right answer, and very quickly, and that for every question where there is no right answer, every subject chose to keep the pattern of a single element, −2, which repeats indefinitely.

This sequence—which we included in the battery to set a baseline—looks utterly trivial, but actually, it shows us something interesting about human cognition.

Consider that the *Online Encyclopedia of Integer Sequences* lists many sequences that fit the subsequence −2, −2, −2. Almost none of them would occur to a human being. The *Online Encyclopedia of Integer Sequences* has an enormous database of sequences, and performs intensive searches to locate a match when the user enters any subsequence. Many of the matches look wild or incomprehensible.

A computer could produce the sequence −2, −2, −2…by doing the following computation: To find the term for each n, where n = 1, 2, 3, 4, 5…, compute $0n−2$. The computer figures as follows: "I am at the first step, that is, n = 1. So what is the value at the first step? The value is $0(1)−2 = −2$. Great! Now I move my counter from the first step to the second. So now I am at n = 2. What is the value at the second step? The value is $0(2)−2 = −2$. Great! Now I move my counter…"

A person confronted with −2, −2, −2 does not compute this way. How do we know that? Perform the following exercise. Say to someone, "Here is the beginning of a sequence: −2, −2, −2, −2, −2, −2, −2, −2, −2, −2, −2, −2, −2, −2, −2, −2, −2, −2, −2, −2, −2, −2, −2, −2, −2. What's the next term?" The human being will say, "−2." Great! But if we then ask, "And what step were you at in the sequence?" the human being will not know, or will have to take a broad guess. The computer always knows what step it is at. The reason the person does not know the current place in the sequence is of course that the person is not computing by tracking steps n = 1, 2, 3…and then computing $0n−2$ to determine the value at that step. The computer is managing the sequence by calculating each step. The person, by contrast, blends the entire infinite sequence to one thing by mapping every element in the sequence to that one thing in the blend and adding the notion of repetition. The computer does not know the 9,873rd element until it computes it. The human being grasps the entire sequence in the blend and knows instantly, without computation, what the 9,873rd element is. It's −2, of course. Duh!

The person is always just *repeating* the previous term, and knows that the previous term must be −2, and so is always giving the same answer: −2. The person understands that we are facing an infinite sequence and that no infinite sequence can be stated explicitly, as a list, in working memory. But the human being conceives of the sequence as a *cycle* web: Just keep repeating −2. Blend all the input steps together as a single entity, −2, and just keep repeating the blend. Second verse, same as the first. Start with −2, repeat ad infinitum.

In this cycle web, we blend all the terms of the infinite sequence into *one repeating term* in the blend. All the potential analogies, across all the infinitely many terms of the sequence, are compressed to a single entity in the blend: -2. And all the potential disanalogies (we are at step n, but now we are at step $n + 1$, but now we are at step $n + 2 \ldots$) are compressed to *change* for that entity: The entity *repeats*. Mathematicians call such a sequence "periodic." We would say that this is an infinite periodic sequence of period 1.

In the inputs for this cycle web, it is not true that there is only one term. On the contrary, there is a countable infinity of terms. And it is not true in the inputs that the term repeats itself in any dynamic sense. The -2 at step n is quite a different entity from the -2 at step $n-1$, even though they have the same value.

We create in the blend both the *single entity* and the *repetition* in order to grasp the infinite sequence. The single entity and the repetition are new stuff in the blend; they are not in the infinite sequence itself. When we create this blend with its new stuff, it becomes so easy for our working memory to hold onto the web, and to give all the right answers, that the performance seems trivial. It seems like a mindless exercise to us, but it is highly inventive in its creation of a cycle web, and provides us with great innovative skill.

In conceiving of sequences by creating cycle webs, we can use other inputs to the blend. One of the most basic, portable, congenial, embodied human concepts is the feeling of a rhythm that repeats. Long before the fetus has detailed experience of the visual field, or experience—or even perception—of moving along a path toward a goal, especially self-locomotion along a path, it has rich experience of *temporal* rhythms. Tapping out a beat—1, 2, 3, 1, 2, 3, 1, 2, 3, 1, 2, 3, 1, 2, 3, 1, 2, 3 ...—is universally easy for all normal human beings. This kind of temporal cycle of repetition can consist of a single repeated unit: 1 (pause) 1 (pause) 1 (pause) 1 (pause) 1 (pause) ... The fetus has experience of its own heartbeat, of mother's heartbeat, of mother's gait in walking, of the rhythm of mother's breathing, and of the muffled sounds of family members' speaking. These days, the fetus has experience of music with cyclic rhythms. And all this experience of temporal rhythmic cycles is richly reinforced after birth, and long before the infant can move itself along a spatial path.

Our counting systems typically depend upon a cycle web: They have a *base*. The base is the cycle that repeats. We tap out 10 and then repeat and repeat and repeat, so as to have cycles of 10. Our words and numerals mark out both the cycle and which repetition we are on. Twenty-seven is the point at which we have gone through the full cycle of 10 twice and then launched upon it a third time but stopped at 7; 7 is the first time we come to 7; 17 is the second time we come to 7; 27 is the third time we come to 7.

It is intriguing that 0 and the negative numbers came up so very late in the historical development of the concept of numbers. Spatially, it is easy to think of a container with nothing in it and to use this idea as a way to conceive of the number 0—first there is the empty container, then we put one thing in it, then another, then another. It is also easy to have a starting point on a path and to take this as a 0 point—first we are at the start, and then take one step, and then another—and accordingly it is easy to think of walking backward from 0—first we take one step back (−1), then two steps back (−2), etc. Why did it take so very long to conceive of these numbers by constructing blending webs using spatial experience? One possibility might be the absence of rhythmic grounding. Although it is easy to tap out positive integers in cycles, how would we tap out 0? How would we tap out −3?

Another input mental space available for cycle webs is our idea of an object that is moving along a circular path in space: We can blend together each of the individual full trips around the circle to have a *spatial* cycle in the blend. When we use *temporal cycle* or *circular motion along a path* as an input to the blend, or both as inputs to the blend, then the mental projection from our idea of either one to the blend is selective and creative. Often, only some elements of the temporal activity of rhythmic beating or only certain elements of the spatial activity of moving along a circular path end up in the blend. In temporal activity, it may be that all moments in time count as distinct temporal moments, but in the blend, we can think of only the beat as counting, and distinguish only the temporal moments of the beats. For example, in 1 (pause) 1 (pause) 1 (pause) 1 (pause) 1 (pause)…, only the moment of the beat counts for the sequence 1, 1, 1, 1, 1, in the blend. The pauses do not count as elements of the sequence. Just so, on the circular path, all the spatial points may have the same weight: They are just points. But in a cycle web for a single repeating term, often the only position that counts on the path is the place from which we *start* and to which we *return* in order to *start again*. Here is a diagram (figure 26).

If we base the blend for such a cycle web on a rhythmic beat, then we have one beat that we perform *again* and even *again and again*. If we base the blend on moving along a circular path, then we come back to the *same spot* and do so *again* and even *again and again*. Obviously, in the infinite sequence itself—more specifically, in the inputs to the blend—there is no unique beat we perform or spot to which we return. In the infinite sequence itself, we always have lots of beats and lots of spots. In the infinite sequence itself, we

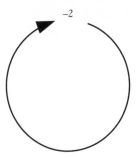

FIGURE 26   Cycle of One Repeating Element

always move to a *different* location in the order, and always to a *new* term, even if the value of that term is the same as the value of a prior term. But in the blend, we return to a unique beat, a unique term. The cycle is not technically an abstraction: It does not arise by taking just something that everything in the category has. Instead, the blend has *repetition*.

One of the most pressing open questions in cognitive science is how our extended conceptions of time, space, and motion arise developmentally. The ability to speak with anything like a rich vocabulary comes up very late in human life: first words around a year, a vocabulary explosion around a year and a half. If we add to that year and a half the 40 weeks of gestation, then we have a span of 2¼ years between conception and the kind of language use that shows us rich control of words. For someone who wants to investigate the early development of concepts,[2] 2¼ years is an eternity. By 2¼ years after conception, the infant has already had vast experience of space and motion. Researchers have noticed for many centuries that human languages often make use of expressions having to do with space in order to construct a vocabulary for talking about time, but it is not clear what inferences we can draw from those late linguistic behaviors about the early formation of the concepts themselves. As many have noticed, the concept of motion along a path, seemingly so spatial, already must include temporality if it involves any notion of pace or speed, so it may be circular to say that ideas of time originate from ideas of motion in space. By the time we can test infants for the formation of concepts, they have already exploited their remarkable ability for blending to create compressed, congenial, masterful ideas. How to peek into the early stages of the formation of such concepts in human beings presents one of cognitive science's toughest methodological challenges.

What's Going on Inside?

Consider another sequence: Blue, Red, Green, Blue, Red, Green, Blue, Red…People are very good at answering questions about this sequence, but not perfect.[3] They are also very strongly disposed mentally to see the sequence as a cycle with period 3, but not all subjects show that mental disposition for all the questions we ask. The unique entity in the cyclic blend for this sequence is an ordered finite set: Blue, Red, Green. It is one thing, but it has ordered parts.

How do our subjects do? 94% of them see a cycle of period 3 in response to this question: "What is the missing item in the following? Blue, Red, Green, __ " The 5 multiple-choice answers from which they can choose are Green, Brown, Orange, Red, and Blue. 94% of them see a cycle of period 3 in response to this question: "Consider the following sequence: Green, Blue, Red, Green, Blue, Red, Green. The first item in the sequence is Green. What is the twelfth item in the sequence?" The 5 multiple-choice answers from which they can choose are Yellow, Green, Red, White, and Blue. 87% of the subjects see a cycle of period 3 in response to this question: "What is the second missing item in the following? Blue, Red, Green, __, Red, __ " The 5 multiple-choice answers from which they can choose are Green, Orange, Red, Blue, and Black. 100% of them see a cycle of period 3 in response to this question: "Consider the following sequence: Blue, Red, Green, __, Red, __. The first item in the sequence is Blue. What is the twelfth item in the sequence?" The 5 multiple-choice answers from which they can choose are Yellow, Green, Orange, Red, and Blue.

Again, these data are consistent with the hypothesis that subjects have a good grasp of infinite sequences when they can blend the terms of the sequence to create a *cycle* with a short period. In this case, the period is 3. These data are also consistent with the hypothesis that subjects grasp such a sequence as a cycle of the shortest unchanging period they can.

In the blend, this one thing—an ordered set of 3 elements—undergoes dynamic change: It *repeats*, just as −2 repeated in the blend for −2, −2, −2, −2, −2…, but now the thing that repeats has internal parts with an internal order, which we preserve in the blend. Now we can think of the sequence as a sequence of ordered subsequences, all identical. All the ordered subsequences are projected to *one* single ordered finite sequence in the blend. In the blend, this single ordered finite sequence *repeats*. Such a cycle web is so common for conceiving of sequences and processes that many software packages include a utility for "drawing" such cycles, like figure 27.

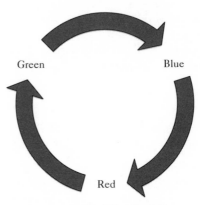

FIGURE 27 Cycle of Blue-Red-Green

Underlying all these specific cycle sequences is a general blending template that we use again and again to manage all kinds of infinity, or rather, to manage webs so conceptually extended as to lie beyond the powers of working memory.

We see that there is flexibility in cycle webs: They can have different kinds of repeating elements. The thing that repeats can have internal structure, which is preserved as we repeat the entity again and again. In the case of Blue, Red, Green…, the repeating element in the blend has 3 parts.

Different Spokes

There are different ways to construe a scene. So it is with cycles. If we tap out a rhythm with our foot, repeatedly, that is a participant viewpoint on the cycle. If we feel the repeating rhythm of percussion in the pressure on our skin and eardrums, that is a witness viewpoint, but when it comes to rhythm, witnessing and participating are not so easily separated. If we see a dog chasing its tail, or a marble rolling around in a circular trough, that is an overview viewpoint. If we see a stationary object being illuminated repeatedly by a "circling" spotlight, that is also an overview viewpoint, but with a sequence of views and expectations somewhat different from our overview viewpoint when watching the dog or marble. If we walk around the outside of a house, that is a participant viewpoint. If we walk around the outside of a house backward, that is also a participant viewpoint, but with a different sequence of views and expectations. If we imagine sitting on a front porch while a child is being chased round and round the outside of the house by a playful dog, that is a witness viewpoint. And so on. Across these construals, there are differences of agency, viewpoint, and focus, yet all of them are structured by the same general idea of temporal repetition or relative motion between an object and a circular path.

Any of these alternatives can be used as an input for a cyclic blending web. We can use a participant viewpoint to think that we are running through the rhythm of the seasons, that summer is coming around again, or that we are coming up on summer again. We can use an overview viewpoint as the basis for inventing a circular clock with hands: At noon, we see in the world only the conditions we associate with noon, but on the clock we see both noon and 6 o'clock and everything else, and we know that although the cycle is currently at noon, it will advance to 6. So the clock prompts us to take an overview viewpoint. Although it is true that we have no experience of actual time "running backward," it is easy to imagine time running backward in a blend by using our idea of walking backward, or, alternatively, by using our idea of staying stationary while a path moves from behind us to in front of us as we stay stationary above the path.

We can use different construals in our cyclic webs for infinite sequences. In the overview viewpoint, we can say that "the sequence" is "cycling" through Red again. In the participant viewpoint, we can say that "we" are coming up on Red again, or that Red is coming up again. We can even say that we should "cycle back" to check the value of the term "5 steps ago." In all these ways, mental webs that are far too large and complex to be held in mind, webs that would otherwise lie beyond our cognitive capacities, can be served by blends that are congenial to human cognition.

Inside Out

For the sequences −2, −2, −2 . . . or Blue, Red, Green, Blue, Red, Green, Blue, Red, Green . . ., we can say what comes next without remembering where we are in the infinite sequence of "repeated" finite subsequences. We know the term −2 is followed by −2, and we know the term Red is followed by Green, regardless of how many instances we have already seen of −2 or Red. But sometimes, the cycle web has additional information, helping us to know not only where we are in the finite subsequence but also where we are in the infinite sequence itself. This does not seem to be an easy task for the human mind—keeping track of where we are in the infinite sequence—and the task is made ever harder as the relationship between the cycle and the input sequences grows complicated. People who count coins sometimes say to themselves, using the auditory loop in working memory: "1, 2, 3, 4, 5, 6, 7, 8, 9, 10, 1, 2, 3, 4, 5, 6, 7, 8, 9, 20, 1, 2, 3, 4, 5, 6, 7, 8, 9, 30, 1, 2, 3, 4, 5, 6, 7, 8, 9, 40, 1, 2, 3, 4, 5, 6, 7 . . ."

People who hand out cards in games often need to provide, say, 7 cards to each of 7 people. That's a lot of cards, and it is difficult to keep all 49 of them in working memory. But the dealer can turn the large sequence into 7 identical subsequences, each of 7 steps, and build a blend in which a simple 7-step sequence repeats 7 times. The dealer can perform the distribution by starting at a fixed spot—say the person to the dealer's left—and restarting the cycle at that spot. There is a common pattern for this counting: "1, 2, 3, 4, 5, 6, 7, **2**, 2, 3, 4, 5, 6, 7, **3**, 2, 3, 4, 5, 6, 7, **4**, 2, 3, 4, 5, 6, 7, **5**, 2, 3, 4, 5, 6, 7, **6**, 2, 3, 4, 5, 6, 7, **7**, 2, 3, 4, 5, 6, 7." This is again a cycle web in which going round the cycle kicks out a piece of information telling us *where we are located in the bigger sequence of "repeated" sequences.* Not surprisingly, this oral counting frequently places its emphasis on the start of each cycle, to create a repeating rhythmic cycle. When learning, musicians often count bars so as to know where they are in, say, an eight-bar sequence that is repeated: 1231 1232 1233 1234 1235 1236 1237 1238 1231 1232...

In fact, cycle webs that produce information about which input to expand are very common. It's how we keep track of years. On January 1, right before we start the cyclic year again, we kick out a new number—*the year*, and this number is always the next integer after the number of the last year: 2012, 2013, 2014. We do something similar with our birthday: Before we restart the cyclic year at our birthday, we project out of the blend a bit of information: *our age.* Our age is just the next integer after our previous age. So if we turn 30 on our birthday, then we go through the cycle once more, and just when we are about to end the year and start again—on our birthday—we project out of the cycle a new piece of information: Now we are 31. These are all cases of keeping a tally outside of the blend of how many times the sequence in the blend has repeated, so that we can have information about how the blend is now connecting to the extensive mental web.

As the cycle in the blend of a cycle web becomes longer or stranger or the relationship of the cycle to the inputs becomes more variable, we have difficulties, and typically turn to external markers to help us keep track of what is going on. One of the advantages of the external markers is that we can look at them in a specific moment to learn "where we were" the last time we changed the marker. We do not need to remember. We just need to read the marker. In that moment of reading, we can then change the marker again, and perform that procedure again and again as needed. For example, we can cross out days in the calendar. We can make tally marks. When counting coins, when we reach 10, we can set those 10 coins apart as a small stack and then move to the next cycle of 10. The result is that we do not need to remember how many times we have cycled through counting 10 coins—the number of stacks that we see is the marker that gives us the answer.

All of the cycles we have considered to this point have a fixed internal structure of a certain sort: The cycle repeats identically every time. Technically, we say that such a cycle is a period, and that the number of steps in the cycle is the number of the period. So, −2, −2, −2… is an infinite periodic sequence of period 1, because there is only one term and it repeats. Blue, Red, Green, Blue, Red, Green, Blue, Red, Green… is an infinite periodic sequence of period 3, because the repetition has three terms: Blue, Red, Green. In these cases, it is assumed that the order of the terms in the cycle does not change. This can be specified formally: An infinite sequence is periodic of period p if there is a fixed integer p such that for every term a_i in the sequence $a_{i+p} = a_i$. So, −2, −2, −2… is an infinite periodic sequence of period 1 because every term is the same as the one before it: $a_{i+1} = a_i$. Blue, Red, Green, Blue, Red, Green, Blue, Red, Green… is an infinite periodic sequence of period 3 because every term is the same as the term 3 steps before it: $a_{i+3} = a_i$. For example, the fourth term is the same as the first; the tenth is the same as the seventh; and so on.

Actually, to be precise, the sequences we have considered have a fixed internal structure only to the extent that we have analyzed them. Consider a leap year.

Inside Job

Here is an example to indicate how hard it seems to be for us to construct cycle webs in which the inside of the cycle changes. Recall that it was fairly easy to go through the same cycle—the day, the year beginning at 1 January, the year beginning on our birthday, the counting of stacks of coins—if all we changed was our place in an integer sequence *outside* the cycle. For example, round and round and round we go, and we age from 40 to 41 to 42, but we do not change the inside of the cycle.

But now, imagine a sequence composed of finite sequences in which each finite sequence has one more step than the previous finite sequence. The first finite sequence is 1. The next is 1, 2. The next is 1, 2, 3. And so on. The infinite sequence is then 1, 1, 2, 1, 2, 3, 1, 2, 3, 4, 1, 2, 3, 4, 5, 1, 2… The structure that changes in this sequence is not some sequential information *outside* the cycle, such as something in the relational structure of the input sequences, but rather something within the cycle itself. The *Online Encyclopedia of Integer Sequences* characterizes this infinite sequence as integers 1 to k followed by integers 1 to $k + 1$ etc. (a fractal sequence). We need a name for it, so let us call it the "sequence of sequences."

People we ask in the lab to work with this sequence seem to have difficulty.[4] They often seem to keep looking for an unchanging cycle. Again, for a computer, this infinite sequence is trivially easy to grasp. We can program a computer in a minute to generate this sequence, check on questions about it, etc. Not so for the person. When we give subjects the rule and ask them to choose which item could appear in the sequence, only 48% can answer correctly.

There is a suite of questions we ask subjects, prefaced by this statement: "The following 3 questions all concern the same sequence. There is a rule that defines this sequence." The first question is, "Consider the following sequence: 17, 18, 19, 1, 2, 3, 4…The first item in the sequence is 17. What is the twelfth item in the sequence?" The second question is, "What is the missing item in 13, 14, 15, 16, __, 18, 19, 20, 1?" The third question is, "Here is the rule that defines the sequence: The infinite sequence composed of successive finite sequences each consisting of the integers from 1 to $n+1$ for $n = 0, 1, 2, 3$…Which of the following subsequences belongs to the sequence?" For this third question, subjects can choose as their answer 7,2; 5,4; 4,1; 28,14; or 3,2. Only 4,1 fits the rule. Only 48% of our subjects answer question 3 correctly.

We see a great deal of varied choice when people try to grasp the underlying sequence. Here is another suite of questions we ask, prefaced by this statement: "The following 5 questions all concern the same sequence. There is a rule that defines this sequence." (1) "What is the missing item in the following? 3, 4, 1, __." 55% pick 2. (2) "What is the second missing item in the following? 3, 4, 1, __, 3, __." 90% pick 4. (3) "Consider the following sequence: 3, 4, 1, __, 3, __. The first item in the sequence is 3. What is the twelfth item in the sequence?" 29% pick 5. (4) "What is the missing item in 4, 5, 6, 7, __, 2, 3, 4, 5 ?" 100% pick 1. (5) "Recall that all five questions in this unit concern the same sequence. Here is part of that sequence: 10, 11, 12, 1, 2, 3. What is the rule that defines the sequence?" The multiple-choice answers for question 5 are:

A. Hours struck by a clock in order

B. The infinite sequence composed of successive finite sequences each consisting of the integers from 1 to $n+1$ for $n = 0, 1, 2, 3$…

C. For whole numbers n, sum of digits n written in base 7

D. For whole numbers n, sum of digits n written in base 13

E. n^7 mod 14

Only 45% choose the sequence of sequences, (B). And here is the surprise: 29% of the subjects chose "Hours struck by a clock in order," even though they had been told that the sequence includes 3, 4, 1 and 4, 5, 6, 7, _, 2.

These subjects knew that at the end of the session they would be paid their earnings, and knew, too, that *every* time they answered correctly, their earnings grew. They were also provided with paper and pencil to record anything they wanted to record and to compute anything they wanted to compute. And they were allowed to take as long as they wanted for each answer. The pull of a cycle web repeating an invariant cycle—1, 2, 3, 4, 5, 6, 7, 8, 9, 10, 11, 12—seems to have been strong. No one chose "n^7 mod 14." Five people chose "For whole numbers n, sum of digits n written in base 7." Three people chose "For whole numbers n, sum of digits n written in base 13." To see the pattern as the sequence of sequences, one must be willing to have a cycle that *changes internally*. Even though that change is as simple as it could be—add one more step to the cycle each time you go around—fewer than half of the subjects, 45%, see it that way.

Again, this investigation is not a memory test. Subjects have all the time they want, the information is in front of them, and they are provided with pencil and paper. Neither is it a math test per se. Our subjects are undergraduates at an elite university and we know their SAT scores. The computer (the *Online Encyclopedia of Integer Sequences*) recognizes these sequences immediately and, for the questions that have no uniquely correct answer, the computer could find acceptable sequences that fit any of the multiple-choice answers. But the human subject is not the robot. These are vast, infinite sequences. None could be held in mind explicitly. Accordingly, the question is: For vast mental webs, which kinds of blends are congenial to the way people think? What makes a vast mental web manageable in limited working memory?

Here is an exercise one can do at home to assess the difficulty of changing the inside of the cycle. Pick a number and tap out that number with your foot, repeating the cycle, with an emphasis each time you come back to 1. For example, 1, 2, 3, 4, 1, 2, 3, 4, 1, 2, 3, 4, 1, 2, 3, 4... This is no problem at all for anybody, until the number you choose gets very big. You can even do it while you are having lunch. But now try changing the cycle as you tap: 1, 1, 2, 1, 2, 3, 1, 2, 3, 4... Good luck!

Blends of Blends

Once blending has created a compressed blend congenial to human thought, that blend can serve as a stabilizing input for a new blending web, to be used in compressing yet other extensive ranges of ideas. A blend resulting from the process of blending can be an input to the process of blending. Blending is recursive.

For example, the cyclic year web is useful all by itself, allowing us to handle thousands and thousands of days in a sequence of cyclic years, but what happens when the sequence of cyclic years itself becomes too hard to handle? One way to handle it is to blend stretches of many years with the cyclic day. That may sound just impossible: Many years are one thing, and a single day is another. What kind of idiot would try to blend many years with just a day? Well, one of candidate Ronald Reagan's most effective ads in the 1984 US presidential campaign began, "It's morning again in America," suggesting that since Reagan's election in 1980, the nation had entered a new phase. In Norway, the period from about 1400 CE to about 1814 CE is often referred to, even in print, even in academic books, as the "400-year night." The string of cyclic years in someone's lifetime is often blended with a day. In such a blend, we can refer to someone's "sunset years." The projection to the blend is selective. We might project to the blend only the part of the cyclic day in which night becomes morning, as in the Reagan ad. We might not project the cyclicity. For example, if Norway had a 400-year night, it is not obligatory in the blend that there will be another night at all. Catullus (poem 5) explicitly points out that a human lifetime blended with a single day has only one cycle: For regular days and nights, night ends and day begins, but *our* night is one permanent sleep.

The time interval in a cyclic blend for time need not, of course, be a year, or any of our other usual measurements, such as a day. In the United States, for example, there is a presidential campaign season every 4 years. We cycle through the campaign season itself, from its beginning to its end, and then we cycle through the rest of the 4 years to the start of the embedded presidential campaign cycle. So one part of the 4-year cycle has a part—campaign season—that is itself a cycle and that does not repeat immediately, but begins again once the 4-year cycle is completed.

When a smaller cycle is embedded as part of a bigger cycle, the bigger cycle of time within which the smaller cycle is embedded need not have a fixed duration. For example, there can be cycles of royal reign, one after another, each ending with the death of the ruler and the next beginning with the new ruler's accession to the throne. But one reign can last 2 months and another 20 years. Cycling through reign after reign organizes the sequence of time.

Cycles Within Cycles Within Cycles

December 31, 1954, December 31, 1955, December 31, 1956…All those days. They can all be compressed to a single day in the cyclic calendric year. Routines can be established at different locations in the cycle.

Establishing a routine at a location in the cycle makes possible another, embedded cycle, because that routine is typically something detailed that we repeat the next time. Consider a weeklong vacation that we take during the same week every year (e.g., the fortieth week). The vacation from work itself would be a routine, but we might in principle do something completely different every vacation. One time, we would hike in the mountains, and the next, take our office work home, and the next, volunteer in a soup kitchen, and the next, look for a new job, and so on, without any repetition of the events inside the routine "vacation."

But there can also be a detailed pattern to the routine. Consider December 31 in the calendric cycle blend. In the evening, there are celebrations, perhaps with certain kinds of fireworks, and a party, and New Year's resolutions. We repeat the cyclic year, and on this day, we repeat the New Year's Eve pattern, and then re-enter the rest of the cyclic year. All the New Year's Eves are compressed to a unity, which we repeat again and again, but those repetitions are not adjacent in the cyclic year. Rather, after one New Year's Eve, we go through the entire cyclic year to get to the next New Year's Eve before we start the New Year's Eve cycle again. Christmas, our birthday, Independence Day, and on and on—each can be compressed to a single routine occasion contained in the cyclic year, and we can repeat that routine pattern on the appropriate occasion. Other parts of the year intervene between successive cycles of that routine. This gives us cycles embedded in the bigger cycle.

The embedded cycle of repetition can be longer than a day, of course. Various religions have particular periods of observance, such as Hanukkah or Advent, Lent, Holy Week, year after year. Instances of the specific period of several days, spread over many years, are all compressed in the cyclic blend to a single pattern, which is repeated cyclically, but the repetitions are separated by other parts of the year. The Western Christian liturgical year, for example, is a cycle that exhausts the calendar year, and within the liturgical year are smaller cycles, repeated every year: Advent, Christmastide, Ordinary Time after the Epiphany, Lent, the Easter season, Ordinary Time after Pentecost. "Ordinary" Time is time that belongs to no particular liturgical season, called "ordinary" because we count the "ordinal" weeks to go through this time before we reach the next liturgical season, which is itself an embedded cycle, repeated annually.

Once we have these compressed cyclic blends, they can seem inevitable, automatic, natural, easy. What's the big deal? Is the origin of ideas so hard? It seems this way because these compressed blends are now at human scale. They have become second nature. But all it takes to disabuse oneself of the idea that they are easy or inevitable is a little study in the origin of ideas of calendars. In glorious and intellectual ancient Greece, each city-state kept a different calendar, and even within relatively advanced Athens at the time of Thucydides, there were at least four different ways of trying to grasp time according to calendars—prytany, festival, *kata theon*, and a seasonal calendar, that is, "by summers and winters."[5] All of these calendars show amazing mental work to create compressed portable ideas at human scale that make it possible for us to get some traction with vast mental webs stretching over vast distances of time, space, causation, and agency. But they all have uncongenial bits that give scholars headaches. Thucydides, in Book 5, section 20 of *The Peloponnesian War*, explains why he rejects calendars other than the seasonal as ambiguous. And yet, for millennia, scholars have conducted long debates over how to interpret the dating in *The Peloponnesian War*, not least because of uncertainty about how one measured when a season began or ended.[6]

We can compress a pattern of elections every n years to an n-year cycle. The election season, or campaign season, is a single thing in the blend, repeated indefinitely, but with multi-year periods of time separating the repetitions.

For all of these cycles-within-cycles, we have analogical and disanalogical connections between the individual instances in the extended web. The analogies are compressed to uniqueness in the blend and the disanalogies are compressed to change for that single entity, as we have seen many times.

Suppose we are considering *the campaign season*. We might propose to *lengthen* or *shorten* it. We might propose to *replace* turkey at Thanksgiving with standing rib roast. Of course, outside the blend, there is no single entity that is being lengthened, shortened, or replaced.

What is a habit? It is not something in the world that one can point to. It is a compressed blend of many activities. To say that we have a "coffee habit" means that we drink coffee at many times. But where is *the habit*? It is an identity created by packing analogies across the vast web of action. Once it is created as an element in the blend, then we can think of acting on it. We can, for example, "kick" it. This is further blending, in which not engaging in an activity is removing an object so that we do not interact with that object. In the blend, when we kick the habit away, we no longer interact with it. The disanalogies—our no longer drinking coffee—are packed to a change for the object—it is kicked away. Accordingly, if one day we do not have coffee, we can say things like *I'm kicking my habit* or *I'm letting go of my habit* or *I'm banishing my habit*. In the compressed blend, we have one thing, and we can change it. We can do things to it. The disanalogies across these spaces are compressed to change. The analogies are compressed to a single entity—the habit.

Processes

A deciduous tree goes through a sequence of conditions during the year, a sequence that happens every year, and we instantly compress it to a cycle web in which the tree is cycling through a process. All those deciduous trees, past, passing, and to come, which form a completely unimaginable and ungraspable expanse of elements, become intelligible by being compressed to a single element that goes through a cycle of change.

But events do not need to be tied to a particular time in order to be compressed to a cycle web. Here is an example. How can there be life? Cells need energy. They get it by breaking down glucose into an energy molecule called ATP. Broadly, carbohydrates and oxygen are turned into water, carbon dioxide, and ATP. Science has modeled this in 3 steps, which "repeat" "again and again." Those 3 steps are glycolysis, the citric acid cycle, and the electron transport chain. The middle step of the 3 is itself thought of as a cycle—the citric acid cycle, also known as the Krebs cycle. Glycolysis turns a glucose molecule into 2 pyruvates, and these pyruvates feed into the citric acid cycle. As long as pyruvates are available to the cell, the cycle will continue to run. As all high school biology students everywhere must memorize, the 2 molecules of pyruvate get turned into 2 molecules of ATP, 6 molecules of carbon dioxide as waste product, and 10 really useful molecules (8 of NADH and 2 of FADH2) that are shipped off to the electron transport chain to produce lots of ATP and some water as waste product. Every biology textbook represents the events in the second step with a picture of a cycle, sometimes in a simple form (figure 28), and sometimes in much more detailed form, which biochemistry students put on their T-shirts.

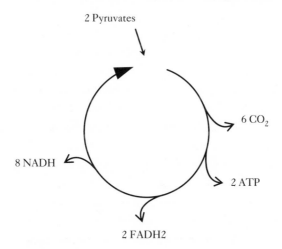

FIGURE 28 Krebs Cycle

But in what sense is it a cycle? New fuel is needed for every citric acid sequence. And come to think of it, that is also true of the deciduous-tree cycle. The citric acid sequence is running all the time, many times, very many times, in very many cells throughout organisms all over the world, and over-lappingly inside the same organism. All of that activity, which lies ludicrously far beyond the power of working memory to grasp in explicit form, is under-stood and managed in virtue of compressing all these sequences to just one, in a round-and-round-and-round-we-go cycle web. This way of understanding events is so common and indispensable that science could not exist without it.

The Myth of the Eternal Return

As we have seen in the case of ritual events such as Christmas, birthdays, and graduations, and in the case of other periodic events such as election seasons and annual seasons, the time periods that are blended into a single cycle need not be adjacent. For example, we go through the cycle of Christmas—pur-chase the Christmas tree, unpack the seasonal decorations, decorate the tree, put the gifts under the tree...open the gifts...prepare and consume the lavish Christmas feast...pack the decorations back up, dispose of the tree...start thinking about New Year's parties. Different families and cultures will have variations in the cycle. At the end of the Christmas cycle, the next cycle does not begin immediately. Rather, it starts again next Christmas season. This is a cycle located at a certain place in the cyclic year.

In *The Myth of the Eternal Return: Cosmos and History,* Mircea Eliade[7] lays out at book length the hypothesis that much of our sense of cultural and personal identity is made possible by the conceptual blending—my words, not his—of different events into one event. Eliade is concerned with what he calls "archaic man," who "acknowledges no act which has not been previ-ously posited and lived by someone else, some other being who was not a man. What he does has been done before. His life is the ceaseless repetition of gestures initiated by others."[8] One of Eliade's most fascinating examples is the "regeneration" of the cycle of time. "Every New Year is a resumption of time from the beginning, that is, a repetition of the cosmogony."[9]

Religions and mythic rituals sometimes reify the cyclic blend. In other words, they view the blend as concretely real. Of course, we do not need to reify the blend for it to be mentally powerful and useful. We do not need to believe that the blend is to be found as such in the world. Rather, we need only find the blend profitable as a tool for managing the mental web it serves. For example, we know that the second set of ten integers (11, 12...)

is not the "same" as the first set. We know that the second subsequence of Blue-Red-Green is not the "same" as the first set. But the cyclic blend in the cycle web is useful for understanding and managing the vast and diffuse web with all these integers or all these subsequences of Blue, Red, Green. We do not need to believe that, on a cosmic plane, we are our ancestors, in order for us to find it useful to think that we are going through the cycle of parenting when we raise our children. Our great-grandparents raised our grandparents; our grandparents raised our parents; our parents raised us; we raise our children; our children raise our grandchildren…This entire mental web of generational descent can be compressed to the cycle of parenting. The cycle is in the blend.

And yet, mythically, these compressions in the blend can result in conceptual relationships not just of similarity and identity, but also of uniqueness. Not only can the bread and wine of the Last Supper be changed in substance if not appearance by Christ into his body and blood, but also, each time the believer goes through the cycle of the Mass, it is, on a cosmic plane, the same time. Mircea Eliade writes, "Indeed, the Christian liturgical year is based upon a periodic and real repetition of the Nativity, Passion, death, and Resurrection of Jesus, with all that this mystical drama implies for a Christian; that is, personal and cosmic regeneration through reactualization *in concreto* of the birth, death, and resurrection of the Savior."[10]

From All Sides

No one imagines that the newborn child holds all of linear time in mind and then, later, packs it into a repeating cyclic day. No one imagines that the undergraduate student holds an infinity of integers in mind and then, later, packs it into a repeating cycle of numbers in base 10: 0-9, 10-19…No one imagines that the mathematician struggles through an indefinite number of Riemann sums, each with a vast number of terms, and at last realizes that the sum of all those terms can be packed into a single concept—the area under a curve.

On the contrary, the compact mental conception that we are calling "the blend" can make it possible to conceive of the input mental spaces and the range of input mental spaces in the first place. After the fact, which is to say, after the elaborate construction of a blending web, the inputs may look as if they are helping to build the blend. But of course, as a matter of process, it may have been that the blend helped us build the inputs. We may well, for example, have a conception of an event without realizing that its structure will be "repeated" many times in the future at particular spots in the year, or that it has been repeated at those spots in the past. In that case, we do not realize that the structure will later come to count as a cyclic blend, once we have done the work to construct the blending web in which it is located as the blend.

Blending always has as its goal the creation of a mental web, but any of the mental arrays in the web can have been used as a basis for building the web. Work can be done on any of the ideas in the web during its construction. There can be multiple inputs and successive and iterated blends. There can be, and usually are, hyper-blends that have blends as inputs. A congenial idea can be unpacked in interesting ways so as to create a mental web in which the original idea comes ultimately, after work, to count as a blend in the web. We can rebuild and revise the inputs to improve the web. New stuff arises not only or even chiefly in the blend, but rather in the entire web.

Advanced blending is constant, complicated, and systematic mental work, but it does not feel that way to us. It is part of human nature. Since somewhere around the onset of the Upper Paleolithic, some tens of thousands of years before the lionman, it has been what we specialize in, the engine of our new ideas.

10

Future Ideas

When we investigate the origin of ideas, we ask *What? Why?* and *How?* The *What?* question asks *What does the mind do? What are its mental processes?* This book has been organized around the *What?* question. It looks at the mental processes that give us the ability to come up with new ideas.

The *Why?* question is about the past: *Why are we the way we are? Why did we end up this way?* This is a question about deep evolutionary time, species time, prehistorical time, historical time, local historical time, and ontogenetic time. The *Why?* question launches the hunt for the causes and influences that led to our present state. An answer to the *Why?* question is very hard to deliver, because we do not have a time machine to take us back 50,000 or 100,000 years or even more to obtain the evidence.

Nor can we dig up data about the evolutionary path that gave us the ability for advanced blending. Unfortunately for us, brains do not survive to become archaeological treasures. We can't tell anything about blending by looking at impressions left by brains on the inside of old skulls. We cannot read the genotype of a living person today in such a way as to inform us about the ability for blending, so of course there is at present little light that can be shed by recovering archaeological genetic material.

The view of mental processes that I offer in this book is the one I take to be the most plausible, or perhaps the least objectionable, on standard evolutionary grounds: Blending, at least rudimentary blending, has been here for a very long time, and human beings, who lack many abilities other species possess, are nonetheless further along the blending gradient than other species. The ability for advanced blending evolved out of a previously existing ability;

advanced blending brought adaptive increased understanding and creativity. Even small increments in that mental ability would have conferred advantage, and so the natural selection story that would take us from more rudimentary forms of blending to full advanced blending is easy to imagine, even if it is impossible, within current science, to prove. One of the problems with such evolutionary imagining, however, is that it is so easy to come up with plausible stories, but so hard to test them.

In our time, science explores the *Why?* question in many ways, but so far, there is no utterly compelling evidence for, and no utterly clear refutation of, stories about the evolution of advanced blending. And yet, there are at least some constraints we should respect on the stories we concoct about how we got this way. We would like our story not to be flatly contradicted by the archaeological record as we have it. We would like our story to follow the patterns of other, well-established, evolutionary accounts, that is, accounts of other biological phenomena we see before us. That way, we would have some reassurance that our story is at least plausible. We would like to be reassured by seeing the mechanisms that supposedly brought us here still at work in our time. But these are only constraints. It is not in the power of science to settle these *Why?* questions yet.

The *How?* question asks *How do biological processes underlie mental work? How do the brain and other systems subtend mind?* The *How?* question is daunting, since our ignorance about the neuroscience of higher-order thought is profound. Answering this question will require many scientific methods that do not yet exist.

Present brain-imaging technology is not even remotely close to allowing us to detect advanced blending as such. Having a brain-imaging lab in the scientific mix can be very useful, but noninvasive brain imaging on everyday people with normal brains who have no neurological issues is still too crude for investigating blending.

If our goal is to detect blending, as opposed to other mental activity, what brain-imaging techniques would we wish for? Consider that blending appears to operate throughout all conceptual domains, and constantly. Very few of the brain's blending attempts ever advance past the initial stage, very few of those achieve good blends, very few of those have an effect on thought, very few of those have access to action, and only the tiniest fraction are ever accessible to consciousness. The seductive colored fMRI images we see in grant proposals and magazines are seductive partly because they look pretty, but they are crude representations of results from crude measures of the paramagnetism of relatively deoxygenated hemoglobin. fMRI is a BOLD response.

BOLD stands for "Blood-oxygen-level dependent." Two of the scientists who helped develop MRI were awarded the Nobel Prize, and MRI is fantastic for detecting what part of the shoulder the weekend warrior blew out swinging for the tennis ball. But when applied to the brain, it is still a measure of blood flow, not neuronal activity. It has very low signal-to-noise ratios. The results presented in those colored images derive from many repetitions and then statistical averaging and smoothing, often involving wholesale subtraction. At present, fMRI has many exceptionally severe limitations and uncertainties.[1] These things move slowly. If we ask, "*Where* does conceptual integration happen in the parts of the neocortex in which fMRI can detect activity?" the off-the-cuff guess would be "everywhere." And if we ask, "*When* does conceptual integration happen in the parts of neocortex in which fMRI can detect activity?" the off-the-cuff guess would be "all the time." It is difficult to see, then, how current fMRI techniques can offer insight into blending.

In the absence of the necessary neuroscience, the effective monitoring techniques, or a time machine, it is not yet clear how answers to our questions will come from the evolutionary depths or the biological processes. It is not even clear how such knowledge would tell us about how blending works.

And yet, there are some interesting speculations about the *Why?* and *How?* questions that I should mention here.

Measuring brain response through electroencephalography. One of the most ingenious and promising techniques in cognitive neuroscience for detecting, not blending per se, but rather the ease, difficulty, or surprise of blending, at least as it is evoked by language, consists of measuring brain responses through electroencephalography. These measurements are called event-related potentials (ERPs). For example, as we saw in chapter 3, human beings routinely blend inanimate objects with animate, minded animals, especially human animals. This kind of blending includes viewing other people as "minded," but goes far beyond it. Language that prompts us for such a blend can be surprising in a context that does not prepare a subject to expect it. Consider, for example, the difference between, on the one hand, "My dog loves me," "My neighborhood loves me," "Paris loves me," "My car loves me," and, on the other hand, "This painting wants me to commit suicide" and "These two peanuts are falling in love." Reading words evokes ERP responses. One of these ERP responses, called the N400, is a negative deflection. It is called N400 because it is negative (N) and shows up about 400 milliseconds after the word is read. The N400 is characteristically small in amplitude when the word is easy to understand. It gets larger as the word becomes harder to understand. Do we see big N400 deflections for sentences that ask us to blend something inanimate with human beings by giving the inanimate objects emotions? Yes, if the blend is unconventional and if the context gives us no warning. But, on the other hand, there is no noticeable N400 at all if we are prepared for the blend. Mante Nieuwland and Jos van Berkum, two neuroscientists who study language and discourse, described in an article in the *Journal of Cognitive Neuroscience* their use of ERP to investigate blending.[2] They found that isolated language that prompts us to attribute animacy to inanimate objects did produce an N400 signature. But when the anomalies were embedded in a supportive context (e.g., a story about an amorous peanut), the N400 effect disappeared completely. The researchers write,

> This process of projecting human properties (behavior, emotions, appearance) onto an inanimate object comes close to what has been called "conceptual blending," the ability to invent new concepts and to assemble new and dynamic mental patterns by "blending" elements and vital relations from diverse scenarios (e.g., Fauconnier & Turner, 2002). Furthermore, most subjects also indicated that they visualized the cartoonlike stories in order to comprehend them, which seems to illustrate the importance of perceptual processes in cognitive mechanisms like language and memory (e.g., Barsalou, 1999). Within such a framework, projecting animate properties onto an inanimate object might perhaps even be understood as "perceptual blending" during language comprehension.[3]

Seana Coulson has also used ERP methods to shed light on the ease of blending in response to linguistic prompts.[4] She and neuroscientist Cyma Van Petten, using ERP methods to test the claim made in blending theory for a continuum between literal and figurative language, conclude that the ERP data support blending theory on this point and challenge standard models of how we make sense of literal versus figurative language.[5]

Mirror neurons. "Mirror neurons" have been thought to help us make blends of self and other.[6] A "mirror neuron" is a neuron that fires when an animal performs or sees an action. One cannot detect a mirror neuron by looking at it. Rather, if a particular neuron functions in the way mirror neurons are supposed to function, it is called a "mirror neuron." The hypothesis that mirror neurons help us imitate motor patterns we see in other people is at present quite popular, and there are many speculations that mirror neurons help us achieve more advanced blends of self and other. One difficulty with the mirror neuron speculation is that the best evidence for mirror neurons (in perception and motor action) comes from non-human species such as macaque monkeys, who lack just the kinds of advanced blending abilities we see so pervasively in human beings and which we are trying to explain. Science is on the hunt for how much ability mirror neurons can deliver.

The existence of mirror neurons usually raises the question of whether the general processes of blending might not be achieved by different neurological activity for different kinds of concepts. Mirror neurons, for example, would help blend self and other.

In general, the idea that similar processes are run by different neurons and neuronal groups is the most basic assumption of neuroscience: Neurons are thought of as "computational," not always in the sense that they are like little computers, but rather in the sense that they run processes that change one state into another. Excitations and inhibitions are summed, and when a threshold is passed, an electrical spike is sent down the neuron's axon. This and other "computational" operations are thought to happen all over the brain, run by lots of different neurons and groups. No one, for example, asks where in the brain the "computation" process occurs. It occurs all over the brain. Similarly, it could be that blending processes are run and blends achieved widely throughout the brain, with different neural correlates. But in looking for them, we would need to remember that connecting ideas that belong to very different conceptual domains is the hallmark of advanced blending. It may seem natural to think that mating is one kind of idea and cooking is another, but blends specialize in creating things like "a recipe for the perfect girlfriend/boyfriend."

Convolution. Paul Thagard and Terrence Stewart have recently proposed an account they describe as "similar to the idea of blending (conceptual integration) developed by Fauconnier and Turner (2002)." Binding and creativity, they write, are based on what they call "representation combination" or "convolution of neural patterns." They propose a hypothetical neural mechanism for this "combination" or "convolution."[7] The examples they cite are right in line with those we have considered in this book:

Many scientific discoveries can be understood as instances of conceptual combination, in which new theoretical concepts arise by putting together old ones. Two famous examples are the wave theory of sound, which required development of the novel concept of a sound wave, and Darwin's theory of evolution, which required development of the novel concept of natural selection. The concepts of sound and wave are part of everyday thinking concerning phenomena such as voice and water waves. The ancient Greek Chrysippus put them together to create the novel representation of a sound wave that could explain many properties of sound such as propagation and echoing. Similarly, Darwin combined familiar ideas about selection done by breeders with the natural process of struggle for survival among animals to generate the mechanism of natural selection that could explain how species evolve.[8]

Generalization of domain-specific integrations. Advanced compression and expansion might have developed through replicating and generalizing some domain-specific, instinctive abilities for blending. During chase play, parent and offspring simultaneously activate motor patterns, attention patterns, and motivational structures that belong to two clashing domains, such as *parent-offspring* and *predator-prey*. Maybe the neural circuitry that supports a particular domain-specific blend was recruited in the evolution of full advanced blending.

Generalization of perceptual integration. One of the kinds of binding mammals do all the time is *perceptual integration,* as when we integrate all the different aspects of our perception of a coffee cup into the perception of the coffee cup. The neural mechanisms of perceptual integration might have been recruited by evolution in the development of advanced blending. There are no accepted theories on how that might have happened.

Synesthesia. The synesthesia approach is related to the perceptual integration approach. Synesthesia, or rather cross-wiring, is an easy candidate for the neural correlate of blending, but blending seems to be much too principled and systematic to be accounted for as a lucky consequence of cross-wiring. Of course, synesthesia itself might be more than cross-wiring.

Neural binding. The neural binding hypothesis to explain our blending ability is the most general hypothesis. It covers a great deal of ground and has different interpretations. In general, the hypothesis claims that mental events are cohesive because of synchrony of neuronal firing. To the extent that there is a pre-existing capacity for mental combination on the basis of synchrony of firing, it might have been recruited and exploited in the evolution of full advanced blending. But any proposal that advanced *blending* could fall out automatically from the capacity for basic neural *binding* runs up against the obvious "3,000-fold problem." Neural binding as described has been present in evolutionary descent since at least mammals, perhaps since arthropods. It has been available in evolutionary descent for at least 150 million years. But human-level blending has been active for perhaps only 50,000 years, give or take some tens of thousands. In other words, mammalian neural *binding* is at least *3,000 times older* than human-level *blending*. Accordingly, by itself, the "binding" speculation does not provide an explanation for advanced blending, although presumably binding is indispensable to advanced blending, as it is to so much else in human life. Binding is necessary but not sufficient. It might be important to entertain the idea that constraints on binding might help the development of blending, because amplifying and pruning a neuronal network are both ways to alter its operation. There are intriguing speculations that unspecified advances in binding might have led to some human-level blending. For example, Antonio Damasio writes, "[C]onstructing the auto-biographical self demands a neural apparatus capable of obtaining multiple core self pulses, within a brief time window, for a substantial number of components and *holding the results together transiently, to boot*" (emphasis added).[9] As we have seen, human higher-order cognition requires more than holding such results simultaneously in mind; it requires compressing them to a human-scale blend, without losing sight of the fact that the blend can be expanded to a mental web with just those inputs. Activating the ideas of a *lion* and a *man* does not on its own give us the origin of the idea of a *lionman*. That takes advanced blending.

The *How?* question is a question of biology and its operation. There is a distant cousin of the *How?* question, namely, *Can we simulate this process algorithmically on a computer?* There are rudimentary attempts to borrow ideas from blending theory for practical applications in computational systems. For example, suppose that an autonomous agent, designed to perform in a certain way in a very limited environment, encounters a difficulty for which it does not have an exact recovery routine. Could it be equipped with some basic blending routines and some general evaluation principles so as to blend its original instructions, or perhaps one of its library scripts, with some details from its current conditions to produce a routine with slightly new structure, emergent structure, and so "invent" a routine with which it was not completely equipped? Can the computer, to this extent, originate a new idea by blending? But these interesting attempts are far from a simulation of blending.

At the beginning of this book, I sketched a conception of the human brain as constantly trying to blend different things, unconsciously, with every human brain engaged at every moment in many attempts at blending. Most of these attempts fail almost immediately, I wrote, because no good blend arises, or if it does arise, attaches to no purpose, and so is allowed to pop, like a little transitory bubble.

This constant attempt at blending puts a strong engine of variation inside our knowledge, our thoughts, our ideas. Almost everything blending produces is selected against by the requirements and constraints of blending, or by pressures and possibilities of our environments, or by the absence of any utility. But some blends, although they blend ideas one might have thought have no business being put together, give us new and powerful ideas. Advanced blending, far from doomed from the start for blending ideas that strongly conflict, is powerful and useful exactly for that reason.

It is all-important that human thought is distributed across people. When a person comes up with a forbidden-fruit blend, other people are right at hand, ready to understand it, incorporate it, and propagate it. Eve plucked the forbidden fruit, tasted it, and handed it to Adam, who also ate. The activity was distributed. In this way, culture is an incomparably larger laboratory of mental experimentation than is the individual brain. Everybody is running forbidden-fruit experiments in a vast laboratory, and this creates wonderful possibilities for sustained, effective, and combined creativity.

But these hypotheses are at the outer limit of what we can at present investigate. An aggressive program of research is needed to explain how the mind performs forbidden-fruit blending. This program of research will require intensive and sustained collaboration across researchers in many different disciplines, to design scientific programs and conduct them to the goals.

During that inquiry, we will continue to find that the human condition is not simple. Evolution did not so much make us human as provide us with the mental abilities we need to make ourselves human, through advanced blending, which is an ongoing and dynamic process, bringing both hope and uncertainty as human thought strives to arch over the vast expanses of time, space, causation, and agency.

APPENDIX

The Academic Workbench

This appendix, written for academics, offers a snapshot of the state and status of blending theory within the academy. Inevitably, the appendix groans under the weight of academic jargon. It considers some issues that only academics could love. A much fuller list of current academic work on blending—theoretical, empirical, and applied—is available at blending.stanford.edu.

The blending hypothesis began when Gilles Fauconnier and I each noticed ranges of similar data that could not be explained using any available theory—data that, taken together, presented challenges to the theories with which we were familiar. We put our heads together and came up with an idea. This idea consisted of a sketch of the processes that might account for this data. Perhaps most theories in the social sciences and the sciences of the mind begin this way. The important thing in science is to have a good idea. Pushing data around by itself does not produce insight.

Our idea was motivated initially by a very tiny data set. We found, to our considerable surprise, often remarked by us and others as the investigation evolved, that the blending model was a useful tool for very many other things, including a great range of classic problems. It turned out to be applicable not only to very familiar data that we could show required new analyses, but also to a vast, open-ended range of completely novel data.

Such progress is standard in science. It is what we find in evolutionary biology, astronomy, and geology. Science proceeds by finding generalizations and reanalyses on the basis of a little data, and then, with luck, those generalizations and reanalyses end up applying to vast ranges of data that were not initially considered. Our proposals were empirical in both directions—based on actual data, and extending to vast ranges of actual data not originally considered. Our generalizations and our predictions about future observations were largely borne out subsequently.

In the brief span of years since the publication of blending theory, it has inspired many books and hundreds of articles by people looking at wide ranges of data that

Fauconnier and I had not considered, often in fields in which we do not work. We branched out to some of these new fields ourselves, as foot soldiers in the blending army. The website at blending.stanford.edu presents long lists of publications on the application of blending theory in computer science, artificial intelligence, decision-making, law, psychology, linguistics, management, organizational behavior, economics, political science, religious studies, art, mathematics, drama and literary studies, neuroscience, discourse studies, gesture, musicology, anthropology, marketing research, and on and on. At least to many researchers, blending theory has achieved the status of a set of important generalizations with wide applicability and explanatory power over many different areas of human behavior.

As in any science, we are perpetually devising ever more ways to test our generalizations. One way to go about this is to locate ever more predictions that our generalizations allow us to make. This is often harder than one might at first think, at least for many sciences. Geneticists do not—indeed, so far cannot—predict what new species will arise in a complicated ecology, although virologists sometimes are lucky enough to put together a simulation laboratory with plenty of carrier animals and to introduce various viruses to see what comes out of the interaction of the viruses and all those animals. That's not a prediction, and blending researchers frequently do something quite similar in introducing material to groups of people to see what blends they do or do not construct.

In the science of the human mind, we run into a major hurdle confronted nowhere else in science: It is in the nature of the case that people are highly flexible and creative in what they come up with mentally, and they have enormous brains with lots and lots going on, and there is no way to know in any thorough way what they are thinking now—even they themselves have little idea what they are thinking, and we researchers have no way to read minds. Accordingly, there is no way to predict in the wild what people are going to do or say next. Worse still, there are no good animal models for the behavior we want to investigate, so we cannot perform tests on the animal models and then draw conclusions for people.

Still, there are yet newer frontiers available for testing the generalizations of blending theory. Most of these have to do with investigating patterns in a large corpus of data. For example, one could predict that, given the grammatical patterns in a language, there will be resistance against blending them in a certain way. One could predict that, if one investigates a large out-of-sample corpus of data, one will find such-and-such patterns with roughly such-and-such frequency. Blending theorists have done some of that kind of prediction.

Here is a (long) example of that kind of prediction, having to do with the study of *viewpoint blending* (which I'll explain in a second). Viewpoint arises inevitably from the fact that we have bodies, and our brains are in our bodies, and in fact our brains are part of our bodies. This condition is referred to as "embodiment." A participant in any scene of communication is embodied, and so has a viewpoint. An individual person is in a particular spot, in a particular time, with a particular perceptual focus and attention.[1] If I say, "I can help you now by looking here," what I have said is unintelligible unless you understand something about my viewpoint, and accordingly what I might mean by "I," "you," "now," and "here," words that could mean many different things in different situations, depending on the viewpoint of the person who says them. All languages have many expressions for expressing viewpoint, but they also have plenty of expressions for expressing *blends* of viewpoint. For example, François Recanati analyzes "the epistolary present," which expresses a blended temporal viewpoint that arises for personal correspondence.[2] In the blend, writer and reader are present in the moment and jointly attending to the letter, although they know that outside the blend in the mental web served by the blend they are in different times and conditions. Recanati's attested examples include "*J'ai devant moi ta lettre, et tu as devant toi ma réponse,*" translated roughly, "I have before me your letter and you have before you my response." The blend provides a human-scale compression: Different times are compressed into one time, just as we saw with the Buddhist Monk. Of course, the writer is not prevented from expressing time differences that exist in mental spaces outside the blend: "By the time you receive this letter, I will already be on my way."

Elsewhere, I analyzed another kind of temporal viewpoint blend, exemplified when the wife, headed to the shower, says to her husband (who has asked how a certain task will be accomplished), "My husband took care of that while I was in the shower."[3] In the blend, the wife's viewpoint recruits much from her embodied viewpoint at the moment she says the sentence, but she also has some of the viewpoint that her future self will have, after the shower. The wife's viewpoint from that future focuses on a mental space—the husband's doing the task—which, from the future viewpoint, lies in the past, and has the certainty of the past. The blend provides a human-scale compression, of time and identity and the status of an idea. Is the idea hypothetical, desired, certain? The past tense belongs to the viewpoint of the future space, where it is grammatical. It is projected to the blend in order to prompt for new meaning in the blend, namely, the certainty of the accomplishment of the task by the husband. Projecting from this new stuff in the blend back up to the mental space of his present moment, the husband understands his wife's absolute expectation of his impending accomplishment as she heads to the shower—or at least her in-jest absolute expectation, which he can read as something close to a playful command, but a command nonetheless. The past tense construction demands a rationale; the husband achieves the rationale by taking what the wife says as a prompt to build a mental web that includes her *blended viewpoint*; the wife uses the past tense construction exactly to prompt the husband to build that mental web and to prompt the husband to take it that the wife intended him to build that mental web. The expression used by the wife calls for a viewpoint blend, drawing on projections from both her viewpoint from the present and her viewpoint from the future. A range of other blended viewpoints prompted for by tense are analyzed by Barbara Dancygier in "Blending and narrative viewpoint."[4]

Kiki Nikiforidou analyzes the role of blending in a construction she calls "past tense + proximal deictic," as in "He *now saw* that he had failed."[5] "Proximal" means "close," as opposed to "distal." "Now" is *proximal* in time but "then" is *distal*. "Deictics" are expressions like "here" and "now" and "I" and "you," whose meaning depends on the viewpoint of the person who uses them. "Saw" is past tense. "Now" is a proximal deictic. The problem with "past tense + proximal deictic" is that the past tense is *distal* but "now" is *proximal*. That's a clash. They should not go together. What is going on? Nikiforidou provides "a detailed blueprint of the blending mappings cued by the [past + proximal deictic] pattern." Essentially, the pattern calls for a blend of viewpoints, in which our overall understanding is stage-managed from the point of view of a narrator but there is some self or consciousness located in a previous time, and the events experienced in that previous time are to be construed, Nikiforidou writes, "from the point of view of that consciousness, as that character's thoughts, speech or perceptions." The blended viewpoint takes on elements of different viewpoints and compresses a time relation. The mental space of the narrator's condition is still the mental space from which the contents of the narration are accessed, put together, and built up, but the experiential viewpoint comes from inside the narrated events. There is new stuff in the blend! In the blend, it is possible to have both (1) knowledge that is available only *at a distance* and (2) experience, perception, and realization that are available only *up close*. In a study of the British National Corpus, Nikiforidou shows that this is a widely used grammatical pattern, even outside of literary genres.

Presciently, Nikiforidou writes that the grammatical pattern has the "effect of zooming in on the events." "Zooming in" caught my attention, because Nikiforidou is talking about what the mind does, not about what we might see on a television screen, for example. So, here comes an example of prediction for a corpus. Francis Steen and I co-direct the Red Hen Lab, which holds more than 200,000 hours of recorded television network news, along with closed-captions and transcripts, so it is possible to search for a linguistic pattern computationally and then see what happens on the screen when some real person actually uses that linguistic pattern.[6] The Red Hen Lab corpus has over 2 billion words; that's big data. To be sure, there is no predicting what someone using the pattern of language Nikiforidou analyzes will actually do (gestures, for example) or what the studio production team will do (background music, for example). But I predicted immediately on seeing Nikiforidou's "zoom in" analysis that we would find many cases in which the camera would "zoom in" on an image of the person with the "past consciousness" when the narrator uses the linguistic pattern *past + now*. And we do find very many. Clearly, coupling the linguistic construction with the visual form is not only possible but natural and even frequent. The TV data played no role in the analysis of the linguistic pattern as a viewpoint blend, but that analysis leads to a hypothesis that can be checked against a vast corpus. The audiovisual zoom turns out to be a pattern of representation that supports the *past + now* grammatical pattern.

There is a hitch in providing this *past + now* visual zoom, because the narrator speaks *at one time* about a consciousness *at a previous time*. That is a mismatch. The consciousness and its experiences are not available in the narrator's immediate environment, or indeed in any of the mental spaces we have for considering the production and broadcast of the narration. The news production team might want to provide some suitable visual representation of that consciousness in the past. There are several ways to resolve the mismatch. The three most common appear to be: (1) have the person who in the past had the consciousness that is now being narrated *re-enact* the events, with the appropriate setting and staging and so on, and film that scene; (2) find archival still photos of that person at the time and present them, for example, with a Ken Burns effect, as the narrator uses the *past* + *now* construction; or (3) find historical film footage containing the person and run that footage as the narrator uses the *past* + *now* construction.

One of the most interesting such cases arises when the narrator and the past consciousness are connected by an *identity* relation, as in a PBS documentary on the Pentagon Papers, in which Daniel Ellsberg, who leaked the secret Pentagon Papers about the Vietnam War to the press, is narrating in advanced age his exploits in the period 1967–1971. There is extraordinary new stuff in this blend, including Ellsberg's ability to speak for his young self in a way that probably would not have been available to him at the time, and of course an enduring, manufactured, compressed character for "Ellsberg" the man: young Ellsberg and old Ellsberg are extremely different things, but the analogies between them, including analogies of viewpoint, can be compressed to a unity of character in the blend.

Nikiforidou writes of the linguistic construction,

> In blending terms... resolution of (apparent) conflict is often achieved through the mechanism of compression, whereby elements that are conceptually separate in the input spaces are construed as one in the blended space. The construction at hand, I suggest, cues a particular kind of compression, namely compression of a time relation. The dynamic, continuously updated character of such blending webs renders them particularly suitable for representing meaning in a narrative, where formal clues may often give conflicting instructions even within the same sentence (as is the case with FIS [Free Indirect Speech]).

Checking Nikiforidou's intuition against the data in the Red Hen Lab is one example of prediction, not an experimental one, and one that runs up against lots of questions: What else can happen on-screen when the expression is used? What else is zooming in used for? That's in the nature of corpus work, and a next step would be to get a full taxonomy and run statistics. Francis Steen and I present some other predictions of this sort elsewhere.[7] Of course, as always in science, what we want to do is find ever more ways of making predictions, to test the applicability of the generalizations. As always, this requires more grant proposals, more postdoctoral researchers, more work.

Here is an example of a new kind of prediction I have not yet tested.[8] Suppose we use a non-invasive eye-tracking machine to see where people are looking as we show them two different videotapes, perhaps of two things moving, such that, if they blend them, they should expect a certain event at a certain spot, and so look at that spot beginning at a certain time, in ways significantly different from people who do not make the blend. Suppose we can separate the people into two groups: those who seem to be doing the blending and those who don't, on the basis of who looks where. Can we devise a set of questions for them to answer (after the eye-tracking task) such that those who got that blend would deliver one kind of answer and those who did not get the blend would deliver another kind of answer? Then our hypothesis would be that those who attended to the all-important spot in the visual field would answer one way and the others would answer another way. As everyone knows, designing such tests to give clear-cut answers is very hard. But in principle, many of these kinds of tests could be devised. Dissertation topic free to a good home.

We need to be a little wise in looking to experiments for insight into blending. For starters, as is standardly analyzed, experiments, whether in physics or in psychology, do not in themselves directly provide explanations; they can be useful for the purpose of distinguishing between competing explanations, but even then, their usefulness depends upon the intelligence of the proposed explanations. An experiment that chooses between two garbage explanations is only picking through garbage, and at best can come up with garbage. Garbage in, garbage out. It's also true that the outcome of experiments, by adding to the observable world, can create total surprises, which then lead to the search for further explanations.

It is also the case that we run up against major impediments in running true experiments on mental operations. In a true experiment, subjects participating in the experiment are randomly assigned to one of two conditions, the "control" and the "treatment," which differ in only one way. Medical examples make the situation clear: Suppose we randomly assign similar individual subjects to two groups, and that everybody in each group takes one little white pill every morning at the same time, and that all the little white pills look and feel and taste the same, but that the white pills for one of the groups are sugar pills with a little additive and the white pills for the other group are just sugar, a placebo. Usually, one prefers that neither the subjects nor the researchers know who is in what group, although the distinction is somehow recorded so it can be known to the researchers after they have done the analysis. Then, so goes the logic, any difference in the outcomes can be caused only by that one additive, because that was the only difference in causes. Of course, there is an immediate flood of difficulty: How do you know it is directly causal? Can there be another unseen variable? What if some of the subjects did not take their little pill every day (this is a problem of "compliance to treatment")? And on and on and on. I run experiments and emphasize that I have the greatest respect for the difficulties involved in designing them.

But now, can we run true experiments on blending? There are immediate reasons to be skeptical. First, human beings in social, communicative situations are not like chemicals in a tube or electrons in a collider: Human beings are geared to think about the social, communicative situation, and this silent and usually unconscious thinking influences their behavior pervasively, as all psychologists know from the many studies of "experimenter" and "demand" effects. It's not like giving them a pill. Second, there's a great deal of activity in any brain at any time, activity we cannot interpret. It may look as if the only difference between the two groups is that in the treatment condition we did one thing but in the control condition we did another. But different people can have great differences in mental activity, so perhaps there are 10,001 differences between them in that moment, not just one. And even if each subject in the experiment experiences both the control and treatment conditions (jargon: this is called a "within-subjects design"), with balancing to mitigate order effects and learning and so on, still, that single subject can have very different mental activity at the two different moments that look so similar, so perhaps again there are 10,001 differences between the control and treatment conditions, not just one. I am not trying to make problems here for running experiments. I don't have to. The problems are obvious, profound, real, and frequently discussed.

There are of course ever more experiments that can be run on blending. I have worked with a team to design some experiments having to do with good versus bad blends, as we saw. The design is simple: We show people parts of infinite sequences (like 2, 2, 1, 2, 2, 2, 1). Because the sequence is infinite, it cannot be held explicitly in mind, as an infinite list of elements. But it can be grasped if one makes a certain kind of blend, a *cycle* blend. I think that some of these blends are easier to get and hold, and others are harder, and that people are mentally disposed toward some of these blends and against others. I could design a battery of experiments for testing subjects on these different sequences, and see how they do. Our inquiries so far are preliminary, but they have a general design that conceivably could lead to true experiments testing a few small hypotheses about easy and hard blends.

The best true experiments about blending of which I am aware come from research using methods of ERP (event-related potentials). ERP values are based on electroencephalographic measurements of electrical activity in brains. There is a certain kind of ERP response, called the "N400," that is associated with the experience of difficulty or surprise in understanding or interpreting something. Experiments seem to show that although a striking blend will elicit an N400 response when said in isolation, it will for the most part not elicit the N400 response when the right context prepares for the presentation of the blend.

A different and frequently asked question about the status of blending theory is, "How important is it?" Blending theory should never be interpreted as suggesting that there is only one component of human thought, and that it is blending. On the contrary, as I have always stressed, advanced blending is only one part of what is needed for human thought, and it is relatively *tiny*. Blending, far from being a catch-all theory, is a tiny part of what goes on in thought and language, but nevertheless a crucial one for art, science, language, religion, mathematics, fashion, social cognition, and all the other activities that characterize cognitively modern human beings. For us, it is tiny, but crucial and ubiquitous. Advanced blending required for its evolution and operation everything that preceded it evolutionarily, and the list is long: bodies, brains, instincts, perception, mammalian memory, attention, viewpoint, and so on. At first glance, we look like just another great ape. What we share with them is enormous. Look at all the non-human species in the world today. All of them seem to be doing just fine without advanced blending. Look at all the species in the world 200,000 years ago. All of them were doing just fine without advanced blending. Life for these species does not require advanced blending, and there is nothing in advanced blending that made its evolution inevitable. The proposal that this one extra step—to a spot higher up on the blending ramp—ushered in a range of distinctive human abilities does not in the least slight the role of any of the others. That step up the ramp to advanced blending was a relatively tiny change, but it had huge effects. One small step altered life for us in a big way.

For example, Fauconnier and I have argued that advanced blending solved the central problem of language, and made full human language at last possible.[9] Language uses "form-meaning pairs," that is, in the simplest case, something like various sounds for "boy" paired with a meaning, *boy*. The central problem of human language is that human language is possible only if a limited number of form-meaning pairs can be used to talk about a vastly larger number of meaningful situations. Blending solves this problem by providing the mental power to blend different mental spaces into a compressed blend, and in the process to project linguistic forms attached to any one of those mental spaces to the blend to express the perhaps new meaning in the blend. Although blending can be highly creative, and although blends can be constructed for any range of meaning, the linguistic forms for expressing blends themselves need not be new at all, and almost never are: They can come from the mental spaces upon which the blend calls. In this way, a limited number of form-meaning pairs can be used to express any amount of meaning. This process makes language "equipotential," that is, it gives language full potential for expressing any new ideas we come up with in any domain. We do not need new language to express new ideas.

This discussion of the origin of language illustrates that it is not so easy to give an answer to the question, "How important is blending?" For language to evolve, we needed vast ranges of abilities and resources, but on the other hand, I think that full human language could not have come into existence until advanced blending had solved some cognitive problems. Advanced blending is a small thing with huge effects.

This discussion of the origin of language also illustrates a central problem we face in trying to think about the evolution, tens of thousands of years ago, of the capacity for advanced blending: There are no good animal models with us now. For many things— like digestion or cardiopulmonary systems or vision or smell—we can look for clues to explain their evolution by investigating how they work in a range of animals. But we cannot do this for art, science, mathematics, language, religion, and so on. We cannot investigate how a range of animals quickly comes up with a cascade of new creative ideas on the fly, because they don't.

One thing we can say definitively about the blending hypothesis is that it is meant to be a fully evolutionary account. The fact that our ability for advanced blending races along at a speed that makes evolutionary biology look as if it is standing still does not mean that this ability did not evolve through those very processes. On the contrary: The human brain evolved to blend.

My own view is that the blending hypothesis, including the analyses of blending that have been proposed, is an explanatory tool that is increasingly reconciled with the latest in a convergence of research results. Some researchers might reasonably object that my view of blending theory is charitable. We'll see. The current status of blending theory comes from the central principle in science that you cannot replace something with nothing, and blending theory is a substantial something. *Vive le sport!*

Notes

CHAPTER 1

1. Fauconnier & Turner 2002.
2. For background on the study of frames, see, e.g., Fillmore 1976 & 1982.
3. Fauconnier 1985.

CHAPTER 2

1. Wynn, Coolidge, & Bright 2009, p. 73.
2. Brooks, David. 2011. An anonymous reviewer observes that less well-known analogues to this kind of cultural blending include the works of Cuban surrealist Wilfredo Lam.
3. Human mental biases and failures in this regard are the subject of considerable scientific research, and there are popular video tutorials presenting them for the purpose of training security officers, guards, police, and, in general, supervisors (see viscog.com). For example, human beings have very selective attention (Posner & Petersen 1990). They are largely blind to change in their environments (e.g., Levin & Simons 1997). They attribute elements to reality that are in fact constructed mentally, such as color (Hubel 1995) and pain (Ramachandran & Blakeslee 1998). They routinely engage in reconstructive memory (Bartlett 1932). Their perceptions change depending on their intentions to act (Vishton et al. 2007).
4. Sherrington 1941; emphasis added.
5. Duncker 1945.
6. Koestler 1964.
7. Turner 2010.
8. Henshilwood et al. 2011.
9. d'Errico 2012; Villa 2012.
10. Steen & Owens 2001.
11. See Fauconnier & Turner 2002 for the initial analysis.
12. Turner 2001.

13. Hare & Tomasello 2005.
14. Fortin, Wright, & Eichenbaum 2004.
15. Clayton & Dickinson 1998.
16. Tomasello, Call, & Hare 2003; Call & Tomasello 2008.
17. Osvath 2009.

CHAPTER 3

1. Hume 2007 [1777], I.xvi:

Next to the ridicule of denying an evident truth, is that of taking much pains to defend it; and no truth appears to me more evident, than that beasts are endow'd with thought and reason as well as men. The arguments are in this case so obvious, that they never escape the most stupid and ignorant.

We are conscious, that we ourselves, in adapting means to ends, are guided by reason and design, and that 'tis not ignorantly nor casually we perform those actions, which tend to self-preservation, to the obtaining pleasure, and avoiding pain. When therefore we see other creatures, in millions of instances, perform like actions, and direct them to like ends, all our principles of reason and probability carry us with an invincible force to believe the existence of a like cause. 'Tis needless in my opinion to illustrate this argument by the enumeration of particulars. The smallest attention will supply us with more than are requisite. The resemblance betwixt the actions of animals and those of men is so entire in this respect, that the very first action of the first animal we shall please to pitch on, will afford us an incontestable argument for the present doctrine.

This doctrine is as useful as it is obvious, and furnishes us with a kind of touchstone, by which we may try every system in this species of philosophy. 'Tis from the resemblance of the external actions of animals to those we ourselves perform, that we judge their internal likewise to resemble ours; and the same principle of reasoning, carry'd one step farther, will make us conclude that since our internal actions resemble each other, the causes, from which they are deriv'd, must also be resembling. When any hypothesis, therefore, is advanc'd to explain a mental operation, which is common to men and beasts, we must apply the same hypothesis to both; and as every true hypothesis will abide this trial, so I may venture to affirm, that no false one will ever be able to endure it. The common defect of those systems, which philosophers have employ'd to account for the actions of the mind, is, that they suppose such a subtility and refinement of thought, as not only exceeds the capacity of mere animals, but even of children and the common people in our own species; who are notwithstanding susceptible of the same emotions and affections as persons of the most accomplish'd genius and understanding. Such a subtility is a clear proof of the falshood, as the contrary simplicity of the truth, of any system.

2. http://en.wikipedia.org/wiki/Lamp_(advertisement)
3. Meddaugh 1996.
4. Meddaugh 1996, p. 4.

5. Smith 1759, 1.1.2.

6. Ekman 1992; Damasio 1999.

7. Smith 1759, 1.1.13.

8. Fillmore 1982.

9. Weizenbaum 1976, p. 7.

10. Disch 1986, p. 5.

11. Camerer, Loewenstein, & Weber 1989.

12. For a review of such studies, see Ross et al. 1977; Marks & Miller 1987.

13. Ross et al. 1977.

14. Ross et al. 1977, p. 280.

15. Wimmer & Perner 1983.

16. Buttelmann, et al. 2009; Baillargeon et al. 2010.

17. Tobin 2009.

18. Newton 1990.

19. Premack & Woodruff 1978. Called a "theory" because it is not observable.

20. Baron-Cohen 1988, 1993, 1995. See also Sigman & Capps 1997.

21. Tomasello 1999, p. 10.

22. Tomasello 1999, p. 14.

23. Tomasello 1999, p. 5.

24. Tomasello 1999, p. 7.

25. Tomasello et al. 2003.

26. Fauconnier & Turner 2002.

27. Yoon, Carol Kaesuk. "Pronghorn's Speed May Be Legacy of Past Predators." *The New York Times*. December 24, 1996. "Science" section, page 1. http://www.nytimes.com/1996/12/24/science/pronghorn-s-speed-may-be-legacy-of-past-predators.html

28. Tobin 2009, p. 171; Kenner 1967, p. 1432.

CHAPTER 4

1. Glenberg 1997, p. 1.

2. Glenberg 1997, p. 1.

3. (1871-1872), chapter 20.

4. I thank D. Fox Harrell for reminding me of this moment in *Star Wars*. Mihailo Antović remarks that the effect is even stronger in the "polished" version of Episode Six: In the original version, the "after-life" Vader is played by Sebastian Shaw, the actor who had played the unmasked living Darth Vader; in the polished version, the "after-life" Darth Vader is played by a younger actor, Hayden Christensen, who had played the role of young Anakin in the prequels. The result is that knowing fans can achieve an additional layer of blending.

5. See McCubbins, Turner, & Weller 2012a, 2012b, and 2012c.

6. See McCubbins, Turner, & Weller 2012a, 2012b, and 2012c.

7. See McCubbins, Turner, & Weller 2012a, 2012b, and 2012c.

8. See McCubbins, Turner, & Weller 2012a, 2012b, and 2012c.

9. See McCubbins, Turner, & Weller 2013.

10. Camerer 2003, p. 22.

11. Camerer 2003, p. 7.

12. *Surfer* April 1995, pp. 46–69.

13. Dennett 1991.

14. Tomasello & Farrar, 1986.

15. Langacker 1985, p. 113.

16. Naturally, a great deal of human communication is dedicated to managing scenes of joint attention, and this has been recognized widely, not least in the work of classical rhetoricians and philologists, but also by structuralists like Ferdinand de Saussure and Roman Jakobson. More specific analyses in linguistics having to do with the nature of the ground include Fillmore 1971; Bolinger 1979; Talmy 1982, 1987; and Rubba 1996.

17. Langacker 1978, p. 857.

18. Other ways in which grammatical structures prompt for some adjustment in the ground are reviewed in Emanation 1991.

19. *Beggars Banquet*, 1968.

20. I thank Gilles Fauconnier for bringing this example to my attention.

CHAPTER 5

1. For an interesting review with new ideas, see Llewellyn 2013.

2. Jouvet & Michel 1959; Jouvet 1979; Hobson 1988; Frith, Perry, & Lurner 1999.

3. Deirdre Donahue, "Book club is spurred to choose 'Seabiscuit,'" *USA Today*, May 23, 2002, p. 1D.

4. Lee 2001.

5. Richardson 1999.

6. Brown 1942.

7. See Turner 1998 for a review.

8. See Fauconnier & Turner 2002. See especially Fauconnier & Turner 2008 for an analysis of how elaborate blending gives rise to what are known as *basic metaphors*, i.e., systematic mappings and compressions such as TIME IS SPACE. See also Coulson 2001 and the talk by Gilles Fauconnier 2008, "How Compression Gives Rise to Metaphor and Metonymy" http://www.youtube.com/watch?v=kiHw3N6d1Js.

9. After Fauconnier and I provided the original analysis (2002), we found editorial cartoons using this kind of compression, as when President George W. Bush on Halloween snatches away a child's trick-or-treat bag. The bag is labeled "kids' health care."

10. See Turner 1991, 1998, & 2005 for reviews of reasons that blends strike us as figurative.

11. Turner 1988; Turner 1991, chapter 6, "Conceptual Connections."
12. Turner 2001, chapter 4, "Analogy."
13. Hofstadter 1996.

<h3 style="text-align:center">CHAPTER 6</h3>

1. Turner, Megan Whalen 1995.
2. Turner 1996.
3. Steinberg 1972, p. 172.

<h3 style="text-align:center">CHAPTER 7</h3>

1. Sherrington, [1941] 1964, p. 178.
2. Damasio 1999, p. 196.
3. Tulving 1985a and 1985b.
4. Tulving 1985b, p. 388.
5. Neisser 1988.
6. Fernyhough 2008.
7. Fauconnier & Turner 2002; Turner 2003, 2008, 2009.
8. Chappatte 2008.
9. The advertisement is available on the League's website at http://www.savebears.org/, under the heading "Grim Reaper Campaign."
10. Analyzed in Fauconnier & Turner 2002.
11. Originally retrieved from http://www.stonescryout.org for April 4, 2005. Archived at http://www.stonescryout.org/archives/2005/04/death_thou_shal.html.

<h3 style="text-align:center">CHAPTER 8</h3>

1. Weyl 1952.
2. For a full review of the following phenomena, with citations, see chapter 4, "The Body of our Thought and the Thought of our Body," Turner 1996.
3. Book XI of the *Odyssey,* lines 170–203.
4. The following discussion of blending sequences draws on McCubbins & Turner 2013.
5. The graphic image of the "Circle of Fifths" is taken from Wikimedia Commons.
6. See, e.g., Dehaene et al. 2008.
7. Kaufman et al. 1949.
8. Núñez 2011.
9. Núñez 2011, pp. 655–656.
10. Núñez 2011, p. 657.
11. Alexander 2011.
12. See especially Pascual 2006, 2008a, and 2008b.

13. Pagán Cánovas 2011.

14. Pagán Cánovas 2011, pp. 573–574.

15. Philo 1854–1890, section 90, pp. 264–265.

CHAPTER 9

1. McCubbins & Turner 2013.

2. See, e.g., Mandler 2004, Carey 2009.

3. McCubbins & Turner 2013.

4. McCubbins & Turner 2013.

5. Pritchett & Van der Waerden 1961.

6. Meritt 1962.

7. 1954

8. p. 5.

9. p. 54.

10. p. 130.

CHAPTER 10

1. Anderson, 2010.

2. Nieuwland and van Berkum 2006. "When presented in isolation, such anomalies indeed elicit a clear N400 effect, a sign of interpretive problems. However, when the anomalies were embedded in a supportive context (e.g., a girl talking to a clock about his depression), this N400 effect disappeared completely. Moreover, given a suitable discourse context (e.g., a story about an amorous peanut), animacy-violating predicates ('the peanut was in love') were actually processed more easily than canonical predicates ('the peanut was salted')." See page 1098.

3. Nieuwland & van Berkum 2006, p. 1109.

4. Coulson 2012.

5. Coulson 2012. To test these ideas, Coulson & Van Petten (2002) compared ERPs elicited by words in three different contexts on a continuum from literal to figurative, as suggested by conceptual integration theory (Fauconnier & Turner, 1998). The graded N400 difference argues against the literal/figurative dichotomy inherent in the standard model, and suggests processing difficulty associated with figurative language is related to the complexity of mapping and conceptual integration.

6. See, e.g., Iacoboni & Mazziotta 2007, Iacoboni 2008.

7. Thagard & Stewart 2010, p. 25.

8. Thagard & Stewart 2010, p. 3.

9. Damasio 2010, p. 212.

APPENDIX

1. See Sweetser 2012 for a review.
2. Recanati 1995.
3. Turner 1996.
4. See also the analyses of viewpoint blending by Eve Sweetser, "Introduction: viewpoint and perspective in language and gesture, from the Ground down" in Dancygier & Sweetser 2012; Barbara Dancygier, "Conclusion: multiple viewpoints, multiple spaces" in Dancygier & Sweetser 2012; and chapters 3, 5, and especially 7 of Barbara Dancygier 2012 *The Language of Stories: A Cognitive Approach,* Cambridge University Press.
5. Nikiforidou 2010 and 2012. The preferred patterns are "was/were + now," as in "It was now possible..." and, for a verb that is not a form of "be," "now + past tense," as in "He now saw that..."
6. Steen & Turner In press. For an introduction to the Red Hen Lab, type "Red Hen Lab" into your favorite web browser or go directly to https://sites.google.com/site/distributedlittleredhen/ or follow the link from http://markturner.org.
7. Steen & Turner In press.
8. I thank Bruno Laeng and Stephen von Tetzchner, in the department of psychology at the University of Oslo, for suggesting an inquiry along these lines.
9. Turner 1996, Turner and Fauconnier 2002.

References

Alexander, J. (2011). Blending in mathematics. *Semiotica, 2011*(187), 1–48. ISSN (Online) 1613-3692, ISSN (Print) 0037-1998, doi: 10.1515/semi.2011.063.

Anderson, M. L. (2010). Neural reuse: A fundamental organizational principle of the brain. *Behavioral and Brain Sciences, 33*, 245–313. doi:10.1017/S0140525X10000853

Aristotle. Περὶ Ψυχῆς (Latin title: De Anima. English title: On the Soul).

Baddeley, A. (2012). Working memory: Theories, models, and controversies. *Annual Review of Psychology, 63*, 1–29.

Baillargeon, R., Scott, R. M., & He, Z. (2010). False-belief understanding in infants. *Trends in Cognitive Sciences, 14*(3), 110–118. doi:10.1016/j.tics.2009.12.006

Balter, M. (2010). Did working memory spark creative culture? www.sciencemag.org. *Science, 328*, 160–163.

Baron-Cohen, S. (1988). Social and pragmatic deficits in autism: Cognitive or affective? *Journal of Autism and Developmental Disorders, 18*, 379–401.

Baron-Cohen, S. (1993). From attention-goal psychology to belief-desire psychology: The development of a theory of mind and its dysfunction. In S. Baron-Cohen, H. Tager-Flusberg, & D. J. Cohen (Eds.), *Understanding other minds: Perspectives from autism* (pp. 59–82). New York: Oxford University Press.

Baron-Cohen, S. (1995). *Mindblindess: An essay on autism and theory of mind.* Cambridge MA: MIT Press.

Barsalou, L. W. (1999). Perceptual symbol systems. *Behavioral and Brain Sciences, 22*, 577–660.

Bartlett, F. C. (1932). *Remembering: A study in experimental and social psychology.* Cambridge: Cambridge University Press.

Bolinger, D. (1979). To catch a metaphor: You as norm. *American Speech, 54*, 194–209.

Brooks, D. (2011). TED talk: The social animal. http://www.ted.com/talks/david_ brooks_the_social_animal.html. Based on Brooks, D. (2011). *The social animal: The hidden sources of love, character, and achievement.* New York: Random House.

Brown, M. W. (1942). *The runaway bunny.* With pictures by Clement Hurd. New York: Harper and Row.

Buttelmann, D., Carpenter, M., & Tomasello, M. (2009). Eighteen-month-old infants show false belief understanding in an active helping paradigm. *Cognition, 112*(2), 337–342. doi:10.1016/j.cognition.2009.05.006

Cacciari C, Gibbs, R., Jr., Katz, A., and Turner, M. (1998). *Figurative language and thought*. New York: Oxford University Press.

Call, J., & Tomasello, M. (2008). Does the chimpanzee have a theory of mind? 30 years later. *Trends in Cognitive Science, 12*, 187–192.

Camerer, C. F., Loewenstein, G. F., & Weber, M. (1989). The curse of knowledge in economic settings: An experimental analysis. *The Journal of Political Economy, 97*(5), 1232–1254.

Camerer, C. F. (2003.) *Behavioral game theory: Experiments in strategic interaction*. Princeton, NJ: Princeton University Press.

Carey, S. (2009). *The origin of concepts*. New York: Oxford University Press.

Carpenter, M., & Tomasello, M. (2000). Joint attention, cultural learning, and language acquisition: Implications for children with autism. In A. Wetherby & B. Prizant (Eds.), *Communication and language issues in autism and pervasive developmental disorder: A transactional developmental perspective* (pp. 31–54). Baltimore: Brookes.

Clayton, N. S., & Dickinson, A. (1998). Episodic-like memory during cache recovery by scrub jays. *Nature, 395*, 272–272.

Coulson, S. (2001). *Semantic leaps: Frame-shifting and conceptual blending in meaning construction*. New York: Cambridge University Press.

Coulson, S. (2012). Cognitive neuroscience of figurative language. In M. J. Spivey, M. Joanisse, & K. McCrae (Eds.), *The Cambridge handbook of psycholinguistics* (pp. 523–537). Cambridge: Cambridge University Press.

Coulson, S., & Van Petten, C. (2002). Conceptual integration and metaphor: an event-related brain potential study. *Memory and Cognition, 30*, 958–968.

Damasio, A. (1999). *The feeling of what happens: Body and emotion in the making of consciousness*. New York: Harcourt.

Damasio, A. (2010). *Self comes to mind: Constructing the conscious brain*. New York: Pantheon.

Dancygier, B. (2005). Blending and narrative viewpoint: Jonathan Raban's travels through mental spaces. *Language and Literature, 14*(2), 99–127.

Dancygier, B. (2012). *The language of stories: A cognitive approach*. Cambridge, UK: Cambridge University Press.

Dancygier, B., & Sweetser, E. (Eds.). (2012). *Viewpoint in language: A multimodal perspective*. Cambridge: Cambridge University Press.

Dehaene, S., Izard, V., Spelke, E., & Pica, P. (2008). Log or linear? Distinct intuitions of the number scale in western and Amazonian indigene cultures. *Science, 320*, 1217–1220.

Dennett, D. C. (1991). *Consciousness explained*. Boston: Little, Brown.

d'Errico, F., et al. (2012). Early evidence of San material culture represented by organic artifacts from Border Cave, South Africa. *Proceedings of the National Academy of Sciences*. doi: 10.1073/pnas.1204213109.

Disch, T. M. (1986). *The brave little toaster: A bedtime story for small appliances.* Illustrated by Karen Schmidt. NY: Doubleday.

Duncker, K. (1945). On problem solving. *Psychological Monographs, 58*(270). Washington, DC: American Psychological Association.

Ekman, P. (1992). An argument for basic emotions. *Cognition and Emotion, 6,* 169–200.

Eliade, M. (1954). *The myth of the eternal return: Cosmos and history.* Translated from the French by Willard Trask. Bollingen Series XLVI. New York: Pantheon Books.

Emanation, M. (1991). Point of view and prospective aspect (pp. 483–495). *Proceedings of the Seventeenth Annual Meeting of the Berkeley Linguistics Society,*

Fauconnier, G. (1985). *Mental spaces: Aspects of meaning construction in natural language.* Cambridge, MA: MIT Press.

Fauconnier, G. (1997). *Mappings in thought and language.* Cambridge, UK: Cambridge University Press.

Fauconnier, G. (2003). Compressions de Relations Vitales dans les Réseaux d'Intégration Conceptuelle. In J-L. Aroui (Ed.), *Le sens et la mesure* (pp. 89–97). Paris: Honoré Champion.

Fauconnier, G., & Turner, M. (1998). Conceptual integration networks. *Cognitive Science,22*(2), 133–187. Expanded web version at http://blending.stanford.edu.

Fauconnier, G., & Turner, M. (2002). *The way we think: Conceptual blending and the mind's hidden complexity.* New York: Basic Books.

Fauconnier, G., & Turner, M. (2008). The origin of language as a product of the evolution of modern cognition. In B. Laks et al. (Eds.), *Origin and evolution of languages: Approaches, models, paradigms* (pp. 133-156). London: Equinox.

Fernyhough, C. (2008). *The Baby in the mirror: A child's world from birth to three.* London: Granta.

Fillmore, C. (1971). *Santa Cruz lectures on deixis.* Bloomington, IN: Indiana University Linguistics Club.

Fillmore, C. (1982). Frame semantics. In *Linguistics in the morning calm* (pp. 111–137). Linguistic Society of Korea. Seoul: Hanshin Publishing Company.

Fortin, N. J., Wright, S. P., & Eichenbaum, H. (2004). Recollection-like memory retrieval in rats is dependent upon the hippocampus. *Nature, 431,* 188–191.

Glenberg, A. M. (1997). What memory is for. *Behavioral and Brain Sciences, 20,* 1–55.

Goguen, J. (1999). An introduction to algebraic semiotics, with application to user interface design. In C. Nehaniv (Ed.), *Computation for metaphor, analogy, and agents* (pp. 242–291). Berlin: Springer-Verlag.

Hare, B., & Tomasello, M. (2005). Human-like social skills in dogs? *Trends in Cognitive Science, 9,* 439–444.

Hart, H. L. A., & Honoré, T. (1985). *Causation in the law* (2nd ed.). Oxford: Clarendon.

Henshilwood, C. S. et al. (2011). A 100,000-year-old ochre-processing workshop at Blombos Cave, South Africa. *Science 334,* 219. doi: 10.1126/science.1211535.

Hobson, R. P. (1993). *Autism and the development of mind.* Hillsdale, NJ: Erlbaum.

Hobson. J. A. (1988). *The dreaming brain.* New York: Basic Books.

Hofstadter, D. (1996). *Fluid concepts and creative analogies: computer models of the fundamental mechanisms of thought.* New York: Basic Books.

Hubel, D. H. (1995). The neural basis of color constancy. In *Eye, brain, and vision* (2nd ed.). Issue 22 of the *Scientific American Library Series.* New York: Henry Holt and Company.

Hume, D. (2007 [1777]) *A treatise of human nature: Being an attempt to introduce the experimental method of reasoning into moral subjects,* D. F. Norton & M. J. Norton (Eds.). New York: Oxford University Press.

Iacoboni, M. (2008). *Mirroring people: The science of empathy and how we connect with others.* New York: Farrar, Straus and Giroux.

Iacoboni, M. and Mazziotta, J. C. (2007). Mirror neuron system: basic findings and clinical applications. *Annals of Neurology, 62*(3), 213–218.

Johnson, C. (1955). *Harold and the purple crayon.* New York: Harper & Row.

Jouvet, M. (1979). What does a cat dream about? *Trends in the neurosciences, 2,* 280–285.

Jouvet, M. and Michel, F. (1959). Correlations électromyographiques du sommeil chez le chat décortiqué et méséncephalique chronique. *Comptes rendus des séances de l'Académie des Sciences,153*(3), 422–425.

Kaufman, E. L., Lord, M. W., Reese, T. W., & Volkmann, J. (1949). The discrimination of visual number. *American Journal of Psychology, 62*(4), 498–525.

Kenner, H. (1967). Artemis and Harlequin. *National Review,19,* 1432–1433.

Koestler, A. (1964). *The act of creation.* New York: Macmillan.

Langacker, R. W. (1978). The form and meaning of the English auxiliary. *Language, 54,* 853–882.

Langacker, R. W. (1985). Observations and speculations on subjectivity. In J. Haiman (Ed.), *Iconicity in syntax* (pp. 109–150). Amsterdam: John Benjamins.

Lansing, J. (1989). *Impersonal you.* Unpublished manuscript.

Lee, M. (2001). Oñate's Foot - a Legend Grows. *ABQjournal,* March 23, 2001. http://www.abqjournal.com/paperboy/text/news/284240news03-23-01.htm.

Levin, D. T., & Simons, D. J. (1997). Failure to detect changes to attended objects in motion pictures. *Psychonomic Bulletin and Review, 4*(4), 501–506. doi:10.3758/BF03214339

Lewis-Williams, D. (2002). *The Mind in the cave: Consciousness and the origins of art.* London: Thames and Hudson.

Llewellyn, S. (forthcoming 2013). Such stuff as dreams are made on? Elaborative encoding, the ancient art of memory and the hippocampus. *Behavioral and Brain Sciences.* doi:10.1017/S0140525X12003135

MacDonald, E. (1991). *John's picture.* Pictures by Dave McTaggart. New York: Viking.

Mandler, J. M. (2004). *The foundations of mind: Origins of conceptual thought.* New York: Oxford University Press.

Marks, G., & Miller, N. (1987). Ten years of research on the false-consensus effect: An empirical and theoretical review. *Psychological Bulletin, 102*(1), 72–90. doi: 10.1037/0033-2909.102.1.72

McCubbins, M. D., & Turner, M. (2013). Concepts of law. *Southern California Law Review, 86*(3), 517–572.

McCubbins, M. D., Turner, M., & Weller, N. (2012a). The mythology of game theory. In S. J. Yang, A. Greenberg, and M. Endsley (Eds.), *Social computing, behavioral-cultural modeling, & prediction* (pp. 27–34). Berlin: Springer Lecture Notes in Computer Science.

McCubbins, M. D., Turner, M., & Weller, N. (2012b). The theory of minds within the theory of games. In H. R. Arabnia, D. de la Fuente, E. G. Kozerenko, P. M. LaMonica, R. A. Liuzzi, J. A. Olivas, A. M. G. Solo, and T. Waskiewica. (Eds.), *Proceedings of the 2012 International Conference on Artificial Intelligence, Vol. I,* (pp. 515–521). Athens, GA: CSREA Press.

McCubbins, M. D., Turner, M., & Weller, N. (2012c). The challenge of flexible intelligence for models of human behavior. *AAAI Spring Symposium Series 2012. Technical Report SS-12-03. pp. 54–60.* Available at http://www.aaai.org/ocs/index.php/SSS/SSS12/paper/view/4273/4647.

McCubbins, M. D., Turner, M., & Weller, N. (2013). Testing the foundations of quantal response equilibrium. In A. M. Greenberg, W. G. Kennedy, & N. D. Bos, (Eds.), *Social Computing, behavioral-cultural modeling, and prediction* (pp. 144–153). Berlin: Springer Lectures Notes in Computer Science.

Meddaugh, S. (1996). *Martha blah blah.* Boston: Houghton Mifflin.

Meritt, B. D. (1962). The seasons in Thucydides. *Historia: Zeitschrift für Alte Geschichte.* Bd. 11, H. 4 (Oct., 1962), 436–446. url:http://www.jstor.org/stable/4434761

Neisser, U. (1988). Five kinds of self-knowledge. *Philosophical Psychology, 1,* 35–58.

Newton, E. L. (1990). The rocky road from actions to intentions. Unpublished PhD dissertation. Stanford University.

Nieuwland, M. S., & Van Berkum, J. J. A. (2006). When peanuts fall in love: N400 evidence for the power of discourse. *Journal of Cognitive Neuroscience, 18*(7), 1098–1111. doi:10.1162/jocn.2006.18.7.1098.

Nikiforidou, K. (2012). The constructional underpinnings of viewpoint blends: The past + now in language and literature. In B. Dancygier & E. Sweetser (Eds.), *Viewpoint in language: A multimodal perspective* (pp. 177–197). Cambridge: Cambridge University Press.

Nikiforidou, K. (2010). Viewpoint and construction grammar: The case of past + now. *Language and Literature, 19*(2), 265–284.

Núñez, R. (2011). No innate number line in the human brain. *Journal of Cross-Cultural Psychology, 42*(4), 651–668.

Osvath, M. (2009). Spontaneous planning for future stone throwing by a male chimpanzee. *Current Biology, 19*(5), R190–R1919. doi:10.1016/j.cub.2009.01.010

Pagán Cánovas, C. (2011). The genesis of the arrows of love: diachronic conceptual integration in Greek mythology. *American Journal of Philology, 132*(4), 553–579.

Pascual, E. (2006). Fictive interaction within the sentence: A communicative type of fictivity in grammar. *Cognitive Linguistics, 17*(2), 245–267.

Pascual, E. (2008a). Fictive interaction blends in everyday life and courtroom settings. In A. Hougaard & T. Oakley (Eds.). *Mental Spaces in Discourse and Interaction* (pp. 79–107). Amsterdam: John Benjamins.

Pascual, E. (2008b). Text for context, trial for trialogue: An ethnographic study of a fictive interaction blend. *Annual Review of Cognitive Linguistics, 6*, 50–82.

Philo (called Judæus or "of Alexandria"). (1854–1890). On the principle that the worse is accustomed to be always plotting against the better, (*Quod Deterius Potiori Insidiari Soleat),* chapter 7 of Yonge, Charles Duke, translator, *The Works of Philo Judæus.* London: H. G. Bohn.

Posner, M. I., & Petersen, S. E. (1990). The attention system of the human brain. *Annual Review of Neuroscience, 13*, 25–42.

Premack, D. G., & Woodruff, G. (1978). Does the chimpanzee have a theory of mind? *Behavioral and Brain Sciences, 1*(4), 515–526. doi:10.1017/S0140525X00076512

Pritchett, W. K., & Van der Waerden, B. L. (1961). Thucididean time-reckoning and Euctemon's seasonal calendar. *Bulletin de correspondance hellénique, 85*, 17–52. doi: 10.3406/bch.1961.1574. url: http://www.persee.fr/web/revues/home/prescript/article/bch_0007-4217_1961_num_85_1_1574

Ramachandran, V. S., & Blakeslee, S. (1998). *Phantoms in the brain: Probing the mysteries of the human mind.* New York: William Morrow.

Ramachandran, V. S., & Hubbard, E. M. (2001a). Psychophysical investigations into the neural basis of synaesthesia. *Proceedings of the Royal Society of Londib B. Biological Sciences. 268*, 979–983.

Ramachandran, V. S., & Hubbard, E. M. (2001b). Synaesthesia—A window into perception, thought and language. *Journal of Consciousness Studies, 8*, 3–34.

Recanati, F. (1995). Le present epistolaire: Une perspective cognitive. *L'Information grammaticale, 66*, 38–44.

Ross, L., Greene, D., & House, P. (1977). The false consensus effect: An egocentric bias in social perception and attribution processes. *Journal of Experimental Social Psychology, 13*(3), 279–301. doi: 10.1016/0022-1031(77)90049-X

Richardson, P. (1999). Making Thanes: Literature, Rhetoric and State-Formation in Anglo-Saxon England. *Philological Quarterly, 78*(Winter/Spring), 215–232.

Rubba, J. (1996). Alternate grounds in the interpretation of deictic expressions. In G. Fauconnier & E. Sweetser (Eds.), *Spaces, worlds, and grammar* (pp. 227–261). Chicago: University of Chicago Press.

Sherrington, C. S., Sir. ([1941] 1964). *Man on his nature.* [The Gifford Lectures, Edinburgh, 1937–1938. New York: The Macmillan Co.; Cambridge: The University Press, 1941]. New York: New American Library.

Sigman, M., & Capps, L. (1997). *Children with autism: A developmental perspective.* Cambridge MA: Harvard University Press.

Smith, A. (1759 [1976].) *The Theory of Moral Sentiments.* Edited by D. D. Raphael and A. L. Macfie. Oxford: Clarendon Press; New York: Oxford University Press.

Steen, F., & Owens, S. (2001). Evolution's pedagogy: An adaptationist model of pretense and entertainment. *Journal of Cognition and Culture, 1*(4), 289–321.

Steen, F., & Turner, M. (In press). Multimodal construction grammar. In M. Borkent, B. Dancygier, &. J. Hinnell (Eds.), *Language and the creative mind*. Stanford, CA: CSLI Publications.

Steinberg, L. (1972). The Algerian Women and Picasso at Large. In *Other criteria: Confrontations with twentieth-century art*. New York: Oxford University Press.

Sweetser, E. (2012). Introduction: Viewpoint and perspective in language and gesture, from the Ground down. In B. Dancygier & E. Sweetser (Eds.), *Viewpoint in language: A multimodal perspective* (pp. 25–46). Cambridge: Cambridge University Press.

Talmy, L. (1982). Borrowing semantic space: Yiddish verb prefixes between Germanic and Slavic. *Proceedings of the Eighth Annual Meeting of the Berkeley Linguistics Society*, 231–250.

Talmy, L. (1987). Decoupling in the semantics of attention and perspective. Presentation at the Pacific Linguistics Conference, University of Oregon, Eugene. Unpublished talk.

Thagard, P., & Stewart, T. C. (2011). The AHA! experience: Creativity through emergent binding in neural networks. *Cognitive Science, 35*(1), 1–33.

Tobin, V. (2009). Cognitive bias and the poetics of surprise. *Language and Literature, 18*(2), 155–172. doi: 10.1177/0963947009105342.

Tomasello, M. (1999). *The cultural origins of human cognition*. Cambridge, MA: Harvard University Press.

Tomasello, M., Call, J., & Hare, B. (2003). Chimpanzees understand psychological states— the question is which ones and to what extent. *Trends in Cognitive Science, 7*(4), 153–156.

Tomasello, M., & Farrar, J. (1986). Joint attention and early language. *Child Development, 57*, 1454–1463.

Tulving, E. (1985a). Memory and consciousness. *Canadian Psychology 26*, 1–12.

Tulving, E. (1985b). How many memory systems are there? *American Psychologist, 40*(4), 385–398.

Turner, M. (1988). Categories and analogies. In D. Helman (Ed.), *Analogical reasoning: Perspectives of artificial intelligence, cognitive science, and philosophy* (pp. 3–24). Dordrecht: Kluwer.

Turner, M. (1991). *Reading minds: The study of English in the age of cognitive science*. Princeton, NJ: Princeton University Press.

Turner, M. (1996). *The literary mind: The origins of language and thought*. New York: Oxford University Press.

Turner, M. (1998). Figure (pp. 44–87). In Cacciari C. et al.

Turner, M. (2001). *Cognitive dimensions of social science: The way we think about politics, economics, law, and society*. New York: Oxford University Press.

Turner, M. (2003). Double-scope stories. In D. Herman (Ed.), *Narrative theory and the cognitive sciences* (pp. 117–142). Stanford: CSLI.

Turner, M. (2003–2014). The blending website: http://blending.stanford.edu.

Turner, M. (2004). The origin of selkies. *Journal of Consciousness Studies, 11*(5–6), 90–115.

Turner, M. (2005). The literal versus figurative dichotomy. In S. Coulson & B. Lewandowska-Tomaszczyk (Eds.), *The literal and nonliteral in language and thought* (pp. 25–52). Frankfurt: Peter Lang.

Turner, M. (2008). The mind is an autocatalytic vortex. In J. Schlaeger (Ed.), *The literary mind*, Volume *24* (2008) of *REAL: Yearbook of research in english and american literature* (pp. 13–43). Tübingen, Germany: Gunter Narr Verlag.

Turner, M. (2009). The scope of human thought. *On the human*. Target article in an online forum run by the National Humanities Center, with commentary by researchers worldwide and a response from the author. See http://onthehuman. org/humannature/.

Turner, M. (2010). Blending box experiments, Build 1.0 Available at SSRN: http://ssrn. com/abstract=1541062.

Turner, M. W. (1995). Aunt Charlotte and the NGA portraits. In *Instead of Three Wishes*. New York: Greenwillow Books.

Undset, S. (1997). *Kristin Lavransdatter. I: The Wreath*. Translated with an introduction and notes by Tiina Nunnally. New York: Penguin Books.

Villa, P. et al. (2012). Border cave and the beginning of the later stone age in South Africa. *Proceedings of the National Academy of Sciences.* doi: 10.1073/pnas.1202629109.

Vishton, P. M., Sephens, N. J., Nelson, L. A., Morra, S. E., Brunick, K. L., & Stevens, J. A. (2007). Planning to reach for an object changes how the reacher perceives it. *Psychological Science, 18*, 713–719.

Weizenbaum, J. (1976). *Computer power and human reason: from judgment to calculation*. San Francisco: W. H. Freeman.

Wells, H. G. (1895). *The Time Machine*. London: William Heinemann.

Weyl, H. (1952). *Symmetry*. Princeton, NJ: Princeton University Press.

Wimmer, H., & Perner, J. (1983). Beliefs about beliefs: Representing and constraining function of wrong beliefs in young children's understanding of deception. *Cognition, 13*(1), 103–28.

Wynn, T. (2002). Archaeology and cognitive evolution. *Behavioral and Brain Sciences, 25*, 389–403.

Wynn, T. & Coolidge, F. (2003). The role of working memory in the evolution of managed foraging. *Before Farming, 2*(1), 1–16.

Wynn, T. & Coolidge, F. (2004). The expert Neanderthal mind. *Journal of Human Evolution, 46*, 467–487.

Wynn, T., Coolidge, F., & Bright, M. (2009). Hohlenstein-Stadel and the evolution of human conceptual thought. *Cambridge Archaeological Journal, 19*, 73–84.

Zeki, S. (1999). *Inner vision: An exploration of art and the brain*. New York: Oxford University Press.

Zeki, S. (2001). Artistic creativity and the brain. *Science, 293*(5527), 51–52.

Index

The annotation of an italicized "*f*" indicates a reference to a figure on the specified page.